ISLE OF MAN STEAM PACKET HEYI

by Adrian Sweeney

Published by Mainline & Maritime Ltd
3 Broadleaze, Upper Seagry, near Chippenham, SN15 5EY
Tel: 07770 748615
www.mainlineandmaritime.co.uk
orders@mainlineandmaritime.co.uk
Printed in the UK
ISBN 978-1-913797-06-5

Front Cover: *MANXMAN* (II) approaches Douglas on a sunny summer's day.

Back Cover: *MONA'S QUEEN* (V) in the Mersey.

Above: The first generation car ferry *MANX MAID*, approaching Douglas.

All: The late Laurie Schofield

1

INTRODUCTION

In 1935 the fleet of the Isle of Man Steam Packet Company consisted of seventeen vessels. It would be no exaggeration to say that it was a very mixed fleet indeed, consisting of steamers built by the Company, steamers bought second hand, coal burners, oil burners, steam turbine engines, steam reciprocating engines, passenger vessels and cargo only ships. It was certainly not a standardised fleet in any sense of the word and of course one of the main causes of this diversity was the losses that the Company had suffered in the Great War. These had included **THE RAMSEY**, sunk in the North Sea in 1915 by the German minelayer/raider **METEOR**, the crack ship in the fleet **BEN-MY-CHREE** (III), sunk by Ottoman gunfire off the island of Castellorizo in 1917, the paddle steamer **EMPRESS QUEEN** in 1916, wrecked on Bembridge Ledge off the Isle of Wight while trooping and **SNAEFELL** in 1918 which was on her way home but was torpedoed three days out of Alexandria by a German U Boat.

Thus the Company had lost some of its finest vessels and it was found that three of the large paddlers that had survived the war, **MONA'S ISLE** (III), **QUEEN VICTORIA** and **PRINCE OF WALES** were not worth reconditioning. The Company began to replace these by buying second hand vessels and it was not until 1927 that they launched their first purpose built post war steamer, **BEN-MY-CHREE** (IV).

In 1935 the fleet consisted of:

VIKING (I) built in 1905
KING ORRY (III) built in 1913
PEEL CASTLE ex **DUKE OF YORK**, built in 1894
MONA (IV) ex **HAZEL** built in 1907
MANXMAN (I) built in 1904
MONA'S ISLE (IV), ex **ONWARD**, built in 1905

SNAEFELL (IV), ex **VIPER**, built in 1906
CUSHAG ex **ARDNAGRENA**, built in 1908
MANX MAID (I) ex **CAESAREA**, built in 1910
BEN-MY-CHREE (IV) built in 1927
VICTORIA built in 1907
RAMSEY TOWN ex **ANTRIM**, built in 1904
RUSHEN CASTLE ex **DUKE OF CORNWALL**, built in 1898
PEVERIL (II) built in 1929
LADY OF MANN (I), built in 1930
CONISTER (I) ex **ABINGTON**, built in 1921
MONA'S QUEEN (III) built in 1933

*Above: **LADY OF MANN** (I) berthed at Liverpool in the late 1930s.*

Author's Collection

As can be seen the fleet had only three modern vessels, many of the second hand purchases were elderly and apart from **LADY OF MANN**, **BEN-MY-CHREE** and **MONA'S QUEEN** there was little standardisation. The Company began to realise that more new builds were necessary and they were about to embark on a course of action which would be followed for the next 20, if not 30 years.

*Above: **MONA'S QUEEN** (III) anchored in the Mersey on 21 June 1934.*

Author's Collection

FENELLA AND *TYNWALD* OF 1936

On the 16 December 1936 two sister ships glided down the slipways together at Vickers Armstrong, Barrow. Named **FENELLA** and **TYNWALD** they were the latest steamers built for the Isle of Man Steam Packet Company and they were of a brand new design encompassing the very latest ideas for the comfort of their passengers especially during the often arduous sailings to the Isle of Man in the winter months. They were, in effect, the beginning of a renaissance of the Isle of Man Steam Packet's fleet, a process that was to continue after the Second World War when the renaissance needed to be boosted by a considerable resurrection of the fleet, on through **MANXMAN** of 1955 to the final side loading car ferry, **LADY OF MANN** of 1975.

It had been reported to the Board of Directors of the Isle of Man Steam Packet Company on 7 November 1935 that the boilers of the steamer **RAMSEY TOWN** had a serious crack in the central combustion chamber of the port double ended boiler. **RAMSEY TOWN** had been built for the Midland Railway in 1904 and her original name had been **ANTRIM**; she had been bought by the Steam Packet in 1928, continuing their post Great War policy of buying second hand tonnage despite the fact that in 1927 they had taken delivery from Cammell Laird of **BEN-MY-CHREE**, their first post war new build. **RAMSEY TOWN** was bought primarily to use on the many secondary services the Company ran in those days and to be used as extra capacity on the main routes at peak periods.

*Above: **RAMSEY TOWN** in the River Mersey.*
Author's Collection

The Board of Trade would only allow a continuation of the passenger certificate of **RAMSEY TOWN** if the boiler pressure was reduced from 185 lbs per sq inch to 170 lbs per sq inch. It was considered imperative that the repairs were carried out as the Company would need the vessel the next summer, especially at peak periods, and therefore Cammell Laird at Birkenhead were instructed to carry out the repairs at a cost of £700. However, the Chairman, Mr G Fred Clucas reminded the Board that even with these repairs the ship would have to be withdrawn at the end of the 1936 season and it was essential to plan a new build now to replace her. He also

pointed out that between 1934 and 1942 no less than 7 ships would be nearing the end of their useful lives, the results of "*....the purchase of second hand ships to carry on our services after the war*". It was decided that as this was not a full Board meeting and the English directors were not present, they would need to be consulted about such an important matter. During this period and before, the fairly regular meetings of the Directors of the Company mainly in Douglas to oversee the day to day functioning of the Company, were attended mostly by the Directors of the Company who were Manx based but these meetings were not regarded as Full Board Meetings at which the big strategic decisions would be made, unless the Directors who were based in England were present.

*Above: **PEEL CASTLE** at the Cammell Laird Shipyard at Birkenhead. She is in one of the flooded up dry docks.*
Author's Collection

The Chairman raised the matter of fleet replacements again at a meeting in Douglas on 21 November 1935 and he emphasised the necessity of having a new ship ready for the 1937 summer season. It was notable that two other Board Members, Mr Waddington and Mr Dodd urged the Company to look into the possibility of installing oil engines for any new vessel, the first occasion that this question was raised. The Chairman however was not in favour of this idea stating that oil engines were unsuitable "*for vessels in our service*".

On the evening of 11 December 1935 the full Board of the Isle of Man Steam Packet Company met at the Victoria Hotel in Barrow and the main item on the agenda was the fleet replacement programme. The Chairman had already circulated a memorandum outlining the necessary building programme from 1935 onwards. According to the Marine Superintendent, Mr Kelly, six of the present fleet would soon have to finish service: **RAMSEY TOWN** in 1936, **PEEL CASTLE** in 1939, **MONA** in 1939, **MANXMAN**, **SNAEFELL** and **RUSHEN CASTLE** all in 1940.

Above: Another view of RAMSEY TOWN at anchor in the Mersey.

Author's Collection

The only way of coping with this situation, according to the Chairman was to dispose of some of the vessels prior to these dates and endeavour to extend the lives of some of the others. The Board agreed that the Board of Trade ultimatum as regards **RAMSEY TOWN**'s passenger certificate was a problem and the Chairman stressed the need to give serious consideration to "*….. placing an order for two ships of 1,700/1,800 passenger capacity, to be ready for the season 1937.*" This would enable the disposal of **RAMSEY TOWN** in 1936 followed by **PEEL CASTLE** in the spring of 1938. After 1938 the Chairman suggested that the Company sell **MANXMAN** and **RUSHEN CASTLE** and replace them with one ship capable of carrying 2,600 passengers. As for the 1937 ships, the Board was informed that money was available for one now and money would be available for the second vessel by her delivery date in the early summer of 1937. He thought it would then be possible for a new build every two years "*provided we continue to place £100,000 to depreciation every year.*" Provisional plans drawn up by the Superintendents were studied which provided for a vessel which could replace **RAMSEY TOWN** in the summer and "*….be very serviceable in the winter time*".

Above: MONA (IV) off Douglas Head in July 1935.

Author's Collection

The following yards were to be invited to tender for the order:

Vickers Armstrong at Barrow
Cammell Laird at Birkenhead
Denny Brothers at Dumbarton
Fairfield Shipbuilding and Engineering Company at Govan
Harland and Wolff of Belfast and Glasgow

The vessel to be tendered for was to be a twin screw geared turbine vessel capable of carrying 1700/1800 passengers with a service speed of either 21 or 20 knots depending on engine specification. The yards were also asked to quote for two sister ships to be built at the same time and to advise the Company on the possibility of oil engines replacing steam.

By the time of the next Board Meeting on 25 February 1936 all the shipbuilders who had been asked to quote had done so. Significantly however, none had quoted for a ship equipped with oil engines, all expressing the opinion that… "*internal combustion engines are not suitable for cross channel ships of high speed on account of noise, vibration and cost of maintenance.*"

The lowest tenders were from Vickers Armstrong at Barrow and Cammell Laird at Birkenhead. The former had proposed a ship measuring 310 feet by 47 feet by 18 feet whereas the Birkenhead Company proposed a vessel 1 foot narrower at 46 feet with less draught at 17 feet 6 inches. Both companies quoted for water tube boilers though Vickers Armstrong did say that if the vessel had cylindrical boilers it could reduce the beam by 1 foot.

In the event Cammell Laird quoted £211,300 for one 21 knot ship whilst the Barrow Company quoted £209,010. For two 21 knot ships Cammell Laird quoted £412,500 whilst Vickers Armstrong quoted £408,120.

The Steam Packet expressed surprise that the costs were more than they had expected but it was agreed that the dimensions suggested by Vickers Armstrong were the ones that were necessary, as was a speed of 21 knots. Telephone conversations were held with both Companies before a decision was reached which was to invite the representatives of Vickers Armstrong to Douglas on Wednesday 27 February. At this meeting the first thing the Steam Packet Chairman asked for was a reduction in the costs of the proposed vessels. Much discussion and negotiation ensued and eventually the Vickers Armstrong representatives, after speaking to their Managing Director by telephone, said they were authorised to reduce the tender to £407,100 for the pair. Still the Steam Packet held out for a reduction to £405,000 but the Barrow Company resisted and said they could go no lower. The Isle of Man Steam Packet Company then made a formal order to them to build the two ships, the second to follow not more than two months after the first.

The names for the two new Steam Packet vessels were discussed at the Adelphi Hotel in Liverpool on Friday 3 April 1936. One of the Directors, Colonel E Gordon Thin proposed **FENELLA** and **TYNWALD** and these suggestions were seconded by Mr Edgar. The rest of the Directors thought the names to be most suitable and they were approved. A few weeks later however a difficulty arose. The Company were informed that the Board of Trade had accepted the name **FENELLA** but had rejected **TYNWALD** on the grounds that there was already a vessel of that name registered in Douglas.

The Directors of the Steam Packet Company were very unhappy to hear that the vessel in question was their former **TYNWALD**, the third of the name, which had been sold to a Mr Colby Cubbin of Douglas in 1933 who proposed converting her into a steam yacht. He had not removed the vessel from the Douglas register, as had been agreed as part of the sale, so the Steam Packet Board decided to write to him urgently, demanding that he do so forthwith. However some weeks later they received a letter from Mr Cubbin stating that he was unwilling to do this as it would involve him in considerable expense. He would have to replace the names on bow and stern and this would result in having to replace some of the plating on which the brass letters were attached as they were badly corroded. He was asked for estimates for these tasks which worked out at £362 plus a £10 survey fee. Mr Cubbin advised the Steam Packet that he would accept £215 from them if they would agree to move, at their expense, a spare shaft and two propellers belonging to his **TYNWALD** from Cammell Laird's at Birkenhead to his own warehouse in Liverpool. He also wanted the Steam Packet to reimburse him the Board of Trade fee for changing the name of his vessel! As Mr Cubbin had paid the Company £500 over the shipbreakers price for the vessel in 1933 the Isle of Man Steam Packet Company agreed to his demands and later in the year Mr Cubbin renamed his vessel **WESTERN ISLES**.

Above: The former **TYNWALD** *(III) in Liverpool Docks, now named* **WESTERN ISLES**, *in 1938.*
Author's Collection

Meanwhile there had been a slight design change for the new vessels. They had originally been intended to carry eight oar propelled lifeboats but after the Marine Superintendent had inspected the Heysham steamer **DUKE OF YORK** it was decided **FENELLA** and

TYNWALD would have, like **DUKE OF YORK**, the newer Fleming lifeboats and thus would need only six.

Considerable trouble was gone to by the Company to make sure that the new vessels offered new standards in passenger comfort. By 20 August 1936 Vickers Armstrong informed the Steam Packet that the designs for the panelling, upholstery and furnishings were all ready for inspection and the Chairman plus other board members visited Barrow on 26 August to have a look and approve the selections. Board members decided that although the two vessels were sisters they needed their own personalities, especially inside and different designs were approved for each vessel. By January 1937 the Company had approved the cabin outfittings for both steamers and their cost.

Meanwhile **RAMSEY TOWN** was put up for auction by C W Kellock and Co the firm of shipbrokers used by the Steam Packet at that time. The reserve price was £6,000 but she eventually went to T W Ward for scrap at a price of £4,750.

Above: **KING ORRY** *(III) on her approach to the Landing Stage at Liverpool in the 1930s.*
Author's Collection

It had originally been hoped that the launching of **FENELLA** and **TYNWALD** would be in October 1936 but on the 27 August Vickers Armstrong advised the Steam Packet that a delay in delivery of the two stern frame castings would result in a delay to the launching of both ships. Initially they were aiming for 16 November but by October the builders had to advise a further delay and 16 December was confirmed as the definite launch date.

The launch arrangements were decided upon at a meeting in Douglas on 21 October 1936. The guests of the Company were to depart from Douglas on 15 December aboard **MONA** at 1000 hours. They would arrive in Barrow at 1400 hours and the launch of both vessels would take place at noon on the 16th. After the launch, lunch and speeches the party would return to Douglas aboard **MONA** at about 1500 hours.

The builders meanwhile had informed the Steam Packet that the completion of the ships might be delayed by possible industrial action at the shipyard. Notwithstanding the Steam Packet authorised the third payment instalment to the builders of £81,420. **FENELLA** and **TYNWALD** were duly launched together at the yard of Vickers Armstrong, Barrow, on 16 December 1936.

On 21 January 1937 a report from the Marine Superintendent, Mr J R Kelly, described the progress being made with the new steamers. **FENELLA** was the more advanced of the two and would be delivered first. Her three water tube boilers had been fitted the previous week and the boiler uptakes were now being erected. The first set of turbines had been set in position and the second set had been tested in the workshops and would be placed on board in a few days' time. **TYNWALD**'s turbines were being built and her boilers were in an advanced stage of construction. Bad weather had caused a delay in laying the decks and time was very short if the builders were to deliver the ships by 31 March. Rather than hurry the job the Steam Packet decided to waive the late delivery penalty and agreed on delivery of **FENELLA** at the end of April.

Proposed arrangements for the trials of **FENELLA** due to take place on the River Clyde on Thursday 22 April suggested that Directors and Officials of the Steam Packet would join the new ship at Barrow at 2000 hours on Tuesday 20 April and sleep on board. The ship would depart Barrow early on the 21st, adjust compasses in Morecambe Bay and "...*proceed under easy steam to the Clyde*". After trials on the 22nd the ship would call for the first time at Douglas to disembark the Isle of Man party and then proceed back to Barrow for engine inspection.

Prior to the commencement of the first sailings and speed trials of **FENELLA**, the Steam Packet Board held a full meeting at Barrow on 19 April. It appeared that all was not well with the new ship. Concern was being expressed about the draught of the vessel as she was some four feet lower at the stern instead of only one foot six inches as per the specification although there were no suggestions concerning cancelling the speed trials. The Company would review the situation after the speed trials. The upcoming trials of **TYNWALD** were also discussed. It was proposed by the builders that the ship would leave Barrow on 5 June and call at Douglas for the first time to embark directors and officials of the Company and then, like **FENELLA**, would proceed to the Clyde for trials on 6 June. She would then return to Douglas and then on to Barrow for her engine inspection.

The speed trials of **FENELLA** were duly completed on the Clyde on 22 April and the arrangements went well. However a few days later, on 28 April, Company officials stated they were still not satisfied by the draught and trim of the new steamer. Representatives of the builders replied that the requirements of the Steam Packet had governed the design of the new ships as regards the draught and trim. Captain Kinley, the master of the vessel during the trials and Mr J R Kelly the Marine Superintendent, were particularly concerned with the ship berthing at Fleetwood, especially at low water on spring tides. "*A long exchange of views took place, during which neither side would concede that the other was in the right*".

Above: **TYNWALD** (IV) on 17 June 1937 anchored off the Cammell Laird Shipyard, River Mersey.

Author's Collection

After further discussion the Steam Packet Company decided to accept **FENELLA** and that this acceptance would be on 30 April. The representatives from the builders, no doubt relieved, informed the Steam Packet Board that if there were any problems running the vessel in the first season, then they would be only too glad to help put things right. The next day, 29 April, Mr R B Moore, Engineering Superintendent, and Captain Kinley reported on the trials of **FENELLA**. Apart from the draught and trim, the trials had gone very well and a top speed of 21.523 knots had been achieved over the measured mile. It was decided that the maiden voyage of the new steamer would take place from Liverpool to Douglas on Saturday 1 May at 1045 hours.

Meanwhile completion of **TYNWALD** was well in hand and her trials on the Clyde took place as planned on 6 June. Captain Kinley reported that the **TYNWALD**'s trials were very satisfactory and she achieved 21.68 knots over the measured mile:

"*Owing to the **TYNWALD** being more easily driven than the **FENELLA** there was slight reduction in the fuel consumption which worked out at 0.879 lbs per SHP per hour*".

TYNWALD was taken over on 7 June but her maiden voyage was not until 18 June, from Liverpool to Douglas. It was at this time that the possibility was discussed of operating just one steamer in the winter instead of the two. Although the Steam Packet liked the idea, the Post Office did not, and so it was decided to stick with the two ship winter service and **FENELLA** and **TYNWALD** began their careers as planned.

*Above: Another view of **TYNWALD** (IV) in the Mersey inbound from Douglas on 23 March 1938.*

Author's Collection

FENELLA - INTO SERVICE 1937 TO 1939

As we have seen **FENELLA** was launched, with her sister on 16 December 1936 and as far as the Steam Packet Company was concerned they were built for all year round work on all the Company routes and to improve the standard of the Liverpool to Douglas winter service. Comfort was the order of the day and their furnishings and public rooms were of a high standard and the sisters soon became popular with the travelling public. Compared with the older ships that the Company had used on the winter service, **FENELLA** and **TYNWALD** must have seemed like the last word in cross channel luxury!

The statistics of **FENELLA** were as follows:

Gross tonnage:	2376
Length:	314 feet 6 inches
Beam:	46 feet
Draught:	18 feet
Service speed:	21 knots
Engines:	Two sets of single reduction geared turbines
Passengers:	1968
Crew:	68
Total cost:	£203,550

After her trials the first sailing of **FENELLA** for the Steam Packet was a light sailing from Barrow to Liverpool on Friday 30 April. She departed Barrow at 1420 hours, sailed past the Bar lightship for the first time at 1642 hours and was off the Rock at 1819 hours. She berthed at Liverpool Landing Stage for the first time at 1834 hours. It had been a fine day with a light south-westerly breeze with a slight sea and hazy visibility. **FENELLA** was ready for her maiden voyage, which was due to take place the next day.

The maiden voyage of **FENELLA** took place on 1 May 1937. She departed Liverpool landing stage at 1048 hours, was off the Rock at 1102 hours and was sailing past the Bar Lightship at 1148 hours. There was a light northerly breeze and the sea state was slight. On board were a total of 292 fare paying passengers plus 14 members of the Territorial Army. The passengers on board held a variety of the tickets that were then available from the Steam Packet Company. They comprised:

Weekend Saloon tickets	9½
Weekend Steerage tickets	32½
One month Saloon tickets	21½
One month Steerage tickets	57½
Single Saloon tickets	5
Single Steerage tickets	33½
Return Saloon tickets	71½
Return Steerage tickets	46
Passes	15

The ship berthed at Douglas for the first time at 1426 hours.

Above: **FENELLA** (II) in Douglas Bay in 1938.
Author's Collection

The first season was a busy one for **FENELLA**. Total sailings between the end of April and 31 December were:

Liverpool to Douglas	107
Douglas to Liverpool	103
Fleetwood to Douglas	5
Douglas to Fleetwood	7
Douglas to Dublin	6
Dublin to Douglas	6
Douglas to Belfast	6
Belfast to Douglas	6
Peel to Belfast	1
Belfast to Peel	1
Douglas to Ardrossan	10
Ardrossan to Douglas	10
Llandudno to Douglas	2
Llandudno to Douglas	2
Heysham to Douglas	1
Local Manx Cruises	6
Round the Island Cruises	5
Light Sailings	13

The Liverpool route was by far the most dominant for the ship in her first season, as indeed it was for her entire short life. However the first deviation from Liverpool was quite an unusual one. On 10 June 1937 the ship sailed light at 0532 hours from Douglas to Peel. She boarded 859 passengers at Peel and sailed at 0927 hours for Belfast, passing Copelands at 1116 hours and berthing in Belfast at 1250 hours. There was a light south-westerly wind and the sea was smooth. It is presumed that this was a charter sailing as present on board was the Vicar of Rushen and it is stated that £312-2s-6d worth of tickets were sold by the Peel Advertising Board. The return sailing left Belfast at 2027 hours and arrived back at Peel at 2345 hours. The wind had by this time swung round to a north-westerly and the sea was by now moderate. The ship returned light to Douglas. It is interesting to note that this sailing also took place in 1938, on 9 June.

On Thursday 17 June the people of Fleetwood saw **FENELLA** for the first time. She sailed light from Douglas to take the 0200 hours sailing from Fleetwood on Friday the 18th. This was a Temple Press Excursion and there were 1745 passengers on board. In a north-north-westerly light breeze, the ship sailed past the Wyre Light at 0220 hours and proceeded to Douglas on a slight sea, berthing at 0535 hours. The return sailing was at 2003 hours. The ship berthed back at Fleetwood at 2310 hours. There were 1766 passengers on board this time, so they had picked a few up during the day! After disembarkation **FENELLA** sailed light back to Douglas.

Dublin had to wait till 21 June for their first sight of the new steamer. She departed Douglas at 0835 hours. The wind was light and the sea was smooth as she crossed to Ireland, passing the Bailey at 1220 hours and berthing in Dublin at 1325 hours, with 207 passengers on board. When she returned to Douglas at 1705 hours, 263 passengers were taking the trip, and they arrived in Douglas at 2129 hours.

The very next day the ship returned to Ireland, to Belfast. The sea was slight but the north-westerly wind was freshening as the ship left Douglas at 0834 hours and called at Ramsey, for the first time, at 0928 hours. She berthed at Belfast at 1332 hours, disembarking 159 passengers. The return sailing was at 1632 hours and she called once again at Ramsey at 2018 hours. The sea by this time was choppy and Douglas was reached at 2114 hours.

On Sunday 27 June **FENELLA** took her first sailing to Ardrossan. With 228 passengers on board she departed Douglas at 1105 hours. She did not call at Ramsey on this occasion. She was off Ailsa Craig at 1530 hours and arrived at Ardrossan at 1717 hours. The six hour sail had taken place in a westerly breeze which became stronger as the day progressed although the sea remained only slight. Visibility had been good throughout.

The return sailing to Douglas was not until the next day. The departure from Ardrossan was delayed because of an accident at Montgomerie Railway Station but **FENELLA** was once again sailing past Ailsa Craig at 1345 hours and was off the Point of Ayre at 1700 hours. She called at Ramsey at 1736 hours and was berthing at Douglas at 1833 hours. The 400 passengers on board had had a choppy passage, the wind being a strong south-westerly.

It has always been somewhat of a tradition of the Steam Packet Company to roster a new ship to do a Round the Island Cruise as soon as possible in her first season. It was the turn of **FENELLA** on Thursday 1 July 1937 when at 1439 hours she departed Douglas with 387 passengers and went north about, calling at Ramsey at 1514 hours. The sea was slight and the breeze was a moderate south-westerly and she got back to Douglas at 1836 hours.

The first visit of **FENELLA** to Llandudno was on Tuesday 20 July. There were 597 passengers on board as she left Douglas at 0938 hours on a fine morning and arrived at Llandudno at 1235 hours. She left Llandudno for the return sailing to Douglas at 1803 hours but by this time the weather had turned showery but the sea was still smooth and the wind was still variable. On the return sailing there were 587 passengers.

Local Manx coastline cruises were popular during the season in this era and sailings to Port Erin Bay appear to have been particularly popular in 1937. **FENELLA** took four of them altogether, all in the evening. For example, on 22 July she left Douglas at 1937 hours, steamed to Port Erin Bay and was back at Douglas by 2215 hours. There were 398 passengers on board on that occasion but the next one on 12 August, 1024 passengers enjoyed the cruise. Further cruises were made on 18 August and 1 September.

Two cruises were also made to Ramsey Bay in 1937. The first was on Thursday 22 July, when with 923 passengers aboard, she left Douglas at 1940 hours for a leisurely cruise passed Onchan Head, round Clay Head into Laxey Bay, into Dhoon Bay and round Maughold Head into Ramsey Bay. It was a non-landing cruise and the ship was back in Douglas at 2208 hours. On 19 August, 447 passengers enjoyed the same cruise.

FENELLA only paid one visit to Heysham in 1937. She sailed light from Douglas on the evening of Friday 23 July and so was ready to take the next morning's sailing to Douglas. This she did at 1028 hours in a north-westerly moderate breeze. Some 2,114 passengers disembarked at Douglas at 1340 hours.

FENELLA had to abort her morning sailing to Belfast on 7 September due to mechanical failure and returned to Douglas at 0930 hours just one hour into the sailing. Passengers were transferred to **VICTORIA**. **FENELLA** sailed light to Liverpool at 1331 hours for dry docking. She did not return to service until Wednesday 15 September with a Liverpool to Douglas sailing.

On the night of 18/19 November the ship sailed once more to Port Erin Bay but this time it was not an evening pleasure cruise but to take shelter from "*the stress of the weather*".

Above: **FENELLA** *(II), Douglas Harbour, 1937.*
Author's Collection

FENELLA of course, with her sister TYNWALD, was built as a winter boat so the start of 1938 saw her still in service on the Liverpool route. Her second season followed the pattern of her first and when the summer season arrived once more she was rostered on a variety of services and cruises. A most unusual sailing however occurred on 28 January 1938. She sailed from Liverpool to Llandudno at 1330 hours and arrived at the Welsh resort at 1530 hours. The charter sailing was for the burial off Llandudno Bay of the body of Sir Thomas White. Sir Thomas had been a great enthusiast for the Liverpool to Llandudno sailings of the Liverpool and North Wales Steam Ship Company and he had given instructions for his burial off Llandudno Bay. The ships of the North Wales Company, ST. TUDNO, ST. SEIRIOL and ST. SILIO were laid up for the winter, so FENELLA was chartered by the family to perform the task. It cost them £100. FENELLA was back in Liverpool by 1755 hours.

In the year 1939, both the winter service and the summer season followed a very similar pattern for FENELLA as 1937 and 1938 had done until the beginning of September. On 3 September Great Britain and France declared war on Germany and FENELLA was beginning what was to be her final week in the service of the Isle of Man Steam Packet Company.

On Sunday 3 September FENELLA sailed from Liverpool at 1053 hours, was passing the Bar Lightship at 1155 hours and arrived at Douglas at 1453 hours. There were 220 passengers on board on an overcast and showery day, with a fresh north-westerly wind blowing. The sea was moderate.

On Monday 4 September FENELLA paid her last visit to Ardrossan. Departing Douglas at 0900 hours she headed into a slight sea and was off the Point of Ayre at 1009 hours. Passing Ailsa Craig at 1331 hours she arrived at Ardrossan at 1555 hours with 828 passengers on board. She sailed from Ardrossan at 1734 hours and arrived back at Douglas at 2315 hours. There were only 34 passengers on board.

Her final call at Ramsey was the next day when the ship left Douglas at 0836 hours for Belfast. She called at Ramsey at 0935 hours and then steamed into a moderate south-westerly wind with a slight sea. Visibility was good and she arrived at Belfast with 205 passengers on board at 1339 hours. The return sailing left at 1704 hours. The wind had freshened and the sea was now rough as she left Irish waters for the final time. She was off the Point of Ayre at 2032 hours, did not call again at Ramsey and arrived at Douglas at 2148 hours with just 30 passengers on board.

The final Steam Packet sailing for FENELLA was the next day, Wednesday 6 September. The day was fine, there was a moderate southerly breeze blowing and the visibility was good as she departed Douglas at 0904 hours with 528 passengers on board. She arrived at Liverpool at 1304 hours to be prepared for war.

FENELLA left Liverpool the next day on 7 September. Presumably she de-stored at the Landing Stage at Liverpool though it is likely much was taken off the ship at Douglas. Her sister TYNWALD also left Liverpool on the same day and both ships sailed to Avonmouth. There they were converted to troop transports and, with others, made several voyages from the Bristol Channel to the French Atlantic ports in Quiberon Bay. FENELLA sailed from Avonmouth on 11, 19 and 28 September returning from her final trip to France on 5 October. FENELLA was not used again until 28 December by which time she was berthed at Southampton.

FENELLA was again trooping from 28 December making countless crossings from Southampton to Le Havre and Cherbourg until the middle of May 1940. TYNWALD joined her sister on 14 January.

At the end of May 1940 FENELLA along with TYNWALD, LADY OF MANN, BEN-MY-CHREE, MONA'S QUEEN, KING ORRY, MANXMAN and MONA'S ISLE joined in rescuing the British Expeditionary Force from the advancing German Army. Three Steam Packet vessels were not to survive the onslaught at Dunkirk and FENELLA was one of them. She sailed into Southampton for the last time on 19 May and went to Dover. She was there on 28 May ready to sail for Dunkirk, as her sister did, but because of a shortage of fuel FENELLA crossed over to the French port at reduced speed in the early hours of 29 May. She arrived outside Dunkirk harbour at 1300 hours but the German air attack in the approaches had reached a terrifying ferocity. When there appeared to be a lull in the bombing FENELLA slipped into the port and berthed alongside the East Jetty and began to embark troops. However good fortune was not to be with the Manx steamer, as the air attacks resumed. By 1700 hours the ship had embarked over 600 soldiers when she received a direct hit on the promenade deck as did the jetty at which she was berthed. Huge chunks of concrete were blown through the sides of the ship, many below the water line. The engine room began to flood and a third bomb exploding between the jetty and the ship. Fortunately most of the troops and her crew were able to evacuate by jumping over the railings at the bow of the ship. FENELLA sank at her berth shortly afterwards and became a total loss.

THE BUILDING OF
KING ORRY AND *MONA'S QUEEN*

As the Second World War progressed into 1943 the Isle of Man Steam Packet Company was already starting to plan for the need for replacement tonnage. Their three newest vessels, **MONA'S QUEEN**, **FENELLA** and **TYNWALD**, as well as the older **KING ORRY** had all become war losses and so on 9 December 1943 during a Board of Directors' meeting in Douglas, the need for a replacement building programme was first raised by a director, Mr Crellin. The view was taken that it would be advantageous to have two new vessels building even if they could only be delivered after hostilities ceased. Cammell Laird at Birkenhead and Vickers Armstrong at Barrow were then asked about the feasibility of such a proposal.

However it appeared, the Birkenhead Company would not be able to build any new ships for the Steam Packet unless the war finished abruptly and naval orders were cancelled and they also advised the Company on 8 January 1944 that they now had a fixed price for contracts which was 65% - 70% above the pre-war prices. Sir James Callender of Vickers Armstrong at Barrow also informed the Steam Packet that they too were working to capacity with naval orders but were willing to discuss requirements after the war. A decision was made to authorise the Marine Superintendent to prepare a statement of Company requirements with a view to replacing **FENELLA** and **TYNWALD**. It was intended that potential builders would prepare plans and specifications to obtain the benefit of the "...*wider experience and to ensure the embodiment of the most up to date engineering practices.*"

Sir Robert Johnson, the Managing Director of Cammell Laird, suggested that the Steam Packet Company seek the views of the Ministry of War Transport over the prospects of obtaining a permit to "*... contract for, or build new tonnage during the war*".

At a Board Meeting in Douglas on 23 February 1944 the Directors of the Steam Packet Company agreed that they would be in a position to order two new passenger vessels as soon as permission could be obtained. The Marine Superintendent was instructed to prepare "*... leading particulars of the proposed vessels for submission to the Board.*" The following firms were to be tendered: Vickers Armstrong at Barrow, Cammell Laird at Birkenhead, Harland and Wolff at Belfast and Denny at Dumbarton. It was further agreed "...*that the vessels be of approximately similar dimensions to the TYNWALD with a speed of 21 knots and accommodation for about 2,000 passengers of which as far as is practicable 25% should be first class and 75% third class. Builders to recommend the type of propulsion which they consider most suitable for this Company's trade.*"

On 15 April at Douglas plans were perused by the Steam Packet Directors and the Marine Superintendent suggested some alterations which were incorporated and on 16 May 1944 it was decided to send a letter to the proposed shipbuilders with the detailed requirements of the Company.

By 27 May 1944 replies had been received from Cammell Laird and Vickers Armstrong and by 3 June Denny at Dumbarton and Harland and Wolff at Belfast had informed the Company that they couldn't tender for the work as they were at full capacity. Denny did however warn the Company costs would be 70% to 80% higher than before the War. In the meantime Fairfield at Govan had also been asked to tender and they replied that they would give the proposals their full attention in due course. On 1 July 1944 Harland and Wolff informed the Steam Packet Company that they would be unable to tender due to war work. However better news came from Cammell Laird on 26 August 1944 as they submitted a tender for the proposed new vessels. The Steam Packet then wrote to Vickers Armstrong and Fairfield at Govan asking them to reply. At a full Board meeting on 2 September replies were read out from the remaining builders stating that they were too busy but Vickers Armstrong of Barrow did helpfully state that they were willing "...*to pass to the selected builder any information that would be of service in connection with this new construction.*"

Despite not being able to tender for the work Fairfield at Govan and Denny at Dumbarton had quoted a price for the work, as had Cammell Laird:

Fairfield	£380,000
Denny	£370,000 to £380,000
Cammell Laird	£360,000

However because of uncertainty, they would have to be built on a "...*time and material basis, plus charges and profit*".

Cammell Laird had gone into the proposals in some detail however and were obviously keen to secure a contract to build the new ships required. A letter from them dated 22 September 1944 said they would now be able to obtain a licence to construct a ship or ships for the Company. They could lay down the first as soon as plans were approved and the second one could be laid down in April 1945. They would give the Steam Packet first chance of the two berths available but warned that they do have other "...*friends who are desirous of taking their turn.*" A further letter on the 25th said that they would be able to deliver the vessels in the early spring of 1946 and that if the Steam Packet did order two vessels, Cammell Laird would cut their profit from £32,500 per ship to £30,000 per ship. These proposals were fully discussed by the

Isle of Man Steam Packet Company. Of the directors, Mr Waddington was not too keen on ordering a second vessel as he thought costs might well come down later on. Mr Quayle questioned whether 21 knots was necessary as money could be saved with a 20 knot service speed. However it was finally resolved to order two ships from the Birkenhead yard with a service speed of 21 knots.

At this stage a further and very different proposal was put forward from Swan Hunter on the Tyne. It appeared there was a possibility of purchasing an unneeded frigate and converting her for passenger use. She had reciprocating engines, a speed of 18 knots and water tube boilers and she could be ready for service in the second half of 1945. The Company decided to pursue the matter, especially if a second frigate could be obtained. The Marine Superintendent followed the matter up over the following weeks and visited Swan Hunter and Vickers Armstrong where the engines were being built. By 28 October the Marine Superintendent was reporting that he was not too sure how successful a passenger conversion would be and the Company began to go cold on the idea. It was formally rejected in December of 1944.

Meanwhile it was reported on 31 October that Cammell Laird had not yet got the licences to build the two new steamers and were suggesting to the Steam Packet that they write to the Admiralty and Ministry of War Transport emphasising the difficulties the Company was facing with such high war losses and aging ships in the fleet. By 4 November Cammell Laird had advised the Steam Packet that licences had finally been provisionally granted and the new builds would now be known as Hull 1169 and Hull 1170. The final hull and machinery specifications were approved by the Steam Packet Board on 2 December 1944. It is interesting to note that a letter from the builders to the Company on 21 November had told them that the Admiralty were insisting on the inclusion of "*Defence Regulations*" in the final specifications. These appear to have related to type of materials used in construction.

On 10 February 1945 the keel of 1169 was laid and Cammell Laird informed the Steam Packet Company that the first instalment of £79,000 was now due! On 28 February 1945 it was decided that the names of the new vessels would perpetuate two of the vessels lost at Dunkirk - **KING ORRY** and **MONA'S QUEEN**. Building work progressed through the early part of 1945 and by 14 June the second instalment of £72,000 became due. It was pointed out that the Company would be wise to hold off fitting out the vessels too early as there was the very real possibility that the ships could be requisitioned by the Admiralty as soon as they were completed. Later in the month, on 23 June, the Company was informed that the keel of **MONA'S QUEEN** had been laid and another £72,000 became due. On 4 August 1945 the Company was informed **KING ORRY** had been plated and **MONA'S QUEEN** framed and therefore two further payments were due. Word was received from the builders on 1 September that **KING ORRY** would be launched on Thursday 22 November 1945 at noon.

*Above: **KING ORRY** (IV) at Belfast. A 1950s view from the Author's Collection.*

When the Steam Packet Board met on 15 September a letter had been received from Cammell Laird requesting that a representative from the Steam Packet Board plus Captain Kinley inspect the proposed new designs for the public rooms and furnishings of the new ships. It was agreed that Mr Edgar represent the Board and that "*... he ask his wife to accompany him as it is felt that her advice would be most valuable.*" The third instalment of £72,000 was paid for **MONA'S QUEEN** on 27 October and by 3 November the details of the new ships were being discussed and finalised. For instance Kelly Bros of Port Michael were asked to supply five hundred deck chairs for the new ships at 25s/3d each. This did not include the carpet seats bearing the Company monogram which were to be supplied by the Company and fitted by Kelly Bros. Total cost of this, including Purchase Tax, would be £1293-15s-0d.

Keen to keep up the momentum the Steam Packet Company held a full Board meeting at the Adelphi Hotel Liverpool on 21 November 1945, to which Sir Robert Johnson of Cammell Laird was invited to discuss the building of a third new vessel. It was resolved to build her along the lines of **KING ORRY** but to take into account possible improvements noted after the first year of operation of the two new vessels. The price was not discussed. However on 27 November, Cammell Laird confirmed the order for a third vessel and agreed to reduce their fixed profit from £30,000 to £28,000. Later the Steam Packet Company expressed disappointment to the builders that there had only been a £2,000 reduction in profit on the new steamer as they had been expecting £5,000. Cammell Laird conceded to this wish on 8 December 1945. The next day **KING ORRY** was launched by her builders at a cost of £295-7s-5d to the Steam Packet Company.

On 5 January 1946 at a meeting in Douglas the cabin outfitting of **KING ORRY** and **MONA'S QUEEN** was decided upon. Rugs and blankets were to be supplied by J G Moore Ltd of St Johns, linen was to be supplied by a number of firms including A Browne and Sons of Liverpool and R G Caine of Douglas, crockery was to be supplied by Dunn, Bennett and Company of Burslem and glassware was to be supplied by Stonier and Company of Liverpool. These purchases were to be placed through the builders.

It was revealed to the Steam Packet Directors on 26 January 1946 by the builders that **MONA'S QUEEN** had a defective stern frame casting and the Steam Packet Company were of a mind to reject it. Cammell Laird advised that casting a new stern frame would delay delivery of the vessel until after the summer and suggested fitting the faulty frame after repairs had been carried out would not result in any problems or cause difficulties with the Regulatory Agency or the Board of Trade. If necessary a new casting could be fitted after the 1946 season. The Steam Packet Company insisted that if the proposed repair to be carried out by the Darlington Forge Company (the manufacturers) proved unsatisfactory then a new one would indeed be needed for the 1947 season.

Meanwhile the attention of the Company was being drawn to naming the third steamer. A gentleman by the name of Mr Nurse of Bristol had written to the Board suggesting the name for this new-build should be one of the older ones such as **QUEEN OF THE ISLE**, **ELLAN VANNIN** or **DOUGLAS**. However the name of another war heroine was chosen instead - **TYNWALD**. In the meantime on 5 February 1946 **MONA'S QUEEN** was launched into the Mersey at a cost to the Steam Packet of £338-14s-1d.

The sea trials of **KING ORRY** were held on 11/12 April 1946. They were reported on 13 April as very satisfactory and a further £72,000 was released to the builders. She had reached a speed of 21.493 knots at full power despite unfavourable sea conditions. The six hour run from the Clyde, where trials had taken place, to Douglas showed the required revolutions that were needed for a service speed of 21 knots.

A final demand note had been received from Cammell Laird's on 18 May 1946 for £39183-16s-6d in respect of **KING ORRY**. This final demand put the cost of the ship slightly higher than the original contract price but was due to the national labour pay awards recently passed by the Government. The Steam Packet duly authorised a cheque for the requested amount.

On 21 June and 22 June 1946 **MONA'S QUEEN** carried out her trials on the Clyde and the new ship achieved 21.631 knots which was better than **KING ORRY**. Everything once again was reported to be very satisfactory including the inspection of engines after the trials.

On 4 September 1946 the Steam Packet were presented with a final demand note from Cammell Laird for **MONA'S QUEEN** of £51,397-0s-1d which included oils which had been left on board. This was £12,000 more than **KING ORRY** but the builders pointed out that **MONA'S QUEEN** had been more seriously affected by the higher wages of the employees. There had also been a rise in the cost of raw materials. The Isle of Man Steam Packet Company authorised the cheque for the builders and now were in full possession of their two brand new steamers and could look forward to the delivery of the third, **TYNWALD**.

*Above: An early view of **MONA'S QUEEN** (IV), in the Mersey on 4 October 1947. Note the black paintwork taken up to the windows at Shelter Deck level, similar to **FENELLA** (II). She is being assisted by an Alexandra Towing Company Tug.*

Author's Collection

Meanwhile the old steamers, **SNAEFELL** and **RUSHEN CASTLE** which had both served the Company faithfully during the war were sent to the breakers despite the risk that the operational capabilities of ships returning from war duties could not be relied upon. Most, such as the **LADY OF MANN**, **BEN-MY-CHREE** and **VICTORIA** would be re-conditioned but **MANXMAN** was unlikely to return to commercial service. More new ships would be needed if the Isle of Man Steam Packet Company was to take advantage of the likely tourism boom predicted for the immediate post war years.

*Above: **SNAEFELL** (IV) at speed in the Mersey.*

Author's Collection

*Above: **RUSHEN CASTLE** is towed out of Douglas by the tug **GANGES** for the breakers at Ghent on 9 January 1947.*

Author's Collection

By August 1946 the efforts of the Steam Packet to regenerate their fleet were well under way. **KING ORRY** and **MONA'S QUEEN** were in service and the next vessel in the series, **TYNWALD** was on order. On 21 August 1946 it was confirmed that the keel of the new vessel had been laid and a first debit note of £72,000 had been handed over to Cammell Laird. **TYNWALD**'s hull number was 1184 and the second instalment was paid to the builders once the Steam Packet received confirmation that the new ship had been framed on 2 November.

Above: **MONA'S QUEEN** *(IV) going astern up the River Lagan to Belfast. She is dressed overall so is on an excursion, possibly from one of the Clyde ports such as Ardrossan or even Rothesay in the 1950s.*

Author's Collection

Above: Her sister, **KING ORRY** *(IV) about to berth at Belfast in the early 1960s.*

Author's Collection

Later in the year at a Board Meeting on 7 December there appeared to be some concern as to difficulty sourcing the decking for **TYNWALD**, as a shortage of suitable timber meant licences had to be obtained and it was possible that Cammell Laird might have to use composition decking which nobody thought was suitable for this type of ship. It was decided to leave the builders to resolve the issue and if necessary appeal against any decision that might be taken which did not suit the Company. It was later confirmed the launch would be on 25 March at 1215 hours.

Meanwhile the possibility of more new tonnage was discussed. Some Company officials considered that the ordering of a new cargo vessel was desperately needed to replace either the chartered **SEAVILLE** or their own aging **CONISTER**. It was decided that Management and the Marine Superintendent would submit a report about the matter in due course.

The next new passenger vessel was also a hot topic of discussion at a Board Meeting on 11 December 1946. Concerns were expressed that speedy delivery could not be expected due to all the shipyards working at full capacity. However delivery for the 1948 season was considered to be desirable. Thus six yards were to be asked to tender for the next new passenger vessel: Cammell Laird at Birkenhead, Vickers at Barrow, Fairfield at Govan, Denny of Dumbarton, John Brown at Glasgow, and Harland and Wolff at Belfast. All were to be asked to quote for:

1)   Vessel similar to **TYNWALD**, 2,200 passengers or
2)   Vessel similar to the **MONA'S QUEEN** of 1934 *"but embodying such improvements as may be decided upon and certified for about 2,500 passengers. Speed in each case to be 21 knots on trial"*.

On 21 December 1946 there was a further progress report concerning **TYNWALD**. It appears that the builders had approached the Director of Merchant Shipping with a view to using African mahogany for decking. The request had been turned down as only ships which traded with the tropics were allowed to have such materials. Proposed modifications to the promenade deck of **KING ORRY** were also discussed. This was to be on the starboard side to enable her to carry cars "...similar to those already built on **MONA'S QUEEN**. The cost would be £1060 and the go ahead was given for the alterations when the ship "*...enters dock for overhaul at the end of the month*". A few days later on 18 January a further debit note was received from Cammell Laird for £72,000 and it was authorised by the Board when the Marine Superintendent confirmed that the new vessel had been plated.

*Above: A late 1950s view of **MONA'S QUEEN** (IV) in the Mersey. The cutaway just forward of the aft lifeboat designed to enable the loading of vehicles can clearly be seen. On this ship and **KING ORRY** (IV) it was only present on the starboard side but the later sisters had it on the port side as well.*

Author's Collection

It was learnt on 18 January 1947 that the newest steamer in the fleet had been damaged at the King Edward Pier on 5 January. **MONA'S QUEEN** had been lying on the south side of the pier when a severe SSE gale had blown up and the ship sustained extensive damage between frames 45 and 50 and to the main belting on the starboard side. Repairs were estimated to cost £800 but the Board were relieved to learn that no early withdrawal was necessary and the work could be done during her refit, scheduled for March.

On 25 January 1947 the Board received letters from Vickers Armstrong at Barrow, John Brown at Glasgow, and Denny at Dumbarton all saying that they could not deliver a new vessel by the 1948 season but Browns and Denny did say they might be able to manage 1949. However Cammell Laird had written to offer delivery in June or July of 1948 but "...*she would have to be an exact duplicate of the **TYNWALD**"*. Estimated cost was £463,000 which included £30,000 for profit. It was also stated however that delivery date was dependent on "...*the labour position and the supply of materials, especially steel and timber"*. Lengthy discussion ensued but it was decided to leave the decision to the next meeting of the Board after canvassing the opinion of the English directors.

In Imperial Buildings on 1 February 1947, letters from the English directors were read to the rest of the Board. Mr Waddington thought that the cost of £463,000 was far too much this time. Colonel Thin also expressed the view that it was very expensive but he was in favour of placing the order for a new ship and scrapping some old

ones as soon as possible. He suggested that perhaps Cammell Laird might be persuaded to reduce their profit to £25,000 as with **TYNWALD**.

*Above: **TYNWALD** (V) in her first season goes astern out of Douglas.*

Author's Collection

After a great deal of discussion the Board agreed to place the order for a duplicate **TYNWALD** at the agreed price but hoped Lairds would reduce their profit to the level of the **TYNWALD**. The Board stressed to Cammell Laird that it was the promised delivery in the summer of 1948 that got them the order. A letter from Sir Robert Johnson of Cammell Laird received on 8 February reluctantly offered to reduce their profit to £27,000 and the Board thanked him for this concession.

On 8 March in Douglas it was confirmed that *TYNWALD* would be launched on 19 April at 1315 hours. It was also learnt that the defective stern frame on *MONA'S QUEEN* had been examined by the Marine Superintendent when the ship was in dry dock and found to have no flaws and was therefore satisfactory. Cammell Laird were handed the fourth instalment of £72,000 prior to the launch of *TYNWALD*, the launching of which cost the Steam Packet £343-0s-6d.

The sea trials of *TYNWALD* were carried out on 26/27 July on the Clyde and were highly successful. A mean speed of 21.54 knots was achieved and all recorded speed tests and machinery inspections were satisfactory. The fifth instalment of £72,000 was thus paid to Cammell Laird.

The next new steamer hull was numbered 1192 by Cammell Laird and the Steam Packet received a debit note from them, on 29 May, for the first instalment of £92,600 which was paid once the Marine Superintendent had confirmed that the keel of the new vessel had been laid. At a meeting of 7 June it was decided to ask the Board of Trade permission to name the new ship *SNAEFELL*.

On 26 July 1947 the Directors of the Steam Packet Company discussed the future of the elderly *MONA'S ISLE*. In view of her age and the fact that the ship was only really needed at weekends, which resulted in high lay up costs at Liverpool during the week it was decided to sell the vessel as soon as possible. It was also noted that her speed had recently been low due to a lack of skilled firemen.

At a Board Meeting in Douglas on 30 August 1947 a debit note was received from Cammell Laird for £92,600 which was paid once the Marine Superintendent confirmed that the new *SNAEFELL* had been framed. The question of the upholstery of the new vessel was also discussed. The builders had advised the Steam Packet Company that samples had been prepared for inspection and pointed out that in the past the Board have "...*invited a lady to assist in the selection*". It was agreed that Mrs Quayle be invited to assist.

Sir Robert Johnson of Cammell Laird informed the Company on 11 December 1947 that Thursday 11 March 1948 at 1115 hours would be a suitable time for the launching of *SNAEFELL*.

Meanwhile the proposed sale of the old *MONA'S ISLE* was not going well. Despite the best efforts of all concerned no sale for further service had materialised due to her limited passenger certificate and the price asked for a ship of her age although there had been enquiries both from home and abroad. The Superintendent Engineer, Mr Craine, was called in to the Board and asked if the performance of the ship could be improved and thus be retained in service?

"*Mr Craine intimated that the slow running time was attributable to the human element and not so much to the quality of the coal used...he would not guarantee faster passages than four and a half hours between Liverpool and Douglas*"

Above: **TYNWALD** *(V) approaches her berth at Belfast. A 1950s photo from the Author's Collection*

It was therefore agreed to inform the agents of the sale to drop the price of the vessel to £20,000 and pending her sale no more money was to be spent on her. By 24 February 1948 all enquiries about **MONA'S ISLE** had come to nothing mainly because potential buyers regarded her as uneconomical and the only market "... *appears to be demolition*". Forever optimistic, the Board agreed that the vessel remain for sale as a going concern. This situation dragged on until 14 August 1948 when the agents for the sale of the vessel reported only a sale to the breakers was feasible as foreign markets were now closed to them. At last, and reluctantly, the Board of the Steam Packet resolved to scrap the ship and accept the best offer. On 18 September an offer was accepted from the British Iron and Steel Corporation of £5,750 for **MONA'S ISLE**, a sum far lower than the Company had originally envisaged if the ship had been sold for further trading. She was finally towed from Douglas on Tuesday 19 October 1948 bound for Hayle in Cornwall but was taken into Milford Haven because of bad weather and it was there that she finally was broken up.

Above: **BEN-MY-CHREE** *(IV) in the Mersey off the Princes Jetty on 18 September 1948. Her funnel had been shortened post war but at this time still had the cowl.*
Author's Collection

Above: **MONA'S ISLE** *(IV) in the Mersey on 17 August 1934.*

Author's Collection

It was at a Board Meeting on 8 January 1948 that the Marine and Engineering Superintendents advised the directors of a proposal to extend the upper bridges of **KING ORRY** and **MONA'S QUEEN** along the lines of the flying bridge of **TYNWALD** as built. Cammell Laird had quoted £750 per ship and Captain Kinley agreed the work should be done but thought the price was on the high side. Thus the Board agreed to get the work done but instructed Captain Kinley to try to get a better price and to obtain an estimate for the same work on **BEN-MY-CHREE**.

On the subject of **BEN-MY-CHREE** it was decided to get a quote from Marconi to fit this ship with Sound Reproducing Equipment as fitted on the new **TYNWALD**. It had proved useful for providing radio news and music for passengers as well as having an important role in the case of an emergency. The quote from Marconi of £249-19s-6d was eventually accepted by the Company although it is shown the cost did in the end go up to £420! At a meeting on 24 February 1948 it was decided to fit this equipment to all the steamers including the cargo ships at a cost of £47 per ship per annum maintenance charge.

On the 11 March 1948 **SNAEFELL** was launched into the Mersey. A payment of £92,600 had been made to the builders on 6 March and it was reported on 17 April that the launching ceremony had cost the Company £528-15s-8d. A further payment of £92,600 was authorised on 14 July on condition of satisfactory sea trials of the vessel. These took place on the 19/20 July 1948 but were not without their tribulations. A windlass engine failed when raising anchor on the 20th - a steam piston was broken and a piston rod bent. However the steamer made two full speed runs on the Skelmorlie measured mile attaining a mean speed of 21.493 knots. A five hour endurance trial at 21 knots was carried out on the way back to Douglas. Bow rudder trials were not carried out due to a defect in the steam control valve in the steering engine compartment. These defects were repaired by the builders and **SNAEFELL** was handed over to the Isle of Man Steam Packet Company on 23 July 1948, at 1100 hours at Birkenhead.

The Chairman reported that after consultation with the English Directors during the sea trials of **SNAEFELL** they were all in favour of enquiries as to the building of a new cargo vessel. The Marine Superintendent was thus instructed to submit recommendations to the Board.

In addition the Board of Directors were given a report from Captain Corkhill which referred to damage to **MONA'S QUEEN** sustained at 0940 hours on Wednesday 21 July while three miles off Douglas on her way to Liverpool in a SSW gale. Heavy seas had forced the starboard interior bulkhead doors inwards and had snapped their hinges. Windows in the top forward lounge had been shattered and there had been an ingress of seawater. Wooden planks had been fitted over the windows and on arrival at Liverpool men from Cammell Laird had removed the doors for repair. The seaworthiness of the ship had not been affected and she took the afternoon sailing from Liverpool as planned.

PROPOSALS, SALES AND BUILDING

On 14 August 1948 the Directors were given the proposals drawn up by the Marine Superintendent for the proposed new cargo vessel.

The new ship was to be 220' by 37' by 16' 6" to the main deck with a loaded mean draft of 12' 3" and a maximum load draft of 13'. Cargo deadweight was to be at least 600 tons excluding bunkers and she was to have a service speed of 11 knots. The ship could be single or twin screw driven by triple expansion steam engines with cylindrical or water tube boilers to burn oil fuel. Alternatively steam turbines with an electric coupling to the shafts would be considered. Whatever engines were chosen, they were to be positioned amidships.

The new vessel was to have two large hatchways and six winches each with a lift of six tons and the main deck was to be fitted for the conveyance of motor vehicles and/or forty to fifty head of cattle. The shelter deck was to extend from the collision bulkhead to the after end of the bridge deck. Officers and crew were to be housed on the shelter deck amidships but there was to be no provision for passengers. However all this was put on hold at a Board Meeting in February 1949 as a new passenger steamer had been ordered and it was felt that the Company had to put its resources into that rather than a new cargo ship.

Above: **SNAEFELL** *(V) at the Princes Landing Stage on 12 June 1967. Cunard Liner* **CARINTHIA** *is turning in the river.*

Author's Collection

On Saturday 18 September 1948 the final accounts for the new **SNAEFELL** were presented to the Steam Packet Company Board from Cammell Laird.

Cost of Labour, materials etc	£473,420
Agreed profit	£27,500
Total	£500,920

Above: **SNAEFELL** *(V) approaching the Princes Landing Stage on 29 June 1971. Shaw Savill liner* **SOUTHERN CROSS** *is berthed at the Stage.*

Author's Collection

The builders stated that the increase of £38,000 over their original tender was mainly due to the cost of materials and included one pair of spare manganese bronze propellers (£1,152).

Interestingly as a cost saving measure it was agreed to adhere to the previous year's arrangement of running the vessels at reduced speed during winter. Arrival time at Liverpool was to be 1300 hours and Douglas at 1500 hours. It was estimated this would save one ton of fuel oil per trip.

On Thursday 9 December 1948 at Douglas at a full Board Meeting of the Steam Packet Company a report by the Marine Superintendent was presented to the directors concerning the probable life expectancy of the elderly vessels **VIKING**, **VICTORIA** and **MANX MAID**. In November it had been reported that during an inspection of one of **VIKING**'s high pressure turbines it had been found that the rotor drum had wasted away to such an extent that there was hardly anything supporting the blading and renewal was essential if the vessel was to remain in service. This had been sanctioned by the Board and repairs were carried out at Cammell Laird. The Superintendent proposed that **VIKING** be disposed of not later than the end of the 1949 season, **MANX MAID** by the end of the 1950 season and **VICTORIA** be disposed of when her load line certificate expired in 1952.

One of the directors, Mr Robertson, insisted that it was imperative that a new passenger steamer be built in the immediate future. He argued that it was necessary as one of the older vessels could become unfit for further service at any time and any repairs would be very costly if they were to be brought up to Regulatory Agency standards. In support of Mr Robertson were the Chairman, Mr Kitts and the General Manager. However other directors such as Mr Edgar, Mr Waddington and Mr Quayle were all against the proposal because of the cost of new builds.

The matter was deferred to a further meeting which took place on Thursday 23 December 1948 at Douglas by which time Mr Waddington and Mr Edgar indicated by letter that they were now in favour of a new steamer as long as fares were raised and the proposed new cargo vessel was cancelled. Mr Crellin reported on a recent meeting with Sir Robert Johnson of Cammell Laird who had intimated that if a new passenger vessel was ordered a slipway would be available by the end of June 1949 and delivery would be in the spring of 1951. He also said that "...*as a result of a weeding out process among his company's workmen, he anticipated the cost of a new passenger ship would not be any higher than that of the* **SNAEFELL**."

It was not until 22 February 1949 that an order was placed with Cammell Laird for the new passenger steamer as a repeat of **SNAEFELL** with delivery for the spring of 1951. The Company stated that they hoped that the builders would once again consider a reduction in their profit on this vessel from the £27,500 they made on **SNAEFELL**. The proposal was made to name this new vessel **MONA'S ISLE**. Mr Edgar and Mr Waddington again pressed for an increase in fares.

Above: **MANX MAID** *(I) in the inner harbour at Douglas on 2nd September 1950.*

Author's Collection

Cammell Laird did offer to reduce their own profit to £25,000 on **MONA'S ISLE** but in April 1949 they sent an estimate for the building of the new ship which was £525,000, higher than that for **SNAEFELL**. They regretted the increase but blamed the price of steel and increased wages. In the meantime the Board of the Steam Packet received a letter from Vickers Armstrong at Barrow regretting that they had not been invited to tender for the new passenger vessel but hoped that they would be invited to tender for the next addition to the fleet.

The Steam Packet Company was concerned for the future of **MANXMAN**. The Company had been informed that **MANXMAN** would cease her service for the Director of Sea Transport on the Harwich to Hook of Holland route about 24 February 1949 and she would thus be available for return to the Company. It had been agreed that she should be sent to Ramsden Dock, Barrow for survey. A letter had been received from the Ministry of Transport enquiring as to the intentions of the Steam Packet regarding the ship. The Ministry asked if the Company would settle for a lump sum in lieu of a full re-conditioning of the ship. The General Manager reported that the ship herself would leave Harwich on 25 February 1949 and arrive at Barrow on the 27th or 28th. The Board agreed that the future of the ship could not be decided before the survey had been carried out and that meetings with the Ministry would then be arranged.

At a Board Meeting in Douglas in April 1949 it was explained that the Ministry had offered the Company £100,000 as a full and final settlement for their liability for re-conditioning **MANXMAN**. This offer was accepted and **MANXMAN** was insured to the value of £25,000. Later in April the old ship was offered for sale for scrapping and an offer of £8,250 from the British Iron and Steel Corporation was accepted and the ship was broken up at Preston later in the year.

Above: **MANXMAN** *(I) on 1 October 1949 at Preston during demolition.*

Author's Collection

A report by the Marine Superintendent on 8 December 1949 stated that the low pressure turbines of **VIKING** thankfully had been passed fit for the 1950 season but would probably not pass for the year after. The only solution was re-blading at a cost of over £30,000 which included new rotor drums. If the work was done **VIKING** would get annual renewals of her passenger certificates for a further four years.

Director Mr Robertson favoured ordering new tonnage instead but the rest of the Board were of the opinion that the economic situation and trading prospects were against this. **VIKING** was examined at Birkenhead in February 1950 and it was found that her hull, frames and plating were in good condition as were her decks, so no major repairs were considered necessary. Her boilers were also good for further service. It was thus decided to retain the ship. It was however decided to dispose of **MANX MAID** at the end of the 1950 season.

Above: **MANXMAN** *(I) in the Mersey on 16 August 1934.*

Author's Collection

The prospect of a new cargo vessel was again raised on 21 January 1950. The Chairman expressed concern at delays in the transit of goods due to the lack of tonnage and there were worries expressed by customers that if **PEVERIL** failed, then **CONISTER** and the chartered **SEAVILLE** were not suitable to take her place. The General Manager said that it was not currently feasible to purchase second hand tonnage at an acceptable cost. There was also the problem of the working hours of the stevedores at Douglas as they did not in future intend to work the traditional half night turn and this could result in further delays.

*Above: Cargo vessel **PEVERIL** (II) at the Office Berth at Douglas in the 1930s. Note she still has an open bridge.*
Author's Collection

Further discussion ensued on 27 February 1950 when it was pointed out that only **PEVERIL** could carry livestock, heavy vehicles and dangerous goods. The Chairman pressed once again for consideration of a new cargo vessel suitable for the carriage of all types of traffic to be delivered as soon as possible. The Board agreed that specifications be prepared. Draft specifications were submitted to the Board by the Superintendents on 18 March 1950 and it was decided tenders were to be invited from among others Cammell Laird at Birkenhead, Aisla at Troon and Thornycrofts at Southampton. However once all the tenders and specifications were returned to the Steam Packet Company they were all so different that a commitment could not easily be made. The Company therefore, on 6 May 1950, decided to draw up detailed specifications themselves and ask the yards to re-tender.

A detailed discussion by the Directors, on 17 June 1950, was held on the merits of steam or oil propulsion for a vessel similar to **PEVERIL**, which was of course steam. The Superintendent Engineer said that oil engines were more economical in operation but "*... overhaul costs are estimated to be about 2% higher.*" The Directors were told that oil engines take up less space and allow more capacity for cargo carrying and they needed fewer crew and no firemen. The Marine Superintendent however "*... favoured a twin screw steam vessel on the grounds that our past experience has proved the reliability of steam engines, whereas he understood there seemed to be a divergence of opinion among shipping people regarding the performance of diesel engines.*" He also said that a

twin screw vessel would be more suitable for turning in the confines of Douglas harbour and "*... would give a better cargo stowage in the after hold than would a single screw type of ship.*"

Much discussion followed but it was the Engineering Superintendent who won the day and thus, prior to the agreement of the English Directors, selected builders would be tendered to build a single screw oil engined cargo vessel for the Company.

On Saturday 22 July 1950 at a Board Meeting it was agreed to place **MANX MAID** in the hands of the brokers B W Kellock & Co Ltd, as a going concern and the brokers were to be advised that as the ship was still in service she could be inspected by prospective purchasers at Douglas or at Birkenhead. It was thought likely that she would be laid up at Douglas at the end of August and would then be available for immediate delivery.

However, the plans of the Company to sell **MANX MAID** for further service were not to be realised. Late in August 1950 the Board were advised by Kellocks that a couple of tentative enquiries had been made for the vessel but they needed to know from the Steam Packet Company what sort of price they were looking for. As the scrap value of the ship was about £6,000 the brokers were instructed to look for a price of not less that £15,000. The local Board were authorised to deal with this matter including any decision to scrap the ship "*... due to the absence of suitable offers.*"

As it turned out there was an absence of suitable offers, which is not surprising given the age of the ship. Of the two tentative enquiries, one had been from Mediterranean interests but because of the age of the ship, they had been unable to get an import licence, while the second had been from buyers in India, whose interest had stalled because of the lack of sleeping accommodation and cargo space aboard the ship. The Company were advised by Kellocks that "... *they had induced the British Iron & Steel Corporation (Salvage) Ltd to offer the sum of £9,000 for MANX MAID subject to the vessel being handed over afloat and substantially intact at Douglas.*" The Manager reported that suitable tides for transferring the vessel from the Tongue would be from 9 November to 12 November so there would be no difficulty in handing her over afloat at a berth. The Board accepted the offer and the fate of **MANX MAID** was sealed.

In the event **MANX MAID** left Douglas on Friday 10 November under tow for Barrow. She was delayed at sea by bad weather but arrived at noon on Sunday 12 November. The Steam Packet received a cheque from Kellocks for £8,775 from the £9,000 sale price.

The Steam Packet Company had been keen to reinstate for the first time since before the war regular day excursion opportunities between Douglas and Dublin. A report on 22 July 1950 from the Marine Superintendent presented to the Board of the Steam Packet Company concerned a special day excursion that had been operated from Douglas to Dublin and back on 19 July 1950. The Marine Superintendent reported that 1,087 passengers had been carried, giving receipts of £915. On arriving back in Douglas Customs examinations had taken less than an hour and all passengers had been off the pier by 2300 hours. The Board were very pleased to hear this as Customs delays had been a major concern in reinstating these sailings and so two further day excursions to Dublin were sanctioned for Wednesday 9 August and Wednesday 23 August. These were also successful and at a later Board meeting two further sailings were sanctioned for September, on Wednesday 6 and Thursday 21st.

It was the success of these day excursions which prompted the Company to restore a full passenger service for the 1951 season. A meeting in Douglas on Saturday 30 September decided to restore a full regular passenger service "...*along the lines of those of pre-war days.*" After a full discussion and subject to the approval of the English Directors, it was decided to restore full passenger sailings to Dublin as follows:

Fridays 22 and 29 June
Wednesdays and Fridays 4 July to 14 September
The steamer was to leave Douglas at 0830 hours and Dublin at 1700 hours

The fares that would apply were:

	1st Class	3rd Class
Return (3 months)	36/-	26/-
Single	23/6	15/-
Day Excursion	17/-	13/-

Later an agreement was reached with the British and Irish Steam Packet Company so that the Irish company would receive 5% commission for each booking they made on the Manx Company's behalf plus an agency fee of £5-5s-0d per trip. The Isle of Man Steam Packet Company thus set aside between £500 and £600 for publicity purposes for the Dublin service that year.

The question of advertising both the Isle of Man as a holiday destination coupled with the Steam Packet Company's services to the Island, were discussed on Saturday 4 November 1950. Firstly the summer services booklet quote from the Isle of Man Examiner to supply 120,000 copies of the 24 page booklet at a cost of £711-5-0d was accepted. A meeting with Mr J D Qualtrough, the Chairman of the Isle of Man Publicity Board followed and it was argued that the Isle of Man would need intensive advertising over the next few years and Mr Qualtrough pointed to the joint advertising that the Publicity Board and Steam Packet had pursued in pre-war days as the way forward. A 50-50 deal was proposed on a £5,000 advertising scheme. The sum of £2,750 was later authorised for a joint bill posting campaign with the Publicity Board in England, Scotland and Ireland while £300 and £200 was to be spent on newspaper adverts in Glasgow and Belfast respectively.

Mr Qualtrough expressed his delight at the re-opening of the Dublin service and then raised the possibility of re-opening the Heysham service as well. The Steam Packet was not too keen on this. Mr Crellin argued that a Heysham service could only be operated at weekends as the Company could not schedule a steamer on a regular basis due to shortage of tonnage and commitments already made to Liverpool and Fleetwood. Mr Crellin stated; "*We could not afford to take the risk of leaving passengers at either of these ports because of sending a steamer to Heysham.*"

Meanwhile the passenger services for the 1951 season were approved on Saturday 21 October 1950. Two sailings per day to Liverpool and Fleetwood were scheduled to commence on Friday 11 May and run through to Monday 17 September. Ardrossan to Douglas sailings were to commence on Friday 1 June and terminate on Friday 14 September while the Belfast service was to commence on Thursday 31 May and run through to Friday 14 September.

Meanwhile the Company Directors heard on Thursday 24 August 1950 via a letter from Sir Robert Johnson of Cammell Laird that progress on the new **MONA'S ISLE** was continuing apace and a suggested launch date for the new steamer was Thursday 12 October at 1145 hours.

Above: **MONA'S ISLE** (V) at the Landing Stage at Liverpool on 2 June 1968.

Author's Collection

MONA'S ISLE was duly launched from the Birkenhead yard of Cammell Laird on that date and fitting out of the ship was completed swiftly so that the ship was ready for trials by March 1951. The new ship left the Mersey on Thursday 15 March 1951 and put into Douglas to pick up a party of Company officials who were to be on board for her trials on the Clyde the following day.

On Saturday 24 March 1951 the Marine Superintendent reported to the Board that the trials of **MONA'S ISLE** had been successful. A mean speed of 21.78 knots had been achieved over the Skelmorlie measured mile at maximum revolutions on her final two runs. The full power endurance trial from the Clyde back to Douglas at 21 knots had also been successful. Afterwards the machinery had been opened up and inspected and was found to be in a satisfactory condition. The ship was handed over by her builders at midnight on 20 March 1951 and the ship which was to become affectionately known as "*The Yacht*" throughout the Steam Packet fleet, joined her four near sisters.

Meanwhile on Thursday 24 August 1950 at Douglas at a Full Board Meeting, the Directors were informed of the progress made in the tendering process for the new cargo vessel. Tenders had been received from the selected shipbuilders and the Superintendent Engineer had recommended that the new vessel should be equipped with British Polar oil engines. Tenders were:

1)   Ailsa Shipbuilding of Troon who quoted a fixed price of £158,000 for a British Polar diesel engine vessel with decks of Oregon pine with a 12 months delivery.

2)   Ardrossan Dockyard Ltd who quoted an approximate price of £151,000, delivery in 14/15 months and decks of teak, with Oregon pine substituted if teak was unavailable at a saving of £4,650.

The Superintendent Engineer did not like an electric generator proposed by Ardrossan and also didn't like the proposed fitting of fuel tanks under the engine room as these were not part of the original Steam Packet specification. Ailsa had largely adhered to the specification and had offered a fixed price and so the contract was awarded to them. Should any problems arise, it was felt they "*...could be amicably settled by consultation with their representatives.*" On 30 September 1950 it was decided to make an application to the Board of Trade to name the new ship **FENELLA**, thus perpetuating the name of the ship which had been at the forefront of the modernisation of the Steam Packet fleet in 1937.

Happily on 7 October 1950 the Superintendent Engineer reported that a meeting had been held with the builders and all matters had been resolved but the cost had gone up to £159,000, the extra one thousand pounds being needed for the "*...additional generator power required by the Superintendent Engineer.*"

The first payment instalment for **FENELLA** of £31,800 was authorised on 18 November 1950 when it was reported that the keel of the ship had been laid. In early December modifications were proposed to winches and generator sets and these had altered the cost of the vessel. Modifications to the engines in order to maintain critical speeds were also pushing up the cost of the vessel. Captain Kinley, the Marine Superintendent, also reported that the builders were not using teak for the wheelhouse but a cheaper substitute. Captain Kinley was instructed to insist on teak being used as per the specification.

On Tuesday 27 February 1951 the directors were advised that the ship would be ready for launching in July although this was delayed until August. Captain R Clucas was appointed master of the vessel and to be present at her trials. He had previously been master of **PEVERIL**.

At a Board meeting on Saturday 2 December 1950 a report was read to the directors from Captain Cubbon, master of **KING ORRY**. It transpired that while on passage from Liverpool to Douglas in a WSW gale with a heavy beam sea the chocks of No 5 lifeboat had carried away causing damage to the keel and fendering of the boat. Further examination of the boat showed that it had been holed and would need to be removed for repairs which would take about 6 weeks, resulting in a reduction of the passenger certificate by 352 persons. To alleviate the inconvenience it was decided to replace the damaged boat as soon as possible.

The marine insurance value of each ship in the fleet is always interesting to see as it rested solely with the age of the ship and not its size or passenger carrying capacity. For the 1951 season the passenger steamers in the Steam Packet fleet were valued, for insurance purposes, as follows:

MONA'S ISLE	£550,000
SNAEFELL	£500,000
TYNWALD	£500,000
MONA'S QUEEN	£480,000
KING ORRY	£480,000
LADY OF MANN	£350,000
BEN-MY-CHREE	£300,000
VIKING	£120,000

Strangely, there was no mention made of the value of **VICTORIA**. However on 9 May 1951 there had been a fire on board **VICTORIA** in the first class smokeroom. The ship was not in service and the fire was caused by a faulty cable to a generator used to supply lighting in the smokeroom during the winter lay-up. The smokeroom was used during the winter as a living room by the Chief Officer. The cost of repairs was estimated to be between £600 and £1,100.

The Company, at the end of 1951, had five modern passenger ships in service as well as the large and speedy **BEN-MY-CHREE** and **LADY OF MANN** of pre-war vintage. However they also had two aging vessels, **VIKING** and the **VICTORIA**, which were reaching the end of their careers.

Above: **FENELLA** *(III) leaves the Liverpool Dock system and enters the River Mersey on her way to Douglas.*
Author's Collection

TWO OUT, ONE IN

At the end of 1951 increased costs made increases in passenger and vehicle fares inevitable for the 1952 season and at a Board Meeting held at Douglas on 6 December 1951 it was decided to increase single fares by 6d, return fares by 1/- and the day excursion fares also by 1/-, except the day excursion fares to Dublin and Belfast which would remain the same. It was also decided to increase the fares charged for motor cars and motor cycles. Car and motor cycle combination fares would rise by 10/- and motor cycles by 2/6d. Freight rates were also increased by 10%.

It was also decided to increase the rates for chartering the vessels of the Company as follows:

Liverpool/Fleetwood to Douglas:
LADY OF MANN or **BEN-MY-CHREE**
Rates increased from £1,200 to £1,300
Other vessels increased from £1,000 to £1,100
Belfast to Douglas:
Increased by £50, making a minimum charge of £750 and a maximum of £1,150
Belfast to Rothesay:
Increased by £50, making a minimum charge of £800 and a maximum of £1,200
Belfast to Dunoon:
Increased by £50, making a minimum charge of £850 and a maximum of £1,250
Workington to Douglas:
Increased by £50
KING ORRY class to £1,150 and **VICTORIA** to £1,050
Garlieston to Douglas:
Increased by £50
KING ORRY class to £1,000, **VICTORIA** to £850
Heysham to Douglas:
Increased by £100 to £1,100

All increases in charges were to begin on 1 April 1952.

Interestingly it was also decided to start the season earlier in 1952. The Assistant Manager pointed out that the Car Races were to begin on 29 May and TT practices were to begin about the same time. As the summer timetable of double daily sailings from Liverpool and the Fleetwood service did not commence until 30 May, this could cause considerable difficulty as the Company would not have enough steamers in service to transport the expected heavy traffic. It was thus decided to start the summer season of sailings on Friday 23 May.

At the end of 1951 the Steam Packet Company had a tragic situation to deal with. For many years the volume of freight traffic from Coburg Dock at Liverpool to Douglas had necessitated the chartering of a third cargo vessel to supplement the sailings of **PEVERIL** and **CONISTER**. The entry into service of **FENELLA** was in part designed to make the chartering of a third cargo vessel unnecessary. It had been the practice of the Steam Packet Company to charter some vessels from the old established Irish Sea concern of John S Monks Ltd, a Company which had been founded in 1907 as J H Monks (Preston) Ltd and owned a total of 38 coasters before its liquidation in 1963. In November 1951 the Steam Packet Company had on charter from John S Monks the 1918 built **SEAVILLE**. This ship had been built by A Jeffrey & Co Ltd at Alloa as **CROSSHANDS** for Cleeves' Western Valleys Anthracite Collieries Ltd of Swansea, which was her first port of registry. She had in fact been ordered by Howden Brothers of Larne as **ISLANDMAGEE** but had been sold to the Welsh Company before launching. She was classed as a coaster/collier and was of 717 gross tons and 190 feet in length. She was powered by a three cylinder triple expansion steam engine aft with a single shaft and screw. She had been sold in 1925 to John Kelly Ltd and then in May 1927 to Wilson & Reid Ltd of Belfast who sold her on to John S Monks & Co in January 1931 and it was they who renamed her **SEAVILLE**.

While under charter to the Isle of Man Steam Packet Company towards the end of 1951 she was on passage with general cargo from Douglas to Liverpool on 20 November she collided in thick fog with **HOPPER NO. 30** in the Queen's Channel near the Q15 buoy and sank with the loss of one crew member.

The sea trials of **FENELLA** took place on the 11 December 1951 and were successful with a mean average speed of 12.785 knots being achieved on the last two runs over the Skelmorlie Measured Mile. The ship was then put on an endurance trial at full speed but deteriorating weather led to this being curtailed after two hours. However, everything was deemed to be satisfactory and the fuel consumption was within specification. Stopping and starting trials of the main engines as well as anchor trials all proved satisfactory after which **FENELLA** returned to Troon. She left Troon on Saturday 15 December at 1600 hours and sailed for Ramsey Bay where she anchored for the night and arrived at Douglas the next day at 1115 hours. During this passage the engines were run at 225/230 revolutions per minute which gave a resultant speed of 10 knots. The Marine Superintendents considered the ship "...*had been built in accordance with the terms of the specifications as far as practicable having regard to the difficulty the builders experienced in obtaining the necessary materials. FENELLA was handed over by builders to our superintendents on behalf of the Company at midnight on the 14th instant at Troon.*"

The number of accidents, heavy weather damage and "*bumps*" reported to the Board involving the vessels of the Company are quite numerous, especially in winter. For example on 27 December 1951 **TYNWALD**, when leaving Douglas at the start of her 0900 sailing to Liverpool, came into contact with the south end of Victoria Pier. Captain W Cubbon reported later that as the ship was backing away from the Edward Pier using the bow rudder, in a strong SSW gale the ship failed to respond to the helm and engine movements and struck the pier. Damage was done to the main belting on the starboard side and hull plating as well as two deck beams in the vicinity of the Chief Steward's room and the third class dining saloon. Damage had been surveyed and repair costs were estimated at £1,500. However **TYNWALD** was declared seaworthy and the repairs were to be carried out during her spring overhaul.

TYNWALD was in the wars again on New Year's Day 1952. Captain Whiteway reported that while the vessel was securely alongside the Princes Stage at Liverpool, she was hit by the tug **FLYING BREEZE** which was attempting to come alongside the stage. The port bow of **TYNWALD** had been damaged although repairs were not urgent and would only cost £25.

On the same day **MONA'S QUEEN** suffered heavy weather damage at about 1415 hours while on passage from Liverpool to Douglas. She was steaming at only 8 knots due to "...*the severe westerly gale and mountainous seas, a hinged doorway was set in and damage sustained to a telegraph casing on deck head and wooden lifebelt locker, all on the port side.*" Repairs were carried out the next day at Liverpool and cost £140.

Above: **TYNWALD** *(V) off the Bar Lightship on 23 June 1959.*

Author's Collection

TYNWALD was in trouble again on 4 February 1952. As she was being towed through the entrance of South Alfred lock at Birkenhead by two tugs at 0630 hours, a fresh northerly wind "...*set the vessel's starboard shoulder on to the south wall and although a fender was placed in position, the third frame, beam and shell plate in the forward lower saloon were slightly damaged.*" Repairs estimated at £130 were once again deferred until the spring overhaul.

On 6 February 1952 **PEVERIL** had come into contact with the North Pier Head at Ramsey. Captain Crellin reported

to the Board on 9 February that as she was being backed out of Ramsey the starboard side touched the North Pier Head. She proceeded on passage to Liverpool but at 1045 hours "...*it was discovered she was taking water freely in the stokehold.*" Accordingly she was taken into Douglas for examination and a crack, twelve inches long was found in the plating below the stokehold. Repairs were carried out "*in situ*" by the crew who welded a plate over the damaged part and **PEVERIL** left for Liverpool at 2000 hours on 7 February.

On 13 February 1952, Captain Cubbon reported that **TYNWALD**, at 12 noon while "... *proceeding out of the Mersey on passage to Douglas, a collision occurred with the Imperial Chemical Industries' steam flat ELEANOR near the Canada Wreck Buoy, visibility at the time being about 400 yards. The latter vessel, which crossed the TYNWALD's bow from port to starboard sustained damage which caused her to sink, the crew of three being rescued by our ship.*"

It was ascertained however that the steam flat was stationary at the time of the collision but because of the poor visibility she had been carried on to the bow of **TYNWALD** by the flood tide. The stem of **TYNWALD** was damaged and the bow rudder was out of action. It was decided however to keep the ship in service until the beginning of the next month when **SNAEFELL** was due to take her place. It is apparent that the Company were worried by this accident as their solicitors "...*have been informed of the mishap and are watching the Company's interests.*"

After investigating all the relevant facts, including radar plots of the Manx vessel, the Steam Packet's solicitors Batesons and Company, believed that any enquiry into the incident would find **ELEANOR** to be two thirds to blame and the **TYNWALD** one third to blame. The advice of the solicitors was that because there might be more evidence forthcoming from the owners of **ELEANOR**, it might be best not to press any claim at this time and that it would be best to arrive "...*at a settlement on terms not less favourable than the proportion of blame they have indicated.*" The Company decided to heed the advice of the solicitors.

In due course ICI, owners of **ELEANOR** issued a writ against **TYNWALD** for £10,000 as their vessel was now a constructive total loss. Bateson's advised the Steam Packet Company to pursue their view that **TYNWALD** was only 25% responsible for the accident and thus any damages should be considered in light of this. The Steam Packet agreed to the solicitor's recommendations. Further meetings as the year went on indicated that ICI saw the apportioning of blame far differently to the Steam Packet Company and in fact considered **TYNWALD** 75% to blame, the exact opposite of the Manx Company. At a meeting on 29 November 1952 the Company decided to follow the advice of their solicitors and take the case to court.

Meanwhile **MONA'S QUEEN** suffered further damage when she came into contact with Douglas breakwater on 28 March 1952. Captain Whiteway reported that as the ship was being backed out from the south side of Victoria Pier at the start of her 0900 hours sailing to Liverpool in a strong ENE wind and rough seas the "*…vessel fell down on the edge of the breakwater, sustaining damage to about 18 feet of the port main belting, shell plate above the main belting and three deck head beams, plating and frames, while two forward boatguards and two pedestals, several tiles and the flooring in the 1st class gent's lavatory had been broken.*" Damage had been surveyed and was estimated to cost £2,000 to repair although once again the ship did not need to be taken out of service. The Marine Superintendent was of the opinion that the Master was to blame as he had not been on the flying bridge at the time and thus did not appreciate that the wheel of the bow rudder needed to be put over in sufficient time. The Company took a dim view of this and decided that the Master and Second Officer Cubbon appear before the Board on 26 April. When questioned by the directors at this meeting Captain Whiteway exonerated his Second Officer stating he had the helm hard over and could not be faulted and conceded that, although it was not common practice to be on the upper bridge "*… for such a short distance of going astern he realised now it would have been better for him to have done so.*" The matter ended reasonably amicably, Captain Whiteway was not disciplined because of his past good record although the Company would insist from now on that the upper flying bridge must be used in such circumstances. Captain Whiteway thanked the Board for their consideration and it was decided there was no need to interview Second Officer Cubbon.

TYNWALD was struck by the Wallasey ferry **LEASOWE** on 27 April 1952 while moored at the south berth of the Princes Landing Stage, Liverpool. She was struck astern on the port quarter. Yet again, the damage did not need her to be taken out of service.

Meanwhile **KING ORRY** had broken down while going astern down the River Liffey on 1 June 1952, in readiness to take a charter to Douglas the following day. It appeared that the starboard low pressure pinion after bearing had become overheated and had been damaged. "*By working through the night, the engineers had affected repairs which enabled the vessel to sail from Dublin to Douglas on the 2nd June but on account of the serious nature of the mishap it was considered it would be unwise to allow the vessel to run on service without further investigation….*"

KING ORRY was thus taken to Liverpool and the damage was investigated. The fault was traced to the time of her survey in Barrow in January when the low pressure pinions had not been refitted properly after their inspection. The Second Engineer had supervised this task and it was deemed he was at fault. He was thus reprimanded by the Board.

Meanwhile during the spring of 1952 **SNAEFELL** had been damaged going through Alfred Lock at Birkenhead and **LADY OF MANN** had damaged Princes Landing Stage slightly, but **TYNWALD** was in the wars again by grounding at Dunoon on the Clyde on 16 July 1952. Captain Kinley reported that his vessel, which had left Belfast at 0810 hours on charter, arrived off Dunoon at 1255 hours but "*…was held up until several British Railways Steamers had arrived at, and departed from the pier and it was 1330 when he received the signal to come alongside.*" By then there was not enough water at the pier and so the ship grounded slightly and did not berth successfully until 1415 hours. Captain Kinley was at pains to point out that there was a Lower Clyde pilot on board at the time.

Further mishaps occurred during 1953. **MONA'S QUEEN** came into contact with the Mersey Docks and Harbour Board vessel **STANDFAST** on 14 May 1953 and this was reported to the Steam Packet Board two days later. It happened while the Manx steamer was berthing at the landing stage at 1300 hours and **MONA'S QUEEN**'s main quarter belting had grazed the other ship's port quarter causing a slight dent to her quarter bulwark and fracturing the bulwark top rail. There was no damage to the Manx ship but repairs to the **STANDFAST** were estimated to be £20.

KING ORRY came into contact with the wharf at Fleetwood on 1 June 1953. The report from Captain Crellin explained it happened when a very strong NE wind caught the vessel while she was swinging and her port bow was blown on to the quayside causing a wooden piling to break. The situation was not helped by the snapping of one of the ship's hawsers during the process and the estimated cost of repairing the damage to the quay was of the order of £63.

Meanwhile **SNAEFELL** under the command of Captain G R Kinley, also on 1 June, was involved in the rescue of the crew from the yacht **AUSTRAL** about 8 miles off Douglas. **SNAEFELL** responded to distress signals fired from the yacht at about 1408 hours and the motor lifeboat was lowered to bring the crew aboard. The operation was completed by 1500 hours in conditions described as squally, gale force NW wind and rough seas. The motor lifeboat was slightly damaged while being lifted back on board. The yacht herself was later salvaged by the Douglas RNLI.

VICTORIA grounded at Fleetwood on 6 June 1953. Under the command of Captain R Clucas she had just left Fleetwood for Douglas when she "*…sheered to starboard and came into contact with the bank between Nos. 16 and 18 buoys in the Fleetwood Channel.*" She remained fast for over 10 minutes before managing to free herself under her own power. It was later discovered that the bow rudder had sustained damage and she needed to be drydocked for further examination.

Six days later **LADY OF MANN** (Captain Cowley) suffered propeller damage at Fleetwood after passage from

Douglas. As the ship attempted to swing at Fleetwood to facilitate a speedy departure the sound of gravel scraping the ship's bottom was heard. Examination of the ship at Douglas revealed that one blade on the port propeller was twisted and would have to be replaced. Arrangements were made to drydock the ship at Birkenhead on 29 June.

MONA'S ISLE, on 9 July 1953, collided with the ferry boat **LUNEVALE** at Fleetwood. She was leaving for Douglas and came into contact with the Knott End ferry. There was a moderate westerly gale blowing at the time and as the ship left her berth a warning blast on the whistle had been sounded. The master of **LUNEVALE** was apparently unaware that the Manx steamer was underway. **LUNEVALE** tried to take evasive action but still touched the starboard side of the Manx steamer. **LUNEVALE** sustained broken stanchions and railings on her port side. **MONA'S ISLE** was not damaged.

TYNWALD continued to suffer her fair share of mishaps. On 17 July 1953 while leaving Donegall Quay, Belfast, bound for Ardrossan, light, the wash from **TYNWALD**'s propeller caused **ULSTER PRINCE** to move off her berth so that the gangways and cargo chute fell into the river. Captain Corkill of the **TYNWALD** told the Steam Packet Board at a meeting on 25 July at Douglas that the weather was calm and only the starboard engine was being used but the departure "...*coincided with low tide and the lack of water in a narrow channel was such as to cause vessels to range badly when the wash of another ship occurs near them...*" Captain Corkill insisted that all normal procedures were carried out and that **TYNWALD** proceeded slowly and carefully from her berth. However the Belfast Steamship Company suggested **TYNWALD** "...*was taken away at such a speed that the forward back spring wire of the ULSTER PRINCE was broken and the vessel drifted from the quay with the result that both saloon gangways and No 1 cargo chute fell into the river.*" They also pointed out it was fortunate that no passengers were embarking at the time. The Belfast Company wanted the Steam Packet Company to pay for repairs but the Steam Packet's agents reported that in their opinion, **TYNWALD** was properly handled, so it was decided to defer the matter pending further reports. It is interesting to note that the cost of repairs was only £5!

Above: **TYNWALD** (V) heads for Douglas from Liverpool on 26 July 1967.

Author's Collection

The condition of the cargo vessel **CONISTER** was discussed at a Board meeting at Douglas on 29 December 1951. It appeared that her Lloyd's special survey and renewal of her Load Line Certificate were due and repairs and renewals were necessary. Captain Kinley and Mr Craine reported that £8,000 needed to be spent on the hull and a further £1,600 was needed for repairs to the boilers and machinery. The Board of Directors, after much discussion, gave approval for the money to be spent to ensure the ship remained in service. However, if anything unforeseen occurred during the repairs, and more money was needed, then the Board were to be informed immediately and "... *the future of the CONISTER will be further considered.*"

Above: **CONISTER** (I) heading for Douglas in 1955. Note although she had the Steam Packet red funnel, she was never given the black funnel rings common to the rest of the fleet.

Author's Collection

The Captains and their ships for the 1952 season were as follows:

Captain J W Cubbon	**BEN-MY-CHREE**
Captain P B Cowley	**LADY OF MANN**
Captain R Whiteway	**MONA'S ISLE**
Captain P J Bridson	**SNAEFELL**
Captain G R Kinley	**TYNWALD**
Captain T H Corkill	**MONA'S QUEEN**
Captain O Taylor	**KING ORRY**
Captain W H Crellin	**VIKING**
Captain J E Quirk	**VICTORIA**
Captain R Clucas	**FENELLA**
Captain L Callow	**CONISTER**

Captain Cubbon was Commodore of the fleet and interestingly he chose to fly his flag in **BEN-MY-CHREE** and not the larger and faster **LADY OF MANN**. It is understood that at the time some Masters preferred **BEN-MY-CHREE** and she had less windage and was easier to handle in certain sea conditions.

Captain Cubbon had been with the Steam Packet since 1920 when he had joined as a Second Officer. He was the first Chief Officer of **BEN-MY-CHREE** when she came out in 1927. In 1940 he was in command of **FENELLA** at Dunkirk and was rescued from the stricken Manx vessel by the paddle steamer **CRESTED EAGLE**, which in turn was bombed by German aircraft and had to be beached at Zuydcoote. Captain Cubbon was rescued from the beach and returned to England. For the rest of the war he commanded various vessels as and when required. When he retired in 1955 he was the longest serving Commodore of the fleet up to his time. It is interesting to note that at low spring tides the wreck of **CRESTED EAGLE** is still visible on the beach of Zuydcoote and it is possible to walk out to her on these occasions.

The master of **PEVERIL** was not mentioned in this list which was presented to the Board on 12 January 1952 but at a later meeting it emerged that Captain Callow was transferred to **PEVERIL** and Captain E McKeiken was appointed to **CONISTER**.

However before Captain Cubbon could hoist his flag on **BEN-MY-CHREE**, as a result of the annual inspection of vessels, it was found that the ship, laid up at Barrow, needed plating to be renewed "…*in way of the after peak and third class accommodation immediately under the steering engine, which may have to be removed to enable the work to be proceeded with.*"

This work was extensive, and Vickers Armstrong had indicated they would not be able to do the work. However Cammell Laird indicated that they would be able to do it but would need the ship delivered to the Mersey by 20 March if she was to be ready for the start of her season.

The annual survey of **CONISTER** had also thrown up further problems. The boiler inspection revealed serious wasting of the shell plating. The Marine Superintendent informed the Board on 8 March that repairs to the boiler would get her through survey for the coming year but he was not confident about future surveys. A new boiler would cost £5,000 with a further £2,000 having to be spent removing the old one and fitting the new one. It was decided to go ahead with repairs to get her through the year, but the general feeling of all concerned was that "…*there would be no justification for the expenditure which would be incurred in fitting a new boiler in such an old vessel as the CONISTER.*"

The problem of **CONISTER** resurfaced again on 17 May 1952. The Manager had been looking into how it would be possible to retain the Ramsey service with a chartered vessel if **CONISTER** had to be disposed of. The Ramsey service required an arrival every ten days during the quieter periods and weekly during busier times. It would be very difficult to arrange intermittent charters that would be necessary to maintain the service and so "… *the sailings to Ramsey would inevitably be uncertain and cause endless annoyance to Ramsey and Northside traders.*" Another difficulty would be trying to charter a coasting vessel with a lifting power of up to 13 tons, which **CONISTER** had, but which most other coasting vessels of her type did not. Most chartered tonnage would have to be ballasted against heavy lifts common at Ramsey, and this, combined with charter fees, fuel costs, berthing charges stores, sundry incidentals and overtime would

come to a total of £41,900 for operating costs per annum.

The Marine Superintendent had even looked into the possibility of converting **CONISTER** into a motor vessel. A new oil engine would cost in the region of £35,000 plus installation costs. The idea was not pursued. Local Board Members of the Steam Packet Company were of the opinion that **CONISTER** would have to be disposed of and that a charter was out of the question. They also rejected the idea of purchasing a second hand steamer and decided the best way forward was to build another new motor vessel, like **FENELLA**. It was decided eventually that **CONISTER** would have to be replaced in due course but could perhaps be kept in service with her present boiler for another two years if she was taken care of while specifications were drawn up for a new cargo vessel.

On 4 December 1952 the Directors were informed that the Superintendents had inspected various potential purchases to replace **CONISTER** but none had been deemed suitable. The Superintendents were also of the opinion that the machinery and hull of **CONISTER** had received considerable investment in recent years and were in good condition and so it could be appropriate to spend an estimated £10,000 on re-boilering. As the Board at this time were considering a new passenger vessel, a new cargo vessel was off the agenda, and so the re-boilering of **CONISTER** was given approval. Even after this in October 1952 the Company were informed that shipbrokers in Liverpool had indicated they had potential buyers for **CONISTER** if the Company wanted to sell. However the Board decided that it would be unwise to sell the ship at this stage as the Ramsey traffic could not be serviced by chartered tonnage. They indicated to the shipbrokers that the Company may want to purchase a more modern vessel and would be interested in any suitable vessels for sale that had been built between 1940/1945.

Meanwhile a sharp drop in passenger numbers was noted by the Board of Directors on 14 June 1952. Passenger arrivals at Douglas from 1 May to 7 June were 48,952 compared to 75,287 the year before. This was a decrease of 26,335, though the Board was unconcerned as the year before TT traffic had been taken into account whereas in 1952 the TT races were being held a week later. The Board were told at a later meeting that passenger figures between 1 May and 2 August were 326,414 compared to 319,333 the year before. This was an increase of 7,081.

The Board of the Steam Packet Company had also, on 24 May, considered a request for two charters from Dublin to Douglas, one by the Dublin Gas Fitters Social Club on August Bank Holiday weekend for 400 passengers and the other by Hewett's Travel Company of Dublin on Sunday 3 August for a party of at least 500. The Board considered the passenger numbers too low to consider a charter for either but instead decided to put on a day excursion from Dublin to Douglas on the August Bank Holiday and offer the would be charterers priority tickets for this sailing. The Manager was certain that the sailing, leaving Dublin at 0800 hours and returning from Douglas at 2000 hours at a flat one class fare of £1 would be a success.

At a later Board Meeting on 28 June 1952 a charter between Ardrossan and Belfast was approved at a fixed sum of £1,500. Ticket sales for a charter between Belfast and Fleetwood, due to take place on 20 September had gone so well that the charterers had asked if it was possible to substitute *LADY OF MANN* instead of a *KING ORRY* class vessel. This would necessitate the Company keeping *LADY OF MANN* in service for a week longer than anticipated, costing the Company something in the region of £700, so the request was turned down.

At a Board Meeting on Saturday 30 August the future of both *VIKING* and *VICTORIA* was considered in detail. The load line certificate of *VICTORIA* was to expire in May 1953 and thus a load line survey would be necessary. This would include a survey of the hull plating. It was already known that the plating in some places had deteriorated "*...particularly in the forepart in the way of the bow rudder steering compartment and forepeak and along the water line, port and starboard.*" It was also noted that some parts of the main deck were in need of repairs "*...as also is the boat deck generally.*" There were also concerns about the fuel oil bunkers and the residual damage caused when she was mined in 1940. Captain

Kinley recommended to the Steam Packet Board that a shorter two year certificate be applied for rather than the usual five year one as it was possible the Ministry of Transport would not demand such extensive repairs for the shorter duration. By the time the shorter certificate expired, Captain Kinley respectfully hoped the Board would have given consideration to the replacement of *VICTORIA* with a new vessel.

The Superintendent Engineer reported that the boilers and machinery of *VICTORIA* were in good condition but once again, because of the age of the vessel it was thought the Regulatory Agency would require a detailed examination of the ship. He recommended the boilers be cleaned and inspected immediately to ascertain the costs of repair.

The boilers and machinery aboard *VIKING* were still in good condition but it was becoming increasingly more difficult to find firemen for the short summer season required of the vessel. *VIKING* it will be recalled was coal fired until the end of her days. Although turbine rotors had been replaced in recent years the turbines themselves had not been renewed and it was felt that these could become expensive to maintain. He thus recommended to the Board that they consider withdrawing *VIKING* after the 1954 season when her current certificate expired and she will have been in service for 49 years.

*Above: **VIKING** (I), energetically doing her bit for global warming, goes astern out of Douglas.*

Author's Collection

Above: **VICTORIA** *steams purposefully up the Mersey towards the Landing Stage at Liverpool.*

Author's Collection

It was decided that the boiler survey of **VICTORIA** be carried out as early as possible at Douglas after which the ship would sail to Birkenhead for a hull survey. The future of **VICTORIA** would be decided upon once it was known how much it would cost to keep her in service.

The prospect of replacing **VIKING** and **VICTORIA** with one newly built passenger vessel was raised at a full Board meeting on 4 December 1952 by the Chairman of the Company. However Director Mr Synge informed the Board that if further passenger tonnage was required the turbine steamer **EMPRESS QUEEN**, belonging to P&A Campbell Ltd of Bristol, had proved unsuitable for Campbell's services and might be for sale. P&A Campbell operated mainly paddle steamers at this time. The specifications of **EMPRESS QUEEN** were accessed from her builders, Ailsa of Troon and her draft of just over 7 feet 6 inches unfortunately precluded her from even being adapted for Manx duties and the issue was not pursued.

Further discussion about the condition of **VIKING** and **VICTORIA** and the expense that would be necessary to keep the vessels in steam was also forthcoming. Captain Kinley recommended that a two year certificate be requested for **VICTORIA** and the Board were favourably disposed towards the building of a new passenger vessel to replace her in 1955, with **VIKING** to be withdrawn in 1954. The views of the Superintendents as regards new tonnage were to be obtained without delay and what type of vessel would be most appropriate - steam or motor vessel.

On 13 December 1952 the Steam Packet Board agreed that estimates should be obtained for a new passenger vessel which "*… would be a repeat of MONA'S ISLE except that propulsion would be either diesel (with a speed of 20 knots on trial) or steam (21 plus knots on trial) for delivery in time for the 1955 season.*" Tenders were to be invited from:

Cammell Laird, Birkenhead
Vickers Armstrong, Barrow
Harland and Wolff, Belfast
William Denny, Dumbarton
Fairfield at Govan
Thornycroft, Southampton

Denny of Dumbarton came up with some interesting suggestions prior to submitting a tender. Contacting the Steam Packet with a view to having more time to tender, which the Board agreed to, they also suggested certain alternative arrangements both in hull and machinery.

They pointed out their recent experience in building cross channel vessels post war for British Railways and Coast Lines such as the **NORMANNIA** built for the Calais - Dover service and **INNISFALLEN** built for the Fishguard to Cork service. Both ships had been fitted with Denny-Brown stabilisers which had been most successful and that the Steam Packet might profit by arranging to visit these two ships to see how they operated. It was agreed that the Superintendents should do this but Denny's were informed that a **MONA'S ISLE** type of vessel was what was required for this tender but following the visits to the two ships suggested, if they were suitably impressed, then due consideration may be given to Denny's proposals.

Tenders for the new vessel were examined and discussed by the Steam Packet Company's Board on 19 March 1953. Cammell Laird quoted £788,500 for a repeat of the **MONA'S ISLE**, £829,000 for one with superheated boilers, £891,000 for oil engines with delivery in May 1955 while William Denny at Dumbarton quoted £810,000 for a repeat **MONA'S ISLE**, £883,400 for one with superheated boilers and £946,700 for an oil engine version with delivery in April 1956.

Harland & Wolff at Belfast meanwhile quoted only for oil engines at £897,000 for delivery in March/April 1955 whilst John. J Thornycroft quoted £937,250 for a repeat **MONA'S ISLE**, £933,250 for a version of her with superheated boilers but did not quote for oil engines. Delivery was for early 1956. Vickers-Armstrong at Barrow quoted only for a repeat **MONA'S ISLE** at £796,085 with delivery in January 1956.

All of the tenders with the exception of those from Cammell Laird were subject to cost variation clauses. The Company were very concerned that all the "...prices submitted were disturbingly high." Given the condition of the older vessels, **VICTORIA** in particular, the purchase of new tonnage was the only option. Delivery date was considered to be of prime importance as the load line certificate of the **VICTORIA** expired in May 1955.

Both Superintendents offered their views to the Board. Mr Craine, the Engineering Superintendent when questioned, was of the view that machinery in the **MONA'S ISLE** if modified to introduce "... *double reduction geared turbines in conjunction with two boilers generating steam at 350 lbs per square inch superheated to 650 degrees F*" was a more modern concept and would be more fuel efficient saving at least £5,000 per season and there might be considerably more savings to be made due to the smaller and lighter machinery when overhaul costs were taken into account. After much discussion it was decided to accept the quote from Cammell Laird for a sister vessel to the post war new builds but with double reduction geared turbines and superheated boilers, for delivery by the end of May 1955.

*Above: A late 1940s photograph of P&A Campbell's **EMPRESS QUEEN**.*

Author's Collection

THE LAST OF THE SIX SISTERS

Inspections of the vessels laid up at Barrow were carried out by the members of the Board of Directors every year and on 8 February 1953 the Marine Superintendent stated that there were considerable difficulties "… *which arose in loading and unloading motor cars on the vessel and in order to overcome these he had suggested moving the port and starboard aft gangway doors slightly astern of their present positions and the ventilators to alternative places which he had indicated.*"

Consideration was given to these suggestions and it was agreed estimates be obtained for the necessary work, which could be done when the ship proceeded to Birkenhead for drydocking before the summer season began. If time was against all the work being done it was decided that the ventilators be moved in any case as this would greatly ease the situation. It turned out that to move the doors on both sides would cost £350 and moving the ventilators and cowls on the shelter deck aft to alternative positions would cost £80. Approval was given for the work to be carried out.

Above: **LADY OF MANN** (I) off the Princes Landing Stage, Liverpool on 20 July 1948.

Author's Collection

One of the instantly recognisable differences between **MANXMAN** and her older sisters were the four raised aft lifeboats on the 1955 built vessel. This suggestion was first made in April 1953 by the Marine Superintendent. It was in order to give more deck space and "… *prevent passengers from sitting on top of the boats with the resultant risk of falling overboard.*" A quote had been received from Cammell Laird to cover this extra cost, which not only involved a different type of davit but also involved extra teak decking under the raised boats as well as extra steelwork and wood for extended bulwarks in place of inboard rails as fitted to the **MONA'S ISLE**. The extra cost was quoted at £2,176 and the builder also warned the Company that the raising of the boats off the deck would have a "… *slight effect on the stability of the vessel.*" It was decided that as long as the stability issue was not too serious then it was agreed that the new ship be modified in the proposed way.

The vexed question of pleasure sailings on a Sunday was still a bone of contention in 1953. At a meeting in Douglas on Saturday 2 May the Manager reported that 4,000 people were expected to cross to Douglas in connection with the TUC General Congress between 7 and 11 September. As part of the entertainment, during the Congress, the Transport and General Workers Union had expressed a desire to charter **LADY OF MANN** for a Round the Island excursion just before the start of the Congress on Sunday 6 September. The charter was agreed but it was decided passenger numbers should be limited to 2,000 and the ship must be back at Douglas by 1815, "…*that is prior to the commencement of the evening church services.*" One of the Board members, Mr Quayle, voted against the charter even with the latter concession in place, simply because it was a Sunday.

Above: **LADY OF MANN** (I) off Douglas coming in with a Co-op charter sailing in August 1960. On this occasion **BEN-MY-CHREE** (IV) was just behind her.

John Sweeney

Above: **BEN-MY-CHREE** (IV) at rest at Liverpool on a summer Sunday in 1962.

Adrian Sweeney

The Steam Packet was always willing to charter out its own vessels if circumstances allowed it to do so. At a Board Meeting on 15 August 1953 in Douglas, the Board were informed of a request from the Chief Marine Superintendent of British Railways via a telephone call as to whether they had a steamer available at short notice for a sailing from Dun Laoghaire to Holyhead on Monday evening, 10 August as their own vessel, **HIBERNIA**, had developed mechanical problems at the North Wales port. The Manager informed the board that the **MONA'S ISLE** was not scheduled for service at that time and he had thus arranged she should deputise for the Railway vessel which would entail "... *trips from Douglas to Kingstown, Kingstown to Holyhead and return to Douglas in time to sail to Belfast on the Tuesday morning.*" The Manager had worked out the cost of all this as £522, and the Directors were pleased with this action and decided to ask for £800 in payment for the services of **MONA'S ISLE**. (It is interesting to note that in the official minutes of the Board Meeting of 15 August 1953 Dun Laoghaire is still referred to as Kingstown although its name had been changed in 1920).

Meanwhile there had been some ongoing discussion between the Company and Cammell Laird regarding some alterations to the design of the new steamer; the builders had not been happy with the wording of several clauses in the contract and about the conditions attached to the delivery date, which in the contract was stated to be "... *not later than 12th May 1955.*" The builders suggested that the wording should be changed to "...*the builders will do all in their power to maintain this delivery which they hope will be about May 1955 but under prevailing abnormal circumstances cannot give any guarantee in respect thereof.*" In other words, Cammell Laird were hedging their bets, probably worried about industrial action or shortages of supplies of components which were beyond their control. The Steam Packet Company were sympathetic up to a point. They informed the builders that the satisfactory delivery date was one of the reasons they were given the contract in the first place and although they would waive the stipulation of 12 May, they insisted the ship had to be ready for the end of May at the very latest, as she was needed for the majority of the 1955 summer season. The matter did not rest there however. On Saturday 22 August 1953, the Board were informed that Cammell Laird still did not think, due to abnormal circumstances, that they should still have to guarantee a specific delivery date but the Steam Packet were insistent that the contract gave them the right to expect the fulfilment of the terms agreed by the builders when the original contract was signed. The only exceptions were if war or government interference occurred during the building process. All this was of course being handled by the solicitors of both companies and eventually the re-wording of the contentious clauses by the solicitors, Batesons and Co, was deemed satisfactory by the Board of the Steam Packet. They seemed satisfied they would get their ship on time and hoped Cammell Laird felt they were sufficiently protected from unforeseen circumstances over which they had no control.

Meanwhile heavy weather damage was reported to **MONA'S QUEEN** on Saturday 22 August 1953. The ship was on charter to the Merseyside Boilermakers Association and at 0917 hours while passing the Bar Lightship bound for Douglas, she reduced speed due to the WNW moderate gale. Nonetheless she shipped a heavy sea which "...*stove in the port forward bulkhead doors, allowing water to rush along the shelter deck.*" Damage occurred and glass was shattered in one of the windows of the Ladies' Cabin on the port side. "*Several passengers received cuts and bruises and were attended to by St John's Ambulance men travelling with the excursionists. On arrival at Douglas they were taken to hospital as a precautionary measure and were given further treatment, but no one was detained.*" The ship herself received temporary repairs at Douglas before more permanent repairs were carried out after her return to Liverpool. The Board noted that several claims had been received from injured passengers and these had been passed to the Company solicitors, Batesons, for settlement.

Above: **MONA'S QUEEN** *(IV) approaches her berth at Dublin in the mid 1950s. Coast Lines'* **IRISH COAST** *can be seen berthed ahead.*

Author's Collection

It was also reported at the same time that **KING ORRY**, while berthing at Liverpool, at the south end of the Princes Stage on Tuesday 25 August had fractured the bed plate at the inner end of No 5 boom. The wind at the time was reported to be NW moderate.

Above: **KING ORRY** *(IV) races down the Mersey on 20 August 1967.*

Author's Collection

A little later in the year on Saturday 5 September the Directors heard of a breakdown in the steering gear of **BEN-MY-CHREE** on 22 August when the vessel was about six miles from the Lune Buoy bound for Fleetwood at about 0900 hours. Temporary repairs had been carried out but the ship did not berth at Fleetwood till 1100 hours. The Superintendent Engineer reported that the trouble had developed in the main bearings of the steering engine and was caused by a "...*slight defect in the lubricating system which caused overheating...*"

The Steam Packet Company meanwhile continued to have concerns over the performance of the Heysham-Douglas service, which had always been regarded as an excursion route. On 5 September 1953 the Board reviewed the results of the seven excursions from Heysham to Douglas that had taken place during the 1953 season. Fares received amounted to £6,627, operating costs had been £4,213 so a profit of £2,414 had been the result. Sailings during 1953 had been on a Wednesday but the Company agent suggested that because of popular counter attractions held at Morecambe on a Wednesday during the summer, more passengers would be possible if the sailings were moved to a Thursday and started a fortnight earlier. It was thus agreed to operate eight sailings in 1954, on a Thursday from 8 July to 26 August inclusive.

It was reported to the Board on 12 September that passenger traffic from 1 May 1953 to 5 September 1953 totalled 418,400 compared to 459,856 for the same period in 1952, a decrease of 41,456. Updated figures to 19 September, given later showed an inclusive total of 437,215 passengers carried compared to 480,766 the previous year a decrease of 43,551. By 30 September passenger traffic was at 440,514 compared to 484,090 the previous year a decrease of 43,576. This was disappointing news.

Barrow had always been the main port of lay up for the Steam Packet vessels during the winter months but on 12 September 1953 the Company were informed that because of a large number of naval vessels which would be laid up at Barrow during the coming winter there would be a lack of berthing space and the Steam Packet vessels would have to be laid up three abreast, which the Marine Superintendent was against, because of the danger of the spread of fire. Modifications to the usual arrangements were thus necessary and it was reported that, after great difficulty, berths had been secured at Morpeth Dock, Birkenhead for **MONA'S ISLE** and **TYNWALD**, leaving **LADY OF MANN**, **BEN-MY-CHREE**, **SNAEFELL** and **VIKING** at Barrow with **VICTORIA** being laid up at Douglas as in the previous year. This appears to have been the first time the Company used Birkenhead for the winter lay-up arrangements - however in the years to come lay-up at Morpeth Dock during the winter months would become very much the norm for the Steam Packet fleet.

At the Board meeting of 22 August 1953 it had been hoped that Cammell Laird would be satisfied with the response from the Steam Packet as to their concerns about the wording of the clauses in the contract in regard to the delivery dates of the new steamer, but on 26 September 1953 it was revealed that the Birkenhead shipbuilders were not happy with the new wording of the contract. They claimed that the wording left them open to penalties if the ship was delayed because of circumstances over which they had no control. They insisted that "...*the clause suggested by our Solicitors gives them inadequate protection.*" The Steam Packet Company however seemed to be showing impatience over the matter and instructed their Solicitors "...*to enquire from Builders how they reconcile their present attitude with that expressed in their tendering letter, on the basis of which the Directors decided to place the order with them.*"

In the meantime it appeared that the Managing Director of Cammell Laird, Mr R W Johnson had been in telephone contact with the Steam Packet Manager over the point at issue. The Steam Packet Board at a meeting on 24 October at Douglas, did not appear to be in the least impressed by this intervention and instructed the Solicitors to write to the builders "...*and inform them that as the matter has not been advanced by the telephone call from Mr Johnson, we still require an explanation of the variance between Messrs Cammell Laird's present attitude and their letter on which we placed the order.*"

Peace appeared to have broken out between the Steam Packet Company and Cammell Laird after a letter from Mr R W Johnson was read out to the Board at a meeting on 7 November 1953. Mr Johnson insisted that the delivery date of the new steamer, hull number 1259, could be subject to delays due to circumstances beyond the control of the builder, as well as the usual caveats of war or government interference. However Mr Johnson, in his letter, gave the Steam Packet an assurance that "...*working under normal conditions, the ship will be completed by the end of May 1955 and in spite of the fact that this is a fixed price contract they will, if necessary, work overtime and do everything possible to effect delivery.*" He still asks the Company to be reasonable and give the builder some protection against the unforeseen circumstances they undoubtedly fear but that in "... *no way will affect their endeavours to carry out their promise.*"

The Directors at this point were disposed to accept the explanation given by Mr Johnson, especially as he had assured the Company the builders would work overtime to complete the contract on time. However they were still a little concerned that they would not be billed for this overtime and requested assurances that this would not be so. On 14 November the company instructed their solicitors to inform the builders that the contract proceed along the lines agreed.

On 18 November 1953 **MONA'S QUEEN** began to suffer boiler problems. It was reported to the Board on 21 November that while on passage from Douglas to Liverpool it was noticed that "*B*" boiler's automatic feed water regulator had stuck in a closed position and this had allowed the water level to fall. All fires on the boiler were immediately extinguished as repairs were carried out in situ and normal operating conditions appeared to have been restored and the ship resumed her full speed, arriving at Liverpool Landing Stage at 1307 hours, the problems having manifested themselves at 0927 hours. However at 1525 hours, about one hour after the boilers were closed down it was noticed that "*B*" boiler was not returning to normal pressure and steam could be heard leaking into the furnaces. Further inspection revealed later, after the furnaces had cooled down, that several tubes had overheated so much they had become distorted and major repairs would be necessary. Although the ship subsequently had continued in service using the other two boilers only for a short while, it was decided to take her out of service the next week for repairs to be carried out in dock. It was estimated that the repairs would take about a week and while **MONA'S QUEEN** was out of service, the Liverpool - Douglas route would be operated by **KING ORRY** alone, sailing from Douglas at 0900 hours and returning from Liverpool at 1500 hours.

Once the boiler on **MONA'S QUEEN** was stripped down it was found that the damage was more extensive than first thought and it was estimated that over 300 tubes would need to be replaced and it was not easy to source these replacement tubes at short notice. The Company decided to bring **TYNWALD** into commission to run alongside **KING ORRY** as the Board considered a one ship service for longer than a week was not satisfactory. Costs to repair **MONA'S QUEEN**'s boiler were estimated at over £3,000.

Above: With boiler troubles fixed for the moment **MONA'S QUEEN** *(IV) is seen off the Battery Pier Douglas on 23 May 1957.*

Author's Collection

The Company had considered the fitting of radar to its vessels for some time but it was not before a full Board meeting held at Douglas on Thursday 10 December 1953 that the Manager submitted some quotations from various companies interested in supplying them. The quote from The British Thomson-Houston Company Ltd included the fitting of a standard radar cabin was £3,437-10s, cheaper than the quotes submitted by Decca or Marconi. Never a Company to rush into anything, the Steam Packet decided to install radar only on the two winter steamers, **KING ORRY** and **MONA'S QUEEN**, so that its performance could be fully evaluated.

Above: **VICTORIA** *off Woodside on the Mersey in 1955.*

Author's Collection

It is not surprising, given their age, that **VIKING** and **VICTORIA** continued to concern the Directors and management of the Steam Packet Company. On 23 February 1954 the future of both of them was once again discussed at a full Board Meeting in Douglas. The Marine Superintendent, Captain Kinley, was concerned that if **VIKING** was to be kept in service after the coming season, considerable expenditure would be needed for repairs to the main passenger deck and passenger accommodation at the fore end of the vessel and to the lower deck while minor repairs would be necessary on the promenade deck. He said that while the hull was in fairly good condition, considerable expenditure would be necessary to keep her in service. He suggested that **VIKING** be disposed of. Captain Kinley meanwhile stated that in view of the large amount of work done on **VICTORIA** in the early part of 1953 in order to renew the load line certificate for two years it was reasonable to assume that further certificates could be obtained to keep her in service for the 1955 and 1956 seasons without a large financial outlay. However after 1956 he considered the ship would need money spent on her and given her age it would not be worth it.

The Superintendent Engineer stated that the extensive repairs to **VIKING**'s engines during 1949/50 and 1950/51 were only expected to take her to the end of the 1954 season and that as her boilers were as fitted in 1905 they were past their best and generally the ship was not in as good condition as **VICTORIA**. The Board decided that after the coming season, 1954, **VIKING** should be put into the hands of a shipbroker and offered for sale. **VICTORIA** was to be retained until the end of the 1956 season.

*Above: **VIKING** (I) on the River Mersey in a pre-war photograph. A Wallasey Luggage Boat can be seen heading for Seacombe.*

No sooner had the decision been made to dispose of **VIKING** at the end of the 1954 season than the threat of competition was heard from an unlikely source. The Publicity Committee of the Douglas Town Council had come to the conclusion that considering the increasing numbers of visitors coming from Northern Ireland the service to be operated by the Steam Packet between Douglas and Belfast during the 1954 season was considered to be inadequate. Furthermore they suggested that if the Steam Packet could not supply extra services then the Tourist Board should *"...make approaches to the operators of steamship services in other parts of Britain with a view to ascertaining whether any of such companies would be willing to operate a steamer service between Belfast and Douglas this year."*

This was discussed on Saturday 6 March 1954 by the Steam Packet Board and the Directors were rather dismissive of the view of the Tourist Board. They decided to inform them that they had met with representatives of Douglas Town Council in February and had discussed with them their wish for Friday night sailings from Belfast but had explained to them the inability of the Steam Packet to provide them. They also resolved to tell the Tourist Board that the Steam Packet could see no evidence at all in support of their supposition concerning the increase in passengers from Belfast that they were suggesting.

Meanwhile Cammell Laird were continuing to pursue cost cutting measures in the construction of the new vessel. On 20 March 1954, the Steam Packet were told that the builders had sourced a cheaper quote than previously to supply the four horizontal sliding watertight doors which had been fitted to all the previous post war steamers. The original quote from Donkin and Co Ltd had been £1,460 but the new quote from the Westmoor Engineering Co was £1,034. As they fulfilled all the current regulations the Company decided to go with the cheaper quote *"... and thereby effect a saving of £426."* A similar question

occurred a month later when Cammell Laird once again had sourced a cheaper quote than previously for the control gear for the watertight doors. Originally the quote had been £4,161 but the cheaper one came out at £3,663. As the cheaper system fulfilled all current regulations, the Company sanctioned it.

The question of echometers for the passenger steamers was also raised at the meeting on 20 March. Captain Kinley was of the opinion that if radar was fitted to the vessels, then the usefulness of the echometers was limited and the annual rental and maintenance contract was £129. It was therefore decided not to fit one to the new steamer and the ones currently on **KING ORRY** and **MONA'S QUEEN** would be removed once the contract had expired.

The Company were informed on 1 May 1954 that a debit note for £165,000 had been received from Cammell Laird, this being the first instalment payable once the keel had been laid. As the Marine Superintendent had confirmed that the keel of the new steamer, vessel 1259, had indeed been laid the note was passed for payment. It was reported to the Steam Packet Board on 8 May 1954 that on the starboard high pressure turbine on **KING ORRY** serious damage had been discovered when preparing the vessel for survey. It was necessary to remove the complete rotor from the ship to the Cammell Laird engine shed and it was then decided that the whole row of blading needed to be replaced. Cost of this was between £400 and £500 but it was hoped the ship would return to service by 28 May. However she was in the wars again later in the season on 10 August. While on passage from Douglas to Liverpool *"...a heavy knock was heard at the stern and severe vibration was felt throughout the ship."* It was thought the problem was the starboard propeller and after various speeds were tried to lessen the vibration, she proceeded to Liverpool with the port engine full ahead and the starboard engine at dead slow. She was drydocked the next day at Birkenhead but very little damage was in fact found on the propeller apart from "...*some small marks at the root of the blades indicating that the propeller had had very recently contacted some hard object possibly the rope guard fitted on the stern tube boss - which was missing.*" The Superintendent Engineer, Mr Craine, was of the opinion that the rope guard had worked loose and hit the propeller and that had caused the problem. The shaft was undamaged. Once she came out of drydock on the Thursday 12 August she ran trials in the Mersey and all appeared to be in order.

The question of the name for the new steamer was first raised at a Board meeting at Douglas on 5 June 1954. After much discussion it was decided "*... that a final selection could best be made from either **MONA**, **MANXMAN** or **VIKING**. The English Directors views will be sought and they will be asked to submit any names which they have in mind.*"

At a further meeting on Wednesday 28 July 1954 it was resolved to name the new ship **MONA** and application be made to the appropriate authority. The Register General of Shipping informed the Company that the name **MONA** was not available for the new steamer. Thus on 4 September 1954 it was decided to name the new ship **MANXMAN**. No problems were anticipated with this name as an owner had "...*a retaining right to the name of a vessel for ten years after closing the registry and the previous **MANXMAN** was only disposed of in 1949.*"

The soon to be de-commissioned **VIKING** was in trouble on 30 June when she came into contact with a breakwater at Douglas, Captain Quirk in command. She was backing out of No 1 berth on Victoria Pier at 1605 hours on her way to Fleetwood and was almost at the outer end of the pier when "...*the vessel's stern took a sharp cant to port, the weather at the time being light to moderate westerly wind.*"

Although the engines were put full ahead she did not have time to get clear and the vessel's counter stern came into contact with the wooded piles on the Battery Pier. Damage included the stern being set back in two places, transom frames were buckled, wooden deck damaged and iron and teak wooden deck rails were set out of position. It was also found that the hand steering gear had been damaged. However damage was not sufficient to prevent the ship sailing. Repairs were necessary and she went to Birkenhead and was back in service for the 0100 hours sailing from Liverpool on Saturday 3 July. The repairs themselves were admitted to be of a temporary nature but "...*they will suffice during the remaining period of the vessel's service.*"

VIKING was also involved in a "*coming together*" with **BEN-MY-CHREE** at Fleetwood on 27 July. **BEN-MY-CHREE** was berthing at No 1 berth at Fleetwood at 2110 hours after completion of her 1800 hours sailing from Douglas during a strong westerly gale. The ship was swinging to the flood tide on the starboard anchor when it dragged and the port quarter of the ship hit the bow of **VIKING** which was moored at No 2 berth. **BEN-MY-**

CHREE had in fact come into contact with the starboard anchor of **VIKING** and "...*received some damage in the vicinity of No 4 Port in the 3rd class ladies cabin.*"

Meanwhile the Board on 10 July were told by Kellock & Co Ltd, the brokers for the Company, that they had been unsuccessful in finding a buyer for **VIKING** for further service. The broker was instructed to dispose of the vessel for breaking up if no offer for further service was forthcoming. On 17 July the Company was told that it was now possible to export vessels for scrapping as restrictions had been lifted and it was thought the scrap value of the old ship was about £16,000. The Board were informed later by the broker that a number of foreign buyers would inspect the ship during the third week of August but they were only interested in scrapping the vessel. It was decided all offers should be submitted by 31 August.

On 4 September 1954 it transpired that Belgian buyers had offered £26,100 for **VIKING** for the purpose of demolition subject to a permit from the Ministry of Transport. The offer from the British Iron and Steel Corporation was £14,000. The vessel was by this time lying at Barrow and it was decided to accept the Belgian offer without delay. Once the British Iron and Steel Corporation heard of the Belgian offer they put forward a plea to the Steam Packet to reconsider the sale to Belgium on patriotic grounds - and they increased their offer to £23,000. The Steam Packet Company informed their brokers that they saw no reason to accept the lower offer and were instructed to get the necessary permit from the Ministry of Transport for the sale of the ship to Belgium. The result of this was that the British Iron and Steel Corporation increased their offer to £25,700 which was nearly as much as the offer from Belgium. As the Ministry of Transport were unlikely to issue a permit for the vessel to be scrapped in Belgium because the British offer was nearly as good the Steam Packet felt they had no choice but to sell to the British Company. Subsequently the ship was allotted to T W Ward of Barrow where she was broken up.

*Above: **VIKING** (I) laid up at Barrow, 3 April 1948.*
Author's Collection

Although the fitting of radar to passenger vessels was beginning at this time to be seriously considered by most shipping companies the Isle of Man Steam Packet Company were still reluctant to commit fully to the new technology even though it had been fitted to **KING ORRY** and **MONA'S QUEEN**. On 24 August 1954 the directors were told that the new vessel had reached the stage of construction when it was necessary to ask whether the builders should fit heavier girders on the top of the fan room to support radar installation. The Board were loathe to commit to radar installation itself at this stage but thought it prudent to tell the builders to strengthen the fan room roof for possible installation at a later date as it was considered it would be cheaper to do it while under construction rather than at some future time. The Board were told on 18 September 1954 by the Marine Superintendent that the Admiralty were keen to stiffen the vessel by fitting girders and strengthening the plates in five places, one on each side of the Bridge, two on the promenade deck aft and one on the shelter deck aft, in case there was the need to place guns on board, and they also wanted to install degaussing gear around the inside of the hull. As the cost of these modifications was to be borne by the Admiralty the Board gave their formal approval.

On 2 October 1954 the Company were made aware of a letter from the Isle of Man Tourist Board to the effect that the new steamer could have a positive influence on visitor numbers if her entry into service was used for advertising. They suggested that she could be allowed to make visits to Manchester, Liverpool and Glasgow before entering service in 1955. The idea was "…*to put the steamer on exhibition, to which the general public would be invited to attend by means of press and poster advertising.*" If *MANXMAN* was not completed in time then it was suggested that one of the other newer steamers could be utilised. The Steam Packet themselves though were not very receptive to the ideas of the Tourist Board. They intended *MANXMAN* to enter service as soon as her trials had been successfully completed and "…*for that reason alone it would not be possible to arrange for the vessel to visit Manchester, Liverpool or Glasgow for publicity purposes.*" The Directors also took into account that to allow *MANXMAN* to carry out the suggested programme of events it would be necessary to bring another steamer into service three to four weeks earlier than normally would be the case. This would involve extra cost and the Tourist Board were told the whole idea was not feasible.

Preparations for the 1955 season, the first *MANXMAN* would be in service, were well in hand by 23 October 1954 when the following passenger services were approved:

Liverpool and Douglas double daily sailings:
Thursday 26 May to Monday 12 September
Fleetwood and Douglas service:
Monday 23 May to Monday 12 September
Ardrossan and Douglas:
Saturday 28 May to Saturday 10 September
Belfast and Douglas:
Thursday 2 June to Friday 9 September
Dublin and Douglas:
Thursday 9 June to Thursday 15 September
Heysham and Douglas:
Every Thursday from 7 July to 25 August inclusive

The Ardrossan sailings had been changed by substituting Saturday evening sailings from Ardrossan in place of the more traditional Sunday night sailings. After due

consideration at a later meeting on 6 November 1954 it was decided, after due representation from the Glasgow agents, to return to the Sunday evening sailings and so the season would run from Sunday 29 May to Monday 12 September. There were some alterations to sailing times from previous years. The departure time from Dublin went from 1700 to 1730 and on Saturdays the afternoon steamer from Fleetwood would leave at 1600 and not at 1530 as previously.

Cammell Laird were informed that Tuesday 8 February was the most suitable date for the launching of *MANXMAN*. Indeed just prior to the successful launch by Mrs Garside on 8 February the Company handed over the final instalment of £165,800 to Cammell Laird.

At a meeting in Douglas on 27 November the Board were asked to consider the implementation of day excursions to the Island from Fleetwood on a Sunday during the coming season. The idea had come from British Railways who gave assurances that special trains from selected stations in the north west of England would be scheduled and that through booking arrangements would be implemented "…*similar to what they are already doing in connection with the Liverpool and North Wales S.S. Co's Sunday trips.*" It was pointed out by the Manager, Mr Douglas, that there would already be a steamer lying in Fleetwood every weekend and "…*so would be available to take any Sunday sailings that may be arranged.*"

There was much discussion of this proposal and the passenger figures on this route on a Sunday from 1939, the last year they had been run, were produced and proved encouraging. It was agreed to go ahead and operate day excursion sailings on a Sunday from 3 July to 20 August inclusive at fares of 20/- first class and 16/- third class. Departure time from Fleetwood would be 1030 hours and from Douglas at 1715 hours. The only concern was overbooking as it would not be economic to use two steamers on this service and so it was decided to restrict availability of tickets to the complement of a *KING ORRY* type steamer.

The Company had agreed to fit radar of the British Thomson-Houston type, to the two winter vessels, *KING ORRY* and *MONA'S QUEEN* but not to any other ships of the fleet. However the matter was raised again on Thursday 9 December 1954 when the Chairman asked the other Directors to consider fitting radar to the new steamer *MANXMAN* as well as to *MONA'S ISLE*, *SNAEFELL* and *TYNWALD*, leaving *LADY OF MANN* and *BEN-MY-CHREE* to a later date. Surprisingly, given previous attitudes other directors did not like the idea of leaving the latter two ships out if radar was to be installed on the other ships. The General Manager reported that fitting radar on all the other passenger steamers except for *VICTORIA*, would cost in the region of £6,000, while "…*apparatus supplied by the British Thomson-Houston Co Ltd, similar to that already on the two winter ships, would on a hire/maintenance basis cost about £2,200 per annum after allowing for rebates in respect of lay-up periods.*"

Realising that this new technology would be of great benefit the Company decided to fit radar to all of the passenger ships apart from **VICTORIA** but radar was not considered for the cargo vessels **FENELLA**, **PEVERIL** and **CONISTER**.

On 9 March 1955 **MONA'S QUEEN** suffered severe damage to her Port Oil Fuel Settling Tank during cleaning and steaming out which cost around £500 to put right. The Chief Engineer was held responsible although the donkeyman was also reprimanded for not concentrating on his job sufficiently. On 24 March she damaged her shell plating while being towed through the bridges leading to the Morpeth Dock, Birkenhead, in a strong westerly wind. The plating was dented in the third class dining saloon and forward boiler room on the port side. Repairs were subsequently carried out. On 7 April while she was being towed out of Cammell Laird's Graving Dock No 5 by the tug **ALFRED LAMEY**, **MONA'S QUEEN** fell heavily on the dock pier head on the north side, denting the shell plating and two frames on the starboard bow by the stewardesses' accommodation. Three days later on 10 April she was lying on the south berth at Princes Landing Stage overnight. At around mid-night the Wallasey ferry **ROYAL DAFFODIL II** in taking up the berth ahead of **MONA'S QUEEN** backed into her, "*...the edge of the top deck of the ferry aft coming into contact with the stem of MONA'S QUEEN on a level with the forecastle deck head.*" There was some slight damage to **ROYAL DAFFODIL II** in that woodwork at the edge of the top deck aft was affected and a stanchion on the deck was also damaged. There appeared to be no damage to **MONA'S QUEEN**. However the cargo vessel **PEVERIL** was moored at the cargo berth at Coburg Dock, Liverpool when she was struck, on 9 April by the tug **MOORCOCK** and damage was sustained to one plate on the starboard bow, below the main belting. Repairs were to cost about £300 at her next refit, but the tug owners agreed liability. In addition on 25 April **FENELLA** sustained damage to her starboard forward derrick gear and winch while company fitters were making some adjustments and somebody accidently left the steering motor switched on. This resulted in a bent derrick which had to be replaced with a spare one the Company had in stock and with repairs to the motor and winch the costs came to £170.

After her successful launch on 8 February 1955 the progress of **MANXMAN** to completion had been carefully monitored by the Steam Packet Company. On 7 May it was envisaged that sea trials of the new vessel would take place from 11 to 13 May. Details of her formal registration were also confirmed as well as her ownership and Mr Andrew Clarke, General Manager of the Isle of Man Steam Packet Company was appointed formally as manager of the steamship under Seal. Her marine and war risk insurance was also calculated at £830,000.

The results of the sea trials were formally reported to the Board on 21 May 1955. A mean speed of 20.9 knots was attained at full power on the last of three double runs over the measured mile at Skelmorlie. Although this was lower than expected, and lower than that of her older sisters, the Board chose to take into consideration several mitigating factors. The weather conditions had been poor, with a strong WSW wind, of about 32 knots with a moderate sea. Owing to a strike of tug boat personnel the ship had not been drydocked to enable the underwater portion of the hull to be cleaned and painted while a number of lugs used in connection with the launch had not been removed. All these factors were considered to have had an adverse effect on the speed of the ship and so it was decided that the trials had been satisfactory. After bow rudder tests had been completed, stern running and stopping and starting trials accomplished, **MANXMAN** proceeded on a full power five hour endurance trial at 20.5 knots with engine revolutions of 273 per minute. This trial was considered to have been efficient and satisfactory.

MANXMAN drydocked at Cammell Laird on 13 May and several minor adjustments and modifications were carried out on deck and in the engine room while several parts of the main engines were opened up for examination and found to be satisfactory. The bottom of the ship was also found to be in good condition and the underwater part of the hull was cleaned and painted and the offending lugs removed. In the opinion of both Steam Packet Superintendents the building of the vessel "*...has been carried out with the requirements of the Contract.*"

Above: **MANXMAN**'s *(II) maiden voyage was on 21 May 1955 from Douglas to Liverpool. However the day before, 20 May 1955 she had sailed light from Liverpool to Douglas and that is pictured above and below. The photographs were taken from* **TYNWALD** *(V).*

Author's Collection

MANXMAN was handed over by her builders to the Isle of Man Steam Packet Company at Birkenhead on Saturday 14 May 1955 at 1000 hours.

MANXMAN IN SERVICE IN 1960 AND 1964

The year 1960 was typical of the early service of **MANXMAN** with the Isle of Man Steam Packet Company. **MANXMAN** at this time was the regular winter steamer along with **KING ORRY**.

New Year's day, 1960, **MANXMAN** departed Douglas for Liverpool at 0903 hours. There was a light north north westerly wind blowing, the sea was slight and it was a fine and clear day. She was off the Bar lightship at 1147 hours, passed the Rock at 1226 hours and berthed at the Princes Landing Stage at 1245 hours. There were 66 passengers on board. They were made up of:

3 first class singles
7 second class singles
18 first class returns
38 second class returns

Receipts for the voyage were:
Passengers   £50-16s-6d
Parcels   £10-18s-2d

From New Year's Day to Monday 7 March the sailings were quite routine. She did 30 sailings from Douglas to Liverpool and the same in the opposite direction. Tuesday 8 March however was a little more interesting. There was a very strong south easterly wind blowing and the seas were rough. She disembarked her passengers from Liverpool at Douglas and then it was decided to take the ship out of Douglas harbour because of the worsening conditions. This of course was in the days before the Battery Pier extension. **MANXMAN** departed Douglas at 1619 hours and made her way to Langness to seek shelter. She anchored off Langness at 1746

hours. The next morning, Wednesday 9 March, she left the anchorage at 0727 hours and sailed round to the shelter of Peel where she arrived to take on passengers. Departing Peel at 0943 hours she was off the Bar at 1425 hours and berthed at Liverpool at 1526 hours, taking over five and a half hours for the passage. The seas were very rough, there was an east south easterly gale blowing and the visibility was only moderate. The ship was able to resume normal sailings to Douglas the next day and settled down to the usual pattern until 19 March, a Saturday, when she was once again diverted to Peel as Douglas was untenable because of the gale force easterly wind. **MANXMAN**'s final sailing of the winter season was Friday 1 April from Douglas to Liverpool after which she went to lay up at Birkenhead and refit. She had done 81 sailings so far in 1960.

Above: **MANXMAN** (II) dressed overall at Liverpool on 28 May 1960.

Author's Collection

Above: **MANXMAN** (II) with Captain Quirk on the Bridge, in the River Mersey on 20 July 1959 on her way to Douglas with the 1030 sailing. The Mersey Ferry **WALLASEY** is taking an interest.

Author's Collection

MANXMAN returned to service on Saturday 28 May, departing Liverpool at 1503 hours on her way to Douglas. Between 28 May and 30 September she did the following sailings:

On the Liverpool-Douglas route there were 34 sailings in total. On two occasions, 28 and 30 September, she was diverted to Peel
On Douglas-Liverpool there were 32 sailings. On one occasion, 29 September, the departure was from Peel not Douglas
On the Fleetwood-Douglas route there were 24 sailings in both directions and the first Fleetwood sailing was on Tuesday 31 May
The Douglas-Belfast service saw 8 sailings in both directions. The first Belfast sailing was on 2 June
On the Douglas-Heysham route there was only one sailing but the Heysham-Douglas service saw two sailings. The first Heysham sailing was on 6 June
Douglas-Ardrossan totalled 4 sailings in both directions and the first Ardrossan sailing was on 18 June
On the Douglas-Dublin route there was only one sailing in either direction and this sailing rotation was on 29 June
Ramsey-Liverpool saw just one sailing. This was a special sailing taking a large number of London Cadets back to the UK

There were seven charter sailings all told in 1960, some single sailings and some return. These included:

The Dance Teachers' Association from Heysham on 6 June
The Jacobs charter to Dublin on 11 June
The Christian Endeavour charter to Belfast on 14 July
The Workington Town Band on 1 August
The Hawks Shaw charter from Fleetwood to Belfast and back on 9 September

There were 14 light sailings during the summer period, mainly positioning after charters.

MANXMAN did lay-up at Vittoria Wharf, Birkenhead for routine maintenance between the 30 August and 7 September.

The autumn sailings in 1960 started at Peel on 1 October and on the 2nd the gales once again forced her to Peel but from 3 October the weather settled down and there were no more diversions. Up to 31 December the ship did 39 sailings from Douglas and 39 from Liverpool which included Christmas Day, a Sunday. On board that day were 155 passengers. The ship departed Liverpool at 1304 hours, passed the Bar at 1406 hours and arrived in Douglas at 1820 hours, a journey time of nearly 5 hours 20 minutes. The sea was very rough and there was a West North Westerly gale force wind blowing.

The total number of Liverpool to Douglas sailings in 1960 was 112, while she did 111 in the opposite direction. There were 4 sailings out of Peel and 4 sailings into Peel.

It is interesting to examine the number and type of sailings of an Isle of Man Steam Packet vessel during a week in high summer, in this case beginning on Sunday 19 July in 1964 and the vessel being **MANXMAN**.

On Sunday 19 July she departed Ardrossan at 1220 hours and was off Ailsa Craig at 1340 hours, off the Point of Ayre at 1656 hours and arrived at Douglas at 1812 hours.

There was a moderate northerly wind, a slight sea, it was overcast but clear. There were 942 passengers on board.

She had a day off on Monday 20 July berthed at Victoria Pier Douglas but on Tuesday 21 July she departed Douglas at 0601 hours and was off the Great Orme at 0844 hours to arrive at Llandudno Pier sixteen minutes later. This was a light sailing. She departed Llandudno at 1025 hours to arrive back at Douglas at 1306 hours. There was a light wind, smooth sea, with very clear visibility and there were 735 passengers on board.

On Wednesday 22 July she departed Douglas at 0900 hours and was off the Liverpool Bar at 1143 hours to arrive at the Princes Landing Stage just under an hour later. The sea had been calm, overcast but clear and there was a light variable wind. There were 185 passengers on board. She departed Liverpool again at 1540 hours and passed the Liverpool Bar at 1631 hours to arrive in Douglas at 1919 hours. There was by now a moderate north westerly wind, a slight sea, still cloudy but clear. There were 168 passengers on board.

She was back off to North Wales on Thursday 23 July departing Douglas at 0932 hours and arrived at Llandudno at 1221 hours. The wind was light and variable, the sea was calm and it was overcast but clear and 263 passengers enjoyed the sail. She left Llandudno at 1906 hours and arrived back at Douglas at 2159 hours. There was now a west north westerly wind and a slight sea but it was still clear and cloudy.

MANXMAN had a busy day on Friday 24 July. She departed Douglas at 0832 hours and called at the Queen's Pier, Ramsey at 0921 hours departing from there just under twenty minutes later. She arrived at Belfast at 1330 hours. There was a moderate north westerly wind, the sea was calm and it was overcast and clear. There were 1,374 passengers on board of which 51 were day returns. 165 passengers boarded at Ramsey. She left Belfast at 1702 hours and called once again at the Queen's Pier, Ramsey at 2038 hours. She was only there nine minutes and arrived back at Douglas at 2143 hours. There was by now a fresh south westerly wind blowing and a moderate to rough sea had developed. It was cloudy but clear visibility. There were 436 passengers on board of which 90 had disembarked at Ramsey. Her day however was not yet finished as she had a light sailing to Liverpool to do. She departed Douglas for the Mersey and arrived at the Princes Landing Stage at 0118 hours. By this time there was a fresh strong south south westerly wind and a moderate sea.

She had sailed light to Liverpool so that on Saturday 25 July she could take the 0730 hours sailing back to Douglas, She departed Liverpool eight minutes late, passed the Liverpool Bar at 0836 hours and berthed back at Douglas at 1135 hours. There was a moderate southerly wind with a moderate sea and swell. It was cloudy, clear with frequent showers and there were 1,775 passengers on board. It was another busy day for **MANXMAN**. She was back out of Douglas at 1501 hours and was off the Point of Ayre at 1604 hours. There was no call at Ramsey on this occasion. She passed Ailsa Craig at 1910 hours to arrive at Ardrossan at 2031 hours. There were light variable breezes, a calm sea and it was fine and clear. 1,094 passengers enjoyed the sail.

Above: **MANXMAN** *(II) arriving at Douglas in a fresh breeze at 1300 on 11 August 1965, with an 0930 sailing from Liverpool, Captain McMeiken in command.*

Author's Collection

VACILLATIONS WITH *VICTORIA*

Once **MANXMAN** was in service during 1955 it is generally considered that the post war rebuilding programme of the fleet was complete. However there were of course many observers at the time who considered **MANXMAN** to be obsolete before she was launched and with the benefit of many years of hindsight they probably had a reasonable argument. The future conveyance of cars to the Island was already causing concern, even in 1955, and it has been argued that **MANXMAN** should have been designed as a car ferry. The lack of linkspans at any of the ports she would serve was of course the major reason she was built as she was and this difficulty was to plague the Steam Packet until the late 1970s, despite the development of the four famous "*side-loaders.*" The other criticism of **MANXMAN** made at the time and indeed since, is the fact that she was a steamer and not equipped with more economical oil engines. All these considerations and more would be revisited when the time came to continue the modernisation of the Steam Packet fleet towards the end of the 1950s.

However, even as **MANXMAN** finished her first summer season in 1955, the Company were wrestling with the problem of what to do with **VICTORIA**. On Saturday 7 January 1956 the General Manager drew the Board's attention to the Marine Superintendent's recent reports considering the condition of **VICTORIA**. Her Load Line Certificate was due to expire in June 1957 and it was "*… the view of both Superintendents extensive repairs and renewals will be necessary to enable the vessel to continue in the Company's service thereafter*". The Board were reminded that the last full survey of **VICTORIA** had cost some £24,000 and the next one could be in excess of £40,000. As she had been built in 1907 it was considered too much of an outlay on a vessel of her age and approval was given for the General Manager, Mr Douglas, to his "*…making enquiries through Messrs C.W.Kellock & Co Ltd, the Company's brokers, to ascertain if there is a suitable second hand steamer of a more recent age than our vessel, on offer for sale…*". The Company therefore was still thinking of passenger only tonnage and the possibility of another new build was not now being considered, unsurprising really, given that they had built six ships in eleven years. It is also interesting to see that although new tonnage was the norm post war, they would still consider the possibility of purchasing a ship second hand, as they had done, in abundance, after the First World War.

On Saturday 14 January a report from the brokers to the Steam Packet Board concerning the prospects of acquiring a ship to replace **VICTORIA**, was not very hopeful. They informed the Board that most shipowners at the time were not sellers until their vessels were past their prime but they said they would continue to be vigilant. They did in fact furnish the Board of the particulars of passenger vessels on their books, "*…one of which was the former steamer **WORTHING** sold by the British Transport Commission to buyers in Greece last year.*" Whether the Board felt that they could "*hijack*" this sale to Greece of **WORTHING** is unclear but they requested the brokers to furnish plans of this vessel for their inspection.

Meanwhile, as the Board at the beginning of 1956 was wrestling with the usual business of fare increases, charter rates, insurance and audited accounts and the usual incidents at sea continued to cause them concern. For example they were told by Captain L Callow that at 2100 hours on Saturday 28 January **PEVERIL**, while anchored in dense fog of the south end of Woodside ferry stage having left Douglas at noon, was hit by the Everard owned vessel **AUSPICITY**, which caused extensive damage to **PEVERIL** in the port bow area above the water line. There was a large hole between Frame No 1 and the stem and "*…an indent in the shell plate, while the internal structure of the vessel had also sustained damage*". The vessel managed to enter Coburg Dock later to discharge her cargo and then proceeded to dry dock for repairs at Birkenhead, where it was decided to take the opportunity to carry out her annual overhaul. The likely cost was in excess of £600. Later it transpired that a large number of hull plates on **PEVERIL** had had to be replaced, not all of them connected with the incident with **AUSPICITY**. It had also been found during the cleaning of the boiler that there was "*…an excessive leakage of water at rivet heads around the furnace plating and examination had shown that cracks extended between all rivets. A new ring plate was needed, the fitting of which would extend the refit time by about two weeks which meant the Company may have had to consider the chartering of a vessel for a round trip between Liverpool and Ramsey to deal with cargo waiting to be shipped.*"

*Above: **PEVERIL** (II) leaving Douglas on 18 May 1961.*
Ships of Mann Collection

Meanwhile, Kellocks, the brokers, had informed the Company that there was no suitable second hand tonnage on offer to replace **VICTORIA** so at a Full Board Meeting at Douglas on 28 February 1956 much discussion took place about the way forward. It was agreed that to build a new vessel, which would cost over £1million could not be justified and the Brokers were asked to redouble their efforts. However it was also decided to take a look at how much it would cost to keep **VICTORIA** in service for a further four years after her Load Line Certificate expired in June 1957.

The Company were still offering **VICTORIA** to charter parties for the 1956 season. There had been a possible charter for her from Garlieston to Douglas on Saturday 7 July and a charter fee of £950 had been quoted. This had been rejected as too expensive, but anxious to secure the business the Company decided to offer her at a basic rate of £750 rising to £950 only on a sliding scale of passenger numbers carried.

*Above: **VICTORIA** berths at Liverpool ahead of Cunard's MEDIA in July 1956.*

John Collins

The Steam Packet Board of Directors were informed on 28 April 1956 that Kellocks had been advised that the British Transport Commission had sold the trio of Heysham to Belfast steamers, **DUKE OF ARGYLL**, **DUKE OF LANCASTER** and **DUKE OF ROTHESAY** to Greek interests but the sale had fallen through. The Steam Packet was advised that **DUKE OF ROTHESAY** might be a suitable replacement for **VICTORIA** (why her and not the other two is not disclosed) even though some re-construction work would be necessary. The Company decided to thoroughly inspect the vessel at Heysham with a view to her purchase. However it was reported on 12 May that all three "*Dukes*" had been disposed of and so the much anticipated inspection, arranged for 14 May, would not now take place.

On Saturday 26 May at a meeting in Douglas grave concern was expressed at the condition of a large number of plates mainly around the water line and they would have to be replaced, or doubled if the surveyors would permit, if **VICTORIA** was to receive her passenger certificate for the 1956 season, which was not far away. It would not be

possible to have the ship ready for her scheduled sailings over the TT Race period and the surveyors had more or less pointed out that **VICTORIA** would not be granted another passenger certificate after the 1956 season. The ship was needed for the coming season and the work on her to enable her to get her passenger certificate had to be carried out but her future was to be discussed at a later date. The Directors decided to listen to "*… the views of the Surveyors…regarding the granting of future certificates.*"

There was a further attempt, reported to the Board on 7 July 1956, to rekindle interest in the possibility of buying **DUKE OF ROTHESAY**. An approach was made by the brokers to the British Transport Commission because the sale of the three "*Dukes*" to the British Iron & Steel Corporation for scrapping had been put back because of the delay in the delivery of their replacements. However it was made clear that there was no chance of a re-sale and all were destined for the breakers. An attempt to persuade the British Transport Commission to consider selling **ST ANDREW** was also rejected as they had no intention of selling that particular vessel then or indeed in the near future. There is no doubt that the brokers, were doing their very best to find a suitable ship to replace **VICTORIA**, but were making very little progress with the matter. On 27 July 1956 **VICTORIA**, while lying at the breakwater at Douglas "*…a fracture occurred in the steam pipe serving the forward capstans and bow rudder and these could not be used until temporary repairs were affected…*" This had occurred at about 0445 hours but the necessary repairs were done in time for her to take her sailing to Belfast at 0830 hours although more repairs were necessary while she lay over in Belfast. A new pipe was fitted after the completion of her weekend sailings.

In any event on Saturday 11 August 1956 both the Marine and Engineering Superintendents were asked by the Chairman to give their views about the future of **VICTORIA** to the Board. Neither of the Superintendents could ascertain at this stage how much work would be necessary to retain the ship for another four years but both agreed that no matter how much was spent, and it would appear that repairs would have to be extensive, the Company would still be left with a very old ship. Captain Kinley was also concerned about the stability of the ship and stated "*…he was not in favour of her sailing during bad weather and felt very strongly that she should be disposed of at the end of the season.*" Mr Craine, the Engineering Superintendent, also was in favour of her being disposed of but if there was any chance of her being retained she would have to be examined by surveyors from the Regulatory Authority. The General Manager agreed with his colleagues that if a suitable replacement could be found then **VICTORIA** should be disposed of "*…but it would not be possible to maintain the present schedule of sailings if only eight vessels are available.*" He felt she should be examined by the surveyors and it might be better to spend the money on her rather than buy and have to spend a considerable sum of money converting a second hand vessel to the Company's requirements.

Once again the Board of Directors put off the decision about what to do with **VICTORIA**. They realised there was a dearth of suitable second hand tonnage available but clung to the hope that one might turn up. They even revisited the idea of rescuing **DUKE OF ROTHESAY** from the clutches of the shipbreaker's torch or perhaps any other suitable vessel about to be broken up. The British Iron & Steel Corporation were once again to be approached as to a possible sale. Meanwhile **VICTORIA** herself was to be laid up at Birkenhead at the end of her 1956 season.

On Saturday 25 August 1956 it was realised that buying a ship from the clutches of the breakers was not a possibility as the British Iron & Steel Corporation were not empowered to sell on any ship sold to themselves for the purpose of scrapping to any other Company for further service. However at the same meeting the Board was told that the former railway steamer **WORTHING** which had been sold to Greek interests the year before was now no longer any use to the Greek Company that bought her and might prove suitable for the Steam Packet after all. The Board decided "*... to ask the British Transport Commission for a sight of the plans of WORTHING and if they are prepared to disclose the price which they obtained for the vessel when disposed of to the Greek buyers.*"

It turned out that **WORTHING** had been sold to the Greeks for £75,000. They had made some alterations to the vessel such as increasing her bunker capacity and the plans of the vessel were forwarded to the two Manx Superintendents at the beginning of September 1956. It was decided to pursue the matter further and it was ascertained that the ship was now called **PHRYNI** and was lying at Piraeus. Discreet enquiries were to be made into what alterations had been made to the ship and what her general condition was like. Representation was to be made to the Shell Mex representative at Piraeus to see what he could find out. It was decided later to instruct the brokers Kellock and Co Ltd to arrange for a private general inspection of the former **WORTHING** by Lloyds and a full report be submitted as early as possible. However Lloyds informed the Steam Packet that it was not possible for them to inspect a vessel at the behest of a prospective buyer - their rules simply did not allow it.

Meanwhile at a meeting in Liverpool of surveyors the Steam Packet's Superintendents enquired as to the possibility of **VICTORIA** being given a new passenger certificate for 1957 and beyond but that possibility had been greeted with great concern by the Surveyors at the meeting. It was learnt that there would have to be a complete inspection and examination of the vessel, "*... places which had not been disturbed heretofore would have to be opened up and it might well mean that some £400,000/£500,000 would have to be expended to bring the VICTORIA up to the Ministry's requirements.*"

The Steam Packet Board of Directors were told on 27 October 1956 that as **WORTHING** had left the British register when she had been sold to the Greeks, she had lost all her dispensations granted to her over the years and they would no longer apply to her. For the purposes of re-registering her as a British vessel she would be looked upon as new which would mean she would have to undergo extensive and extremely expensive alterations before she could enter service again under the British flag. To compound the issue because of a large number of complaints received concerning the overcrowding on Irish Cross Channel steamers during the 1956 season, the Ministry of Transport were planning new rules and regulations which would inevitably result in all passenger steamers having their passenger certificates reduced to the number of fixed seating accommodation available, which would certainly have a very great adverse effect on a steamer the age of **VICTORIA**. The Board of the Steam Packet finally, after all this disturbing news, decided that **VICTORIA** would have to be withdrawn and the purchase of **WORTHING** was also out of the question. However they still had the problem of not enough steamers available for the peak periods of the 1957 season.

*Above: **VICTORIA** turns in the Mersey in June 1953.*
Author's Collection

One solution to this problem, suggested on 27 October 1956 at the Board Meeting in Douglas was "*... to explore the possibility of chartering the Liverpool & North Wales steamer ST TUDNO for certain Fridays and Saturdays during the season to take the sailings hitherto carried out by VICTORIA.*" Captain Kinley was of the opinion that **ST TUDNO** would be a suitable vessel for Steam Packet service.

*Above: **ST. TUDNO** (II) off the pier at Llandudno in August 1958.*
John Coates

Board Members realised that chartering **ST TUDNO** could only be a temporary measure and they understood that *"…all indications pointed to consideration having to be given to the placing of an order for a new vessel."* It was agreed to put this item, and the final disposal of **VICTORIA**, on the agenda of the next full Board Meeting to be held in Douglas in December 1956. However before this, on 17 November the Board were informed by the General Manager that the Liverpool & North Wales Steamship Company were of the opinion that **ST TUDNO** had been built far too *"stiff"* and they considered she would not be suitable for Steam Packet service and under no circumstances would they charter her for service to the Isle of Man. It was known that **ST TUDNO** was not a good sea-boat and rolled disconcertingly in any sort of swell or beam sea. Her shallow draft at just 9 feet, which was to allow her to navigate the Menai Strait at low water was most likely the cause of this problem. She had been deemed unsuitable as an armed boarding vessel by the Admiralty in October 1939 because of her tendency to roll and she spent most of the war as an accommodation ship at Stangate Creek, Sheerness.

Above: **ST. SEIRIOL** *(II) berthed at the King Edward Pier at Douglas on 26 August 1959.* **TYNWALD** *is on the other side of the pier.*

Author's Collection

The North Wales Company however were prepared to charter out their **ST SEIRIOL** (1,500 passengers) for Saturdays during July and August though the ship would not be available for the TT Race period. The cost to the Steam Packet would be £400 per trip, but might increase if there was an increase in the cost of fuel oil or crew wages within national agreements. Port charges and passenger tolls were to be paid by the charterer but catering and bar receipts were to go to the owners. There was a snag also in that the ship's passenger certificate was limited to daylight sailings only which would preclude her taking the Friday night sailing from Liverpool to Douglas - an exemption would have to be applied for. The charter of **ST SEIRIOL** would be for eight double trips between Liverpool and Douglas. Despite the difficulties it was agreed to accept the charter terms of the North Wales Company. It was also agreed that no useful purpose could be achieved by postponing a decision on the future of **VICTORIA** any longer and so it was decided she should be sold for scrapping as soon as possible. Kellocks & Co Ltd were instructed to find a buyer.

At a full Board Meeting held at Douglas on Thursday 6 December 1956 the question of new tonnage was discussed at length and every Director was invited to give his view on the matter. The General Manager warned the Board that the new regulations likely to be enforced by the Ministry of Transport regarding passenger numbers on short sea vessels would *"…almost certainly lead to a reduction in the carrying capacities of our steamers and so increase the present difficulties experienced handling passengers on Saturdays."*

He pointed out that the absence of **VICTORIA** in 1957 created a *"… situation which could only be overcome by either the purchase of a suitable second hand vessel or the building of new tonnage."* He also drew the attention of the Board to the fact that while the chartering of **ST SEIRIOL** for the coming season was useful it could only be regarded as a temporary measure and as she was a one class vessel only she could *"… only be used for the conveyance of 2nd class passengers and in conjunction with one of our own steamers…although if it is possible to charter for a further year or two it would help to ease the situation temporarily."*

The problem for the Steam Packet was two-fold. They would dearly have liked to buy a second hand steamer but none were available and the financial situation of the Company precluded the ordering of new tonnage. It was therefore decided to defer the question of new tonnage for twelve months but should a suitable second hand vessel become available it would be given immediate attention.

The best offer received for **VICTORIA** it transpired had come from Van Heyghen Frères of Ghent, who had purchased **RUSHEN CASTLE** in 1946. They had offered £42,700 for the old ship, a price which included the 80 tons of fuel oil still on board. The ship did have a seaworthy certificate for towing. Interestingly the lowest bid was from the British Iron & Steel Corporation who had only offered £26,000 and the Steam Packet would have had to remove the fuel oil themselves. It is thus unsurprising that the Company accepted the offer from the Belgians. A week later the Board were informed that the Ministry of Transport were unable to grant an export license for **VICTORIA** to Belgium because the British Iron & Steel Corporation had decided to match their offer. The brokers were thus instructed to draw up a new contract with the British Company which matched the one agreed with Van Heyghen Frères. On 19 January 1957 the Directors were informed that the brokers, C W Kellock & Co Ltd had received a deposit for the ship and they were instructed to proceed with the full sale. The ship herself was allotted by the purchasers to T W Ward Ltd of Barrow-in-Furness, where she arrived for breaking up on Friday 25 January 1957. Remarkably the ship was in her fiftieth year, had served extensively on the English Channel when first built, had served through two world wars and at the end of World War Two she had worked on the Calais - Dover troop ship service for two years, as well as, of course, serving the Steam Packet for nearly thirty years.

A SETTLED FLEET AND THE DEMISE OF FLEETWOOD

The Steam Packet fleet in 1957 thus appeared settled at eight passenger vessels and three cargo ships. The insurance values and masters were:

LADY OF MANN	£362,000 (G R Kinley)
BEN-MY-CHREE	£282,000 (P J Bridson)
MANXMAN	£932,000 (W H Crellin)
MONA'S ISLE	£802,000 (J E Quirk)
SNAEFELL	£687,000 (R Clucas)
TYNWALD	£653,000 (L Callow)
MONA'S QUEEN	£621,000 (W E McMeiken)
KING ORRY	£621,000 (R E Gelling)
FENELLA	£231,000 (F Griffin)
PEVERIL	£50,000 (J D Craine)
CONISTER	£15,000 (A W G Kissack)

The author's first sailing to the Isle of Man, as a six year old boy, was in 1957. It was on Monday 29 July on the 1530 sailing from Liverpool to Douglas on board **TYNWALD**. The master he thus sailed with was Captain L Callow. It is interesting to note an incident involving **TYNWALD** on 24 May. Captain Clucas, who was Master of **TYNWALD** during the early part of the season, reported to the Board of Directors on Saturday 1 June that as the ship was backing away from No 1 berth on Victoria Pier at 1700 heading for Fleetwood, "*...with a strong N.E. wind prevailing, the vessels starboard quarter belting came into contact with the pier, setting in the shell plating on the starboard side abreast the fireman's quarters and 2nd class lounge and buckling the frames.*" Repairs were estimated at £280 but would not be effected until **TYNWALD**'s next overhaul the following winter. It is safe to say that the young six year old boy boarding the ship less than three months later did not notice the damage!

Captain Lyndhurst Callow was one of the most highly respected of the post war Steam Packet masters. He had started with the Company as a seaman during the season in the 1920s but was appointed a Second Officer in 1928. When the war began he was Chief Officer of **VICTORIA** but before Dunkirk transferred to **MANXMAN** where his ship, as well as Dunkirk, took part in evacuations from Cherbourg and St. Malo. In 1946 he had been appointed as Master of **CONISTER** and then worked his way up through the fleet before becoming Commodore in 1969 and 1970, flying his burgee in **LADY OF MANN**.

Above: **TYNWALD** (V) leaving Fleetwood for Douglas in August 1958.

Author's Collection

Above: **BEN-MY-CHREE** (IV) berthed on the King Edward Pier, Douglas on 19 July 1956.

Author's Collection

At a meeting on Saturday 13 December 1958 the Directors were informed of the new regulations pertaining to passenger vessels concerning the number of seats available on vessels. To simplify a complicated situation, basically the Ministry of Transport wanted all passengers to have a seat available. A survey of the Steam Packet ships showed that the situation current at the end of 1958 was worrying. **MANXMAN** had a passenger certificate previously of 2,393 persons but fixed seating for only 1,759. All other vessels were similarly affected. The situation could be resolved by supplying the vessels with extra deck chairs up to the number required but otherwise the capacity of all the steamers would be drastically reduced which would cause serious problems at peak sailing times. The extra deck chairs were problematical as they would take up valuable space and "*...seriously encroach upon the limited space presently available to those desirous of walking around during the passage.*" However, more encouragingly it appeared that the Ministry were prepared to grant exemptions if the surveyors concluded that if an increase in seats is "*...not readily practicable no reduction in passenger numbers will be made...*"

The new regulations would not apply at all to ships over 25 years old so **LADY OF MANN** and **BEN-MY-CHREE**. were exempt However there was still concern about this matter despite the possibility of the exemptions and the Company decided to inform the Ministry through Mr Roy Hill of the Liverpool Ship Owners Association, that "*... our vessels are constructed on the lines of pleasure steamers and that a large proportion of our passengers prefer to walk around on the open decks.*"

If the regulations were not to be modified the Company would have to severely restrict the pleasure its passengers got from the open deck facility or they would have to severely decrease passenger numbers on all ships, both of which were highly undesirable.

Above: **LADY OF MANN** (I) goes astern off the Landing Stage at Liverpool at 1600 on 19 June 1965. Captain Callow is in command.

Author's Collection

The regulations also stated that "*...in no case may motor vehicles be carried in covered spaces measured for passengers, or in sheltered spaces set apart for passengers without prior approval from the Ministry... that spaces set apart exclusively for the carriage of motor vehicles must not be included in the spaces measured for passengers.*" If the Ministry did not give their approval for exemptions, the Company would not be able to transport motor vehicles on its passenger steamers in the future.

Meanwhile by early in the year 1959 concern was being expressed at the future of the port of Fleetwood in relation to sailings to the Isle of Man.

On 7 March 1959 the Directors were informed that although the current berths at Fleetwood would be usable for the 1959 season there was no guarantee they would be usable after that. Current repairs to the berths were to cost £18,000 but there was a limit to the repairs that could be carried out. The owners of the port, British Transport Commission were losing up to £100,000 per year operating the port. The cost of building two new concrete berths with appropriate fenders would cost in excess of £700,000 while a new dredger capable of coping with future difficulties at the port would cost £500,000 to build and £70,000 per annum to operate. Sir Robert Letch, Chairman of the British Transport Commission, was intimating that the port of Fleetwood might have to close to Isle of Man traffic although he was told by the Company of the importance of the route both to the Steam Packet and the Isle of Man in general. Sir Robert had also asked whether the Isle of Man Government might be able to help with the costs necessary to keep the port open and the Steam Packet Board decided to approach the Government to ascertain their view. Discussions on all this continued throughout the rest of the summer of 1959 but the Fleetwood service was included in the 1960 timetable.

The possibility of new tonnage was finally discussed with a positive outcome at a full Board Meeting in Douglas on 3 December 1959. A report had been prepared by the General Manager, Mr A J Fick and his staff and furnished to the Board some days previously, which dealt at some length with the difficulties of conveying cars on the passenger steamers, especially with imminent new regulations. The Board were also worried as to "*...the possible intervention by other concerns interested in the car ferry business.*" The figures for the carriage of motor vehicles since 1953 indicated a steady growth in this sort of traffic. The Board "*...accepted the principle that a passenger/car ferry (with accommodation for, say, 1,400 passengers and 60/70 cars) is undoubtedly necessary although it was recognised that within the next few years the trend of visitors to the Island towards air travel may be such as to necessitate consideration being given to the possible disposal of a unit of our present fleet.*"

The Superintendents and Management were instructed to consult on the type and design of the proposed new vessel and submit their proposals to the Board in due course.

As the Company officials pondered what, for them, would be a revolutionary vessel, the current vessels which they were very familiar with continued to give them plenty to be concerned about. **MANXMAN** had, on 16 January 1959, been in collision with the motor vessel **SEAMEW** in the Mersey but Bateson's & Co, solicitors acting for the Company, had been unable to ascertain the views of the **SEAMEW**'s owners, General Steam Navigation Company of London regarding blame for the collision, and as time was going on, thought it best to try and bring things to a head. The ship was on charter to Moss Hutchison of Liverpool at the time of the incident. An independent witness had been found, an officer on duty at the Wallasey Ferries Radar Establishment who saw the collision occur at 1250 hours although those on **MANXMAN** stated the incident occurred at 1310 hours. The witness stated that **SEAMEW** was stationary to the east of mid-river as **MANXMAN** "...*shaped to pass her port to port and then ported so as to bring about the collision.*" Batesons did not regard the evidence with much enthusiasm but it was the only independent view of the affair who fixed the time and position of the accident. Those on **MANXMAN** and **SEAMEW** "...*being unable to state definitely because no fixed object were in sight. The independent witness therefore throws some doubt on the claim by the officers of the MANXMAN that she was on her right side of the river at the material time.*"

*Above: A rare view of **MANXMAN** (II) berthed on the Wallasey Stage on 11 September 1965.*

Author's Collection

Damage to the **MANXMAN** was put at £2,200 while **SEAMEW** sustained damage of £2,000. As there were so many possible outcomes as to who was to blame - **SEAMEW** perhaps for not observing the approach of **MANXMAN** or the **MANXMAN** for not being aware of her position in the river if the witness statement was upheld - the Solicitors advised the Steam Packet Company to come to an agreement with **SEAMEW**'s owners that each side would bear the costs of their own vessel's repairs. As costs of repairs would be covered by the Steam Packet's own marine insurance, the Board instructed Batesons to negotiate.

At a Board Meeting in Douglas on 9 January 1960 the issue of inflatable liferafts once again came to the fore. Ministry of Transport requirements demanded that before

passenger certificates could be issued for the coming season all of the passenger vessels "... *would have to be fitted with a further 60 - 20 man liferafts (one in six of which will require to have a partial pack consisting of sea anchors, bailer, pump, repair kit, electric torch etc) while glass fibre stowage containers will also be necessary, 37 to be fitted with mounting cradle for use on the 'summer only' steamers and 23 designed for ramp stowage on the 'all-year-round' steamers.*"

Cory Brothers & Co Ltd, who had supplied liferafts for the Steam Packet the previous year had offered a 10% discount on the liferafts and a further 5% discount on the storage containers as the order was so substantial. After consideration the Board placed an order with them for "...*60-20 man Elliot inflatable liferafts and 60 fibreglass stowage containers at a total cost after making allowance for discounts of £17,669.11s.9d.*"

The liferaft matter was further discussed by the Steam Packet Directors on the 3 March 1960 especially on the two main winter steamers, **KING ORRY** and **MANXMAN**. The latter would need 58 of the new liferafts and the former would need 55 but it was the stowage of them which was causing concern. The only feasible way of carrying these extra rafts appeared to be that "...*a skid deck will have to be constructed on the port and starboard sides of each vessel aft of the Bridge and be capable of stowing 38 rafts per vessel - the Ministry of Transport having approved the plans. Accommodation for the remaining rafts will be found on the Bridge and the after end of the Promenade Deck.*"

Cammell Laird had estimated that all this would cost £2,300 per steamer and "...*if side screen windows are fitted under the new liferaft deck the additional cost would be £1,969 in the case of the MANXMAN - which already has five windows fitted - and £3,719 for the KING ORRY.*"

There was hesitancy about spending the money, especially on **KING ORRY**. It was argued that no decision had yet been reached about the proposed new car ferry, "... *the outcome of which could affect the future operation of the KING ORRY...*" so it was decided to spend the money on **MANXMAN** only and store the necessary new liferafts for **KING ORRY** "...*in a number of special seat containers which incorporate two 20 seater liferafts each and cost approximately £30 each.*" The construction of the skid deck for **KING ORRY** was thus deferred.

Unfortunately the Company was told on 19 March that the Ministry of Transport at Liverpool would not dispense with the requirement of a skid deck on **KING ORRY** although they would agree to a shortened one to store the rafts that would be required during 1960 and 1961, that is 12 rafts on each side rather than 19. Cammell Laird had quoted £1,850 for this work. After due consideration "...*it was decided to have constructed on the KING ORRY a skid deck similar to that to be erected on the MANXMAN at a cost of approximately £2,300, as such should meet all eventualities.*"

*Above: **KING ORRY** (IV) departs Douglas at 1600 for Liverpool on 13 July 1966. Note that the "skid deck" on the port side is there but there are no liferafts on it.*

Author's Collection

The matter of liferafts arose again at a later Board meeting on 7 January 1961. To comply with Ministry of Transport regulations and before passenger certificates could be issued for the 1961 season a further 35 twenty man liferafts would need to be fitted to **LADY OF MANN**, **BEN-MY-CHREE**, **KING ORRY** and **MANXMAN**, all other vessels in the fleet now being compliant. In the event Cory Brothers and Co offered the Company 29 twenty five man life rafts at the same price and offered a 10% discount as well on the glass fibre stowage containers and all the paraphernalia that went with them. The offer was accepted by the Steam Packet Company.

Meanwhile the state of the berthing facilities at Fleetwood continued to give considerable concern and a Board meeting held in May 1959 had been told that an approach to the Home Office asking for government support for the reconstruction of the facilities at Fleetwood had not been well received. The Home Office had suggested that all interested parties get together and try themselves to find a solution to the funding problem. Following on from this a sub-committee of the Lieutenant Governor's Executive Council had been set up to pursue the matter and it was decided on Saturday 16 January, that members of the Steam Packet Board would attend a meeting of the sub-committee on Wednesday 20 January and that it would be the intention of the sub-committee to discuss the matter with The Isle of Man Tourist Board, Fleetwood Corporation, British Railways and British Transport Commission. There appeared to be real concern in

Imperial Buildings that if progress was not made, then the route from Fleetwood might have to cease.

The Chairman reported back to the Board on the Fleetwood matter on Saturday 23 January 1960 and informed the members that the sub-committee had wanted to "*...obtain as much information as possible regarding passenger tax and harbour dues payable at Fleetwood and the number of passengers carried on that route.*" In other words there was uncertainty as to whether repairs to the quay were going to be cost effective.

*Above: Berthed at Fleetwood in later years is **KING ORRY** (IV).*

Author's Collection

The sub-committee had had a meeting with representatives of Fleetwood Corporation on Friday 5 February and at a Board Meeting the next day in Douglas reported that they "...were in no position to render monetary assistance but assured us of all possible moral support in an endeavour to retain all steamer services for their port." They would approach the local MP, Captain Stanley, and would also approach the Lancashire and Merseyside Industrial Development Association to see what help might be available.

The position seemed to be even gloomier by 28 May 1960. The Board was told that although moral support was available from all concerned, the granting of hard cash was quite another matter. The Executive Council of the Lieutenant Governor were not prepared to make a financial contribution as they considered the wharf at Fleetwood and its finance was a matter for its owners, the British Transport Commission. It was felt that an increase in passenger tax at Fleetwood was the way forward in respect of paying for repairs to the wharf and "... if there was a contribution of £20,000, which would be the equivalent to a 1/- increase on all fares, that was all that should be expected."

The Council understood that such an increase in fares might very well have a detrimental effect on passenger loadings from Fleetwood but it was possible the Manx Government could alleviate the situation by reducing the passenger tax at Douglas. On 11 June 1960 the Steam Packet Board decided that "...in the event of the construction of a new wharf at Fleetwood the Company would agree to the passenger tax at that port being doubled from $11^1/_4$d to $1s/10^1/_2$d per passenger each way." It was estimated that about £12,000 of extra revenue would be raised per annum. The Board decided that this was as much as the Steam Packet could do towards the construction of a new wharf at Fleetwood. On 22 October 1960 the Directors were told that the Manx Government would not make a contribution towards the cost of a new wharf at Fleetwood and thus the Steam Packet Board was firm in its resolve that it had gone as far as it could.

Matters came to a head at a meeting on Friday 28 October 1960 in Douglas between Sir Robert Letch, General Manager of the British Transport Commission, the Lieutenant Governor and certain members of his Executive Council and representatives of the Steam Packet Company. Two new wharves were proposed at Fleetwood but once again the Steam Packet made it clear it had gone as far as it could financially with the increase in passenger tax arrangements which had been agreed. The Isle of Man Government made it clear that it could not sanction the spending of substantial sums of money on capital projects outside the Isle of Man. Sir Robert Letch made it clear that for the British Transport Commission to do anything "... it would have to be on a commercial basis and they would look to others to meet the interest on the capital outlay."

The only solution it appeared would be to try and persuade the UK Government for financial assistance on the grounds that Fleetwood had an important bearing on the economy of the Isle of Man. What was made very clear was that if the building of the new wharves was not given the go ahead Fleetwood would close to passenger traffic after the 1961 season. The Steam Packet however did suggest to the British Transport Commission that as a cheaper alternative to the plans for two new wharves, it would still be possible for the Company to provide sailings to the Isle of Man if only one new wharf was constructed - "...while not equal to that at present being operated, would at least be preferable to a complete termination of the Fleetwood and Douglas service."

Above: Heading back to Douglas, **KING ORRY** (IV) leaves Fleetwood in the late 1960s.

Author's Collection

Sadly there was no solution to the problem. The Steam Packet Directors were informed at a meeting on 15 July 1961 that the British Transport Commission could not see a way of making the operation of a new single berth financially viable and in fact had spent over £100,000 between 1951 and 1960 in repairs to the No 1 and No 2 berths and had additionally demolished three other berths which were beyond repair. As no financial contributions from the Manx Government were forthcoming the Steam Packet were informed that the berths would not be available for its vessels after the end of the 1961 season and that "...the passenger service cannot be operated from the port next year and onwards." The Directors of the Steam Packet agreed no further steps could be taken and they would have to accept the end of the Fleetwood passenger service.

Nevertheless the new situation had to be managed. The Steam Packet Company made it clear that the ordinary traffic which had passed through Fleetwood could be handled via Liverpool although there would be some attendant difficulties and possible delays especially at peak times and weekends.

PROPOSED NEW TONNAGE

At a full Board Meeting on 23 February 1960 a report prepared by the Manager, Mr A J Fick, his staff and the superintendents regarding the new ship was fully discussed, especially as to what design of car ferry would be best for Steam Packet routes and the Marine Superintendent was called into the meeting to give his views in detail. It was decided that several shipbuilders should be approached and asked to submit designs and specifications with prices by 30 April. The firms approached would be:

Ailsa Shipbuilding Company, Troon
Cammell Laird, Birkenhead
Wm Denny & Bros Ltd, Dumbarton
Harland & Wolff, Belfast
Thornycroft & Co Ltd, Southampton
Vickers Armstrong, Barrow
Samuel White & Co, Cowes

The proposals submitted from the various shipbuilders were examined and discussed on 23 June 1960. A simplified summary of all the proposals are as follows:

Ailsa Shipbuilding Company, Troon (all costings included variation clauses)

Pametrada engines	£890,000
Sulzer engines	£869,000
Mirlees engines	£855,000
Stabilizers	£60,000
Bow Thrusters	£24,000 or £27,900 if a motor ship

Cammell Laird, Birkenhead (all fixed price)

Pametrada engines	£1,030,371
Mirlees engines	£995,277
Stabilizers	£58,227
Bow Thrusters	£21,661

Wm Denny & Bros, Dumbarton

Pametrada engines	£1,218,700, fixed price, £1,158,700 with variation clause
Sulzer engines	£1,163,700 fixed price, £1,118,700 with variation clause
Mirlees engines	£1,133,700 fixed price, £1,088,700 with variation clause
Stabilizers	£55,600
Bow Thrusters	£20,700

Harland & Wolff, Belfast (all fixed price)

Pametrada engines	£1,170,000
Stabilizers	£55,000
Bow Thrusters	£22,000

Thornycroft & Co Ltd, Southampton (all fixed price)

Pametrada engines	£982,600
Stabilizers	£51,000
Bow Thrusters	£16,400

Vickers Armstrong, Barrow (all fixed price)
Pametrada engines

(Babcock & Wilcox Boilers)	£1,170,357
(Foster Wheeler Boilers)	£1,165,347
Sulzer engines	£1,045,738
Mirlees engines	£1,007,659
Stabilizers	£54,398
Bow Thrusters	£9,756

Samuel White & Co, Cowes

Pametrada engines	£1,572,395 fixed price, £1,457,395 with variation clause
Crossley engines	£1,336,835 fixed price, £1,237,835 with variation clause
Pielstick engines	£1,397,835 fixed price, £1,294,835 with variation clause
Stabilizers	£52,992
Bow Thrusters	£19,613 or £19,173 if a motor ship

As can be imagined much discussion about the proposals took place. During the subsequent discussion by the Board it was pointed out that Cammell Laird were the only builders "*... who have developed a system of ramps and designed a vessel which could achieve the loading and unloading of vehicles entirely by ramps at any state of the tide, such a system being preferable to mechanical means which are liable to breakdowns and would involve additional operating costs and annual maintenance.*"

Denny of Dumbarton, Ailsa and Thornycroft had submitted designs which "*... the absence of a lift obviates the necessity of the cutaway hull from the main deck upwards...*" which the superintendents thought would not find favour with the Ministry of Transport while the other builders had had included lifts which operated only from deck level "*...and thus vehicles could not be loaded or unloaded at all states of the tide.*"

It was decided to give Cammell Laird the order for the new vessel - a car ferry propelled by geared turbines of Pametrada design and Babcock and Wilcox steam boilers at a fixed price of £1,005,000 plus certain other items "*... to be the subject of discussion between builders' representatives and ours amounting to £25,371. It was further decided that anti-roll stabilizers be fitted to the vessel at an additional cost of £58,227.*"

Meanwhile on Saturday 12 March 1960 the Directors of the Steam Packet listened to a letter from the clerk of Ramsey Town Commissioners as to whether the Company might consider reinstating a direct service between Ramsey and Liverpool. The Commissioners referred to the direct sailings to Ramsey when Army Cadets were transported for summer camps and that the Steam Packet should consider making a similar service available for summer visitors during the season. In response the Manager's reply told the Commissioners that in 1939, the last season that direct passenger sailings had taken place, there were nine sailings to Ramsey from Liverpool and only 1,973 passengers had been carried while in 1938 there had been eleven sailings and 2,348 passengers had availed themselves of the service. These numbers, in the view of the Manager, did not justify the reintroduction of a direct service and the Board agreed with him.

MANXMAN	Captain R Clucas
	Chief Officer H N Kinley
MONA'S ISLE	Captain L Callow
	Chief Officer J Cannon
SNAEFELL	Captain W E McMeiken
	Chief Officer T H Cubbon
TYNWALD	Captain R E Gelling
	Chief Officer B C Corlett
MONA'S QUEEN	Captain F Griffin
	Chief Officer J R Kinley
KING ORRY	Captain J D Craine
	Chief Officer H E Collister
FENELLA	Captain A W G Kissack
	Chief Officer M Maugham
PEVERIL	Captain A Clucas
	First Officer H A Kinley
CONISTER	Captain T Corteen
	First Officer G Kelly

It is interesting to note that the list for the 1961 season was exactly the same. However, sadly, the Chief Officer of **MONA'S ISLE**, J E Cannon died suddenly on board the vessel during passage from Liverpool to Douglas in the early hours of 20 May. He was 57 years old and had joined the Company in 1930. His death led to a reorganisation of Chief Officers for 1961 with J J Keig being appointed to **PEVERIL**.

Captain J E Quirk on **BEN-MY-CHREE** was another Steam Packet Officer who had been on **FENELLA** when she was wrecked at Dunkirk and like Captain Cubbon had also been rescued by **CRESTED EAGLE** only to be beached again a couple of hours later. He was Chief Officer of **VICTORIA** by the time of D-Day. His first command of a Steam Packet vessel was **RUSHEN CASTLE** for a short time after the war. He was Commodore of the fleet between 1965 and 1969.

Meanwhile the Isle of Man Tourist Board had come up with a 'revolutionary' concept concerning the care of visitors to the Island. This was put to a Board Meeting of the Steam Packet Company on Saturday 21 May 1960. They proposed setting up an information bureau on the steamers with "...the object of giving a service to visitors during the passage...answering enquiries, dealing with hotels, amusement, coach bookings etc."

*Above: **MONA'S ISLE** (V) arriving at Ramsey Pier in July 1965.*

Author's Collection

The approved dispositions of Captains/Chief Officers and their ships were confirmed on Saturday 2 April 1960 for the coming season as follows:

LADY OF MANN	Captain G R Kinley
	Chief Officer F Cannell
BEN-MY-CHREE	Captain J E Quirk
	Chief Officer J Cubbon

They suggested starting the project on just two steamers and targeting at first just the Liverpool and Fleetwood routes. If space was a problem then they suggested having a courier on each of the two steamers who could move among the passengers giving advice. Costs would be borne by the Tourist Board. The Directors promised to consider the proposals and come to a decision as soon as possible which turned out to be a negative one. There was no possibility of setting up a bureau on any of the steamers because of a lack of space and although the courier proposal might be acceptable "...no assurance could be given that sleeping accommodation would be available on board either at Liverpool or Fleetwood if it should be required."

*Above: Commodore ship once again in 1960, this view of **LADY OF MANN** (I) shows her leaving Douglas for Belfast on 13 July 1966 at 2010 with Captain Callow in command.*

Author's Collection

It was perhaps fortuitous that the Company had decided to order a passenger and car ferry for the fleet from Cammell Laird on 23 June 1960 as the passenger loadings for the 1960 season had not been very satisfactory. Passenger arrivals from 1 May 1960 to 30 September totalled 335,292 (266,717 ordinary and 68,575 day) compared with 365,312 (279,678 ordinary and 85,634 day) during the corresponding period in 1959, which was a decrease of 30,020. It would appear that the visitor industry in the Isle of Man was at the beginning of a decline which the Company hoped could be arrested with the introduction of the revolutionary new vessel.

Furthermore, the "*All In Tours*" which had been started in 1957 were also showing a decline. The Steam Packet Company's partners in this scheme were British Railways, the Isle of Man Tourist Board and the Creative Tourist Agent's Conference, all of whom contributed to the advertising costs. The Directors of the Steam Packet Company were concerned and on 30 September 1960 in Douglas discussed their further participation in the scheme. What was irritating the Steam Packet was that the fares charged passengers who had taken up an "*all in*" package was 3/s less than that charged for ordinary passengers and this coupled with the advertising costs, commission to agents and so on caused the Board to state that "*...our receipts from 'All-In' holidays during the past season actually suffered to the extent of 11/2d for every passenger who travelled under the scheme, when compared with the fares paid by other travellers.*"

*Above: Plenty of passengers on board **BEN-MY-CHREE** (IV) as she departs Douglas for Liverpool on 22 June 1963.*

Author's Collection

The Company had warned the year before that unless there was a marked improvement in the bookings during 1960 then they would have to review their position. In the event bookings had totalled 1,318 in 1960 compared with 1,333 in 1959, 1,337 in 1958 and 2,222 in 1957 - so bookings were declining. The Directors concluded that "...the cost of operating...seemed to be out of all proportion with the results achieved...further participation in the scheme was not justified." British Railways were to be told there would be no fare concessions in 1961 and the Company would not participate in any advertising for the scheme from then on. The Isle of Man Tourist Board asked the Company to reconsider its position if some way could be found to alleviate its concerns at declining revenue. The Steam Packet replied that they would be prepared to reconsider and would send the Manager to a meeting in London to discuss the matter. They finally decided they would indeed provide £250 (as in previous years) to the cost of advertising if efforts were made to improve traffic. However the decision to end the fare concession for this scheme would remain - 55/- 1st Class Return for Saturday travel and 45/- 1st Class Return for Tuesday travel.

Meanwhile Cammell Laird had submitted plans for the refrigeration space aboard the new ship in which "... meat, fish and vegetables would be stored in the one compartment... and as this would be similar to the cold chambers on the present fleet which have proved unsatisfactory, and in any event it is doubtful if the Ministry of Transport would accept in the form shown on the specification, builders have been requested to go into the matter with a view to improving the facilities."

Cammell Laird came back with a plan to provide three separate compartments with a total capacity of about 585 cubic feet (the original plan had only envisaged 250 cubic feet) and the extra cost would be £497. The builders were instructed to proceed.

On 22 October 1960 the interior accommodation of the new ship was also discussed and the wishes of the Company concerning the 1st and 2nd Class accommodation on the lower deck and the 1st Class Dining Saloon and Smoke Room on the promenade deck were conveyed to the builders for incorporation into their plans.

Lifeboat Davits, especially those for the two accident boats, were also discussed. The Marine Superintendent expressed a wish that "... the lifeboat davits should be fitted complete with electrically driven hoisting winches for each pair of davits...". The Builders had originally proposed a mechanical winch for these but the Company decided on electrical operation and also "...decided to fit Bi-Luff (double pivot) davits suitable for fibreglass lifeboats at an extra cost of £2,550." It was later decided that all lifeboats would be fibreglass (the original idea had been to fit aluminium ones and mahogany ones were also considered) at an extra cost of £1,467.

As the contract to build the ship had been signed she began to be known as Hull No 1303. Of course just because the contract had been signed did not preclude new clauses being proposed for incorporation into the contract when being discussed. For example Cammell Laird seemed a bit nervous about the speed of the new vessel once on trials - perhaps this was because **MANXMAN** had not actually reached her contract speed in 1955 and although the Steam Packet Company had made allowances and accepted the ship, the builders were no doubt nervous such goodwill would not occur again. They proposed that in the event the new ship did not reach her contract speed, that is falling below 21 knots, they wished "...to retain the same figures as those which applied to the trials of the **MANXMAN**, viz £500 for each one tenth knot deficiency down to 20 ½ knots and £1,000 for each one tenth knot below 20 ½ ..."

The Isle of Man Steam Packet Company rejected this suggestion by Cammell Laird, not least because their figures were based on 1955 valuations and the new ship was costing much more than **MANXMAN**. The builders had also proposed for one coat of paint less on the hull of the new vessel than that recommended by the paint manufacturers. The Steam Packet didn't like this either and instructed Cammell Laird to put on the extra coat of paint even though there was an additional cost of £404.

*Above: **MANXMAN** (II) departs Heysham for Douglas on 31 July 1968.*

Author's Collection

On 28 February 1961 it was proposed that application be made to the Board of Trade to name the new car ferry **MANX MAID** and later in April 1961 the Company was informed that **MANX MAID** was available.

The year 1961 was the final year when all passenger services were to be maintained by passenger only steamers. The services to be operated were approved on 22 October 1960 and their starting and terminating dates were broadly as follows:

Liverpool and Douglas double daily sailings:
Friday 19 May to Monday 11 September, excepting 24, 25 and 26 May when a single service would operate
Fleetwood and Douglas service:
Saturday 20 May to Monday 11 September
Ardrossan and Douglas:
Sunday 4 June to Friday 8 September
Belfast and Douglas:
Thursday 15 June to Friday 8 September
Dublin and Douglas:
Thursday 15 June to Tuesday 12 September
Heysham and Douglas:
Every Thursday from 6 July to 17 August

*Above: Funnel of **MONA'S ISLE** (V) in 1966.*
Author's Collection

*Above: Funnel of **KING ORRY** (IV) in 1964.*
Author's Collection

*Above: Funnel of **TYNWALD** (V) in 1965.*
Author's Collection

*Above: Funnel of **LADY OF MANN** (I) in 1966.*
Author's Collection

During the 1960s and onwards **KING ORRY** could always be recognised at a distance from her sister vessels by her cravat, or cowl, having been removed and her funnel thus appeared to be shorter. The decision to do this was made on 15 April 1961 at Douglas. Following an inspection of the vessel by Cammell Laird it had been revealed that the cravat was in an irreparable condition. To remove it and replace it with a new one and repair the top of the inner casing would cost about £1,250 while just to take off the cravat and just repair the inner casing on its own would cost just £650. Additionally it had been found that three plates on each side of the funnel near the top were also badly corroded and the cost of this essential replacement would be at least £200. The Superintendents assured the Directors that in removing **KING ORRY**'s cravat no adverse effects would be apparent (in fact many observers thought it improved her appearance) and so it was agreed to remove the cravat, not replace it, but carry out the other essential repairs.

*Above: **KING ORRY** at Liverpool Landing Stage on 4 April 1960 - with a rusty cravat!*

Author's Collection

Charters of vessels to other companies were not that common in this era but occasionally they could be a source of unexpected income. One such example was on 31 July 1961 when the Manager, Mr A J Fick received an urgent telephone call from the Manager of Burns and Laird Line requesting to charter one of the Steam Packet's vessels to replace their **ROYAL ULSTERMAN** which had suffered an engine breakdown at Belfast. This would enable them to maintain their Ardrossan/Belfast daylight service. The Steam Packet Manager had arranged for **MANXMAN** to be chartered from Monday 31 July to Friday 4 August, both dates inclusive, for the

sum of £1,050 per day. The Steam Packet Company would pay crew costs and port charges but retain all receipts for catering, cabins and other sales on board, apart of course from the passenger fares themselves. In the event the ship completed the charter sailing daily from Ardrossan at 0930 and from Belfast at 1515.

The comfort of passengers on the new vessel No 1303 was very much uppermost in the minds of the officials of the Steam Packet even to the extent of discussing the type of upholstery in the public areas of the new vessel. In their original tender for the vessel Cammell Laird had allowed for Vynide to be used as the covering material for the settees and chairs in the First Class Top and Lower Lounges, Ladies' Room and Smoke Room as well as in the Private Cabins. The Directors did not like the look of the Vynide material so Cammell Laird had submitted prices and samples of alternative coverings and "...*it was decided that the seating accommodation in the 1st Class Top and Lower Lounges, Ladies' Room and Private Cabins be covered with moquette at an additional cost of £275, that for the latter to be the grey design as selected for the Ladies' Room and not as submitted.*"

The new vessel of course was to be ready for the 1962 season but a major worry of course was the loss of the Fleetwood service and so in August 1961 a meeting was held in Imperial Buildings between representatives of the Steam Packet and "...*Messrs T W Polding (District Passenger Manager, British Railways, Manchester), T C Byron, (District Passenger Manager, Liverpool), W Stewart (Acting Line Operating Officer), and E W Hill, (Assistant District Passenger Manager, Manchester)*" the object of which was to find a way of minimising the effect on the Steam Packet's passenger traffic with the loss of the port of Fleetwood. The British Railways' representatives were confident that they could run special trains into Liverpool on a Saturday just as easily as they had run them into Fleetwood and that transport could be provided between Railway Station and Landing Stage at the Pier Head. The British Railways' people were also "...*prepared to make more use of Riverside Station not only on Saturdays by means of special trains from Wakes towns, but in connection with the TT Races, and it would be necessary, because of the extra cost this would involve, for 1/- to be added to the rail fares...*"

The Company hoped to retain some of the through booked passengers who travelled from the Manchester area to Douglas via Fleetwood and there was a hope that new passengers might possibly be attracted from towns close to Liverpool such as Wigan or St Helens. It was therefore decided that a long day excursion should be introduced on certain Wednesdays leaving Liverpool at 1030 and returning from Douglas at midnight.

IMPORTANT DECISIONS

There was much discussion and important decisions to be made on 2 September 1961 when the full Board of the Company met in Imperial Buildings, Douglas. The Manager, Mr A J Fick and his assistant were in attendance.

Firstly there was some pleasing news about the Passenger Traffic numbers for the main summer season. Arrivals from 1 May to 27 August 1961 totalled 317,919 of which 252,687 were ordinary passengers and 65,232 were day excursionists. This compared with 305,655 (245,857 and 59,808) for the corresponding period the year before. This was an increase of 12,254.

However it was inevitable that discussions would soon revolve around the new ship. It would appear that on the original specifications, the car embarkation doors were to be operated in the traditional manner - that is by means of chains, chain pipes etc. The Marine Superintendent was of the view that this method would be difficult and slow with these type of doors, on the lower deck, considering their size and weight. He therefore suggested to the Board that it was possible to operate these doors hydraulically with one crew member only and that the equipment for doing this was available from Short Bros and Harland Ltd. The extra cost for this, there were four doors in question, was £4,658. This was accepted and the builders were instructed to proceed with this work.

In addition the Marine Superintendent had noted that the capstan controller and the windlass controller on the forecastle head were some distance apart and thus it would not be possible for one man to operate them. To change the design and move them nearer to one another would involve an extra cost of £130 but the advantages, and economy, of one man operation persuaded the Company to instruct the builders to alter the design of these items so one man operation was possible.

An increase in wage costs for the 1962 season inevitably led to an increase in fares. After discussion it was agreed that from 1 January 1962 the following fare increases would come into effect:

Liverpool, Heysham, Belfast, Dublin and Douglas:
Single up by 1/-, return by 3/-
Ardrossan and Douglas:
Single up by 1/-, return by 2/-

It was agreed however that day excursion fares should remain unaltered.

Special Fares, such as those available for members of sporting teams travelling to the Island to compete in competitions were also increased by 3/- and Conference Fares, that is the concessionary fares available to those passengers attending the various conferences that were held on the Island were to be increased from 30/- to 35/- but the Ardrossan Conference fare was to go up from 35/- to 40/-. Contract Tickets were also to increase by 10%.

The Manager reported that "*All In*" Holidays to the Island were also showing a modest increase. In 1961 the numbers totalled 1,485 compared with 1,321 in 1960 and 1,333 in 1959. After discussion it was decided that the fares to be applied to these passengers in 1962 would be the same as those for ordinary passengers - that is, 57/- 1st Class Return on Saturdays and 47/- 1st Class Return on Tuesdays.

As far as fares for motor cars was concerned it was decided that "*...with a view to encouraging as much additional traffic as possible with the advent of the new car ferry, to leave the freight charges on motor vehicles unaltered for 1962.*"

It was inevitable that the Company would decide to dispose of one of the passenger ships for the 1962 season. The Fleetwood route had closed and a new ship was due to join the fleet and the Company considered that eight ships were sufficient to maintain the proposed schedule. The views of the Marine and Engineering Superintendents had been consulted prior to any decision being made. Both had agreed that it should be **MONA'S QUEEN** that should be offered for sale. This reflected her history of boiler troubles but also she could command a higher price than the two pre-war ships, **BEN-MY-CHREE** and **LADY OF MANN**. The Company was aware that the higher passenger certificates held by **BEN-MY-CHREE** and **LADY OF MANN** remained valuable at peak times. It was thus decided to place **MONA'S QUEEN** into the hands of the brokers, Messrs C W Kellock & Co Ltd for disposal as a going concern. It was stated that "*...they will be advised that the vessel is at present on service and can be inspected either at Douglas or Liverpool, that she will be laid up at Barrow-in-Furness on the 17th September and thereafter be available for delivery.*" The brokers were asked to investigate what sort of price could be expected for a vessel of her type.

Later on 23 September 1961 it was reported that the Assistant Manager had received a letter from the brokers that "*...it was practically impossible to put a value on the* **MONA'S QUEEN** *having regard to the limited market. It may be possible to obtain £250,000, but it could be considerably more, or less than that amount depending on the requirements of a prospective buyer.*"

The advice from the brokers was to wait for offers and then discuss rather than suggest a price beforehand and the Board agreed to do this.

Above: BEN-MY-CHREE (IV) at Douglas on 25 June 1964. She had been retained in the fleet when MANX MAID (II) entered service even though she was the oldest vessel in the fleet. Astern of her is LADY OF MANN (I) with SNAEFELL (V) and TYNWALD (v) on the other side of Victoria Pier.

Author's Collection

Above: LADY OF MANN (I) was also retained in the fleet in 1962. Here she is seen on 12 August 1965 entering Douglas with the 1400 sailing from Liverpool.

Author's Collection

Above: MONA'S QUEEN (IV) seen here in April 1960 in the Mersey, was the vessel that made way for MANX MAID (II) in 1962.

Ships of Mann Collection

The question of hovercraft once again was raised on 30 September 1961 at a Board Meeting in Douglas. A Company called Starways Ltd had applied to the Air Transport Licensing Board for a license to operate hovercraft as and when they became available at nearly every port in the country. The Steam Packet Company were informed about this in a letter from the Passenger Steamship Owners' Association and that certain members of the Association had objected to the Licensing Board that Starways should be granted a license *"...for any service on the routes affecting them and one member has applied for a license to operate hovercraft in the Bristol Channel area."* (This was P & A Campbell Ltd)

A meeting of the Association was to be held in London on 6 October and Mr Alexander of the Liverpool and North Wales Steamship Co would be attending. It was decided to ask Mr Alexander to represent the Isle of Man Steam Packet Company at the meeting as well and that the view of the Manx Company was that they would object most strongly to any license being granted to Starways in respect of any proposed service between Liverpool and the Isle of Man.

Meanwhile passenger traffic was continuing to show an increase. Arrivals from 1 May to 30 September totalled 352,076 (277,712 ordinary and 74,364 day trippers) compared with 336,649 (266,717 and 69,932) in 1961.

Early in October 1961 the question of a second car ferry in the Steam Packet fleet was raised, but initially not by the Company themselves. On 7 October 1961 at Douglas a letter from the Government Secretary was read out to the Steam Packet Directors which informed the Company that *"...advising that the Lieutenant Governor and his Executive Council have discussed the need for transporting motor cars from the United Kingdom to Douglas during the summer months. In view of the considerable increase in this traffic in the last few years and the fact that the closing of Fleetwood may well persuade car owners who previously would have left their cars behind and travelled from Fleetwood to Douglas in future to go to Liverpool by car because of alleged poor rail connections and then bring their cars to Douglas, His Excellency and Executive Council consider that a second car ferry will be necessary and it may be that with the cessation of the Fleetwood service would consider converting one of our existing vessels for this purpose."*

The idea of converting one of the passenger fleet into a car ferry was discussed at length but it was decided that it was not really a practical proposition. The conclusion was reached that it would probably be cheaper and easier to build a new ship rather than go through the complications of conversion. It is interesting to consider that if the Steam Packet Company had thought this was a practical proposition, which vessel would have been chosen for this conversion, what alterations both externally and internally would have been necessary and what she would have looked like afterwards.

Ordering a new vessel would of course mean a very great financial outlay once again but the Company were *"… alive to the possibilities of this type of traffic and are closely watching developments in that connection…"* It was pointed out that the fleet of existing passenger vessels did have considerable deck space that could be utilised for the carrying of vehicles and that *"…it would not be prudent - at any rate at this stage - to place an order for a second car ferry."*

Meanwhile the Steam Packet Directors were becoming increasingly alarmed at the ambitions of Starways Ltd. The Company were of the opinion that hovercraft should be regarded as ships, not aircraft, and as such posed a threat to the services built up over many years by members of the Coastwise Passenger Steamship Owners. It was not known whether they had applied to operate on any Isle of Man routes. It was decided to find out as a matter of urgency and if they had applied, to object in the strongest possible terms. Later in October it was revealed that Starways had indeed applied to operate hovercraft, seating from 20 to 100 passengers, between Liverpool and the Isle of Man and wanted the license to be valid for an unlimited period from the date suitable craft would become available and *"…for frequency according to traffic demand, for the carriage of tourist class passengers, freight and vehicles."*

The Steam Packet Company regarded these developments as a serious threat to their operations and decided to object strongly to the Regulatory Authorities at the earliest possible opportunity.

The sad news was received on 14 October 1961 that Captain Alexander Clucas, Master of **PEVERIL**, had died suddenly on board the vessel in Coburg Dock, Liverpool on Monday 9 October. He was only 56 and had suffered a fatal heart attack.

Captain Clucas had been born in 1905 and his father had been Commodore of the Steam Packet fleet in 1936 and 1937. He himself had joined the Company as a seaman in 1932 but by 1935 had obtained his tickets and was appointed Second Officer of **MONA**. By 1939 he had transferred to **FENELLA**, still as Second Officer but because he was on leave to attend his father's funeral in May 1940 he missed Dunkirk. For the rest of the war he served with Coast Lines but came back to the Steam Packet in 1945 as Second Officer of **MONA'S ISLE**, transferring later to the new **KING ORRY**. However from 1948 he served mostly on the cargo vessels and became the first Chief Officer of the new **FENELLA** in 1951. He served on both her and **PEVERIL** and had been appointed Master in 1958. As a result of this untimely death certain rearrangements were necessary with Masters and Officers in the fleet. Captain T H Corteen was transferred from **CONISTER** to **PEVERIL** and the Chief Officer of **MANXMAN**, H N Kinley was appointed to command **CONISTER**.

*Above: Captain H N Kinley's first command, **CONISTER** (I). She is seen here at Ramsey on 24 June 1964.*
Author's Collection

The dates for the various passenger services for 1962 were finalised on 28 October 1961. They were as follows:

Liverpool and Douglas double daily sailings:
Friday 28 May to Monday 10 September inclusive
Ardrossan and Douglas:
Sunday 3 June to Friday 7 September inclusive
Belfast and Douglas:
Friday 1 June to Friday 7 September inclusive
Dublin and Douglas:
Thursday 31 May to Tuesday 11 September inclusive
Heysham and Douglas:
Every Wednesday and Thursday from 4 July to 23 August inclusive

On 25 November 1961 at a Board Meeting in Douglas the embarkation arrangements of the new vessel were discussed by the Directors. The builders had advised that to *"…ensure the successful working of the vessel* at Douglas from the passenger embarkation and disembarkation aspect and to avoid continual moving at her berths, it has been found necessary to arrange for an additional set of sliding doors on the Promenade Deck (port and starboard) and two sets on the Shelter Deck (port and starboard) while the Bridge Deck aft has been carried out to the ship's side to provide a position for a passenger gangway port and starboard."

The extra cost of this work was £2,564 but the Company regarded the work as essential and the go ahead was duly given. It would appear also that Cammell Laird had been asked to look into the possibility of fitting refrigerated shelves in the bars and buffets of the new vessel. However the costs of this were considered to be quite high and so it was agreed to their fitting only in the 1st and 2nd class Smoke Room Bars at a cost of £401.

Meanwhile the brokers had circulated details of **MONA'S QUEEN** world-wide and there had been 37 enquiries. However no offers had been received as the costs of converting her to the particular needs of interested parties were prohibitive. No British Companies appeared to be interested nor were any from France, Belgium or Scandinavia. The brokers suggested reducing the indicated price which had been set at between £200,000 and £300,000. The Company were disappointed but agreed to reduce the price to £175,000.

The Steam Packet Company Directors continued to discuss the hovercraft situation and in December 1961 the Company had made enquiries of Vickers–Armstrong at Barrow regarding their thoughts of the future development of the hovercraft. It appeared that they had been carrying out tank trials of a small craft capable of carrying 24 passengers at 60 knots in sheltered waters and they were in the process of designing larger craft carrying 200 plus passengers and up to 20 cars as well as freight. It was believed by Vickers that the small craft could be in operation by 1963 but the larger ones would not operate commercially until 1967/68. As far as sea conditions were concerned wave heights of over 12 feet would require a very large craft to operate safely but tests in this direction were continuing. Vickers it seems were confident hovercraft would in future contribute to the transport systems of the world and they were investing a lot of money in their design and development. They had invited representatives of the Steam Packet Company to their South Marston Works at Swindon to see the progress that was being made. It was agreed to send the Marine and Engineering Superintendents to the Swindon Works and for him to report back.

At a later meeting on 16 December 1961 the Steam Packet Company Directors were informed that the Isle of Man Airports Board had on 8 September strongly recommended to the Air Transport Licensing Board that the application of Starways to operate hovercraft services to the Isle of Man be rejected. They hoped that Starways "...will apply for a license to operate a service [only] when suitable hovercraft are available and operationally capable of maintaining regular services. If and when such application is made the Isle of Man Airports Board will be pleased to give full support thereto."

Meanwhile bumps and scrapes of the vessels in service continued to occupy the officials of the Company. On 6 January 1962 the Directors were made aware of two mishaps involving **KING ORRY**. The first incident occurred on 20 December 1961 when **KING ORRY** was moored on the south berth on the Princes Landing Stage at Liverpool. The ferry **ROYAL DAFFODIL II**, while approaching her berth, collided with the bow of the Manx steamer "...inflicting considerable damage to the stem casting and shellplating." **KING ORRY** needed temporary repairs to keep her in a serviceable condition and Cammell Laird secured the bow rudder and made tight the hull structure while the ship lay at her berth at the Princes Landing Stage. At the time of the collision "...there was a light S.E. wind prevailing, but nil visibility."

KING ORRY was withdrawn from service on Friday 29 December and was replaced by **TYNWALD**. It was anticipated she would be in dry dock until 12 January and the owners of **ROYAL DAFFODIL II**, Wallasey Corporation Ferries, were informed that the Steam Packet held them fully responsible for the accident.

Above: KING ORRY (IV) on the King Edward VIII Pier at Douglas on the 23 June 1964.

Author's Collection

Before **KING ORRY** could get into dry dock she was involved in another scrape on Christmas Eve at Douglas. Captain Callow reported that when he was entering Douglas Harbour at 0810 hours "...on completion of the midnight sailing from Liverpool, the strong to gale force E.S.E. wind, with rough sea and heavy swell, caused the vessel to sheer against her helm to port and in endeavouring to regain control in order to approach No 1 Berth, Victoria Pier, the vessel fell heavily on the south end of the pier causing extensive damage to the starboard shoulder and main belting and plating."

It was decided that the plating repairs could be done when she entered dry dock for the repairs to the bow but the belting could be done once the vessel was back in service and would probably take about two weeks to complete.

MANX MAID

The launch of the new vessel took place on 23 January 1962 at 1220 hours and the Board Meeting of the Steam Packet Company on 20 January authorised the fourth payment of £212,600 to Cammell Laird.

*Above: Classic view of a classic vessel - **MANX MAID** (II) in Douglas Bay.*

Adrian Sweeney

A few weeks later it was not the new ship but the oldest of the passenger steamers that was concerning the Marine Superintendent. He was worried about the unsatisfactory state of the upholstery in the two 2nd Class Lower Lounges on **BEN-MY-CHREE**. These rooms had never been refurbished since the ship returned from war service in 1945 and it is entirely probable the upholstery was original from when the ship was built in 1927. The Marine Superintendent had obtained estimates and samples from Messrs. John J Ashburner & Co Ltd with a view to refurbishment. It was decided to *"...have the existing coverings stripped off, hair filling recarded and sterilised, new inside hessian cases supplied and covered in Marquette (as per design selected) at a total cost of £914-0-3d."*

Meanwhile on 24 February 1962 the Deck Officers, Engineers and Chief Stewards for the Fleet for the 1962 season were confirmed. Masters and their ships were as follows:

LADY OF MANN	Captain G R Kinley
TYNWALD	Captain J D Craine
BEN-MY-CHREE	Captain R Clucas
KING ORRY	Captain A W G Kissack
MANX MAID	Captain J Quirk
FENELLA	Captain T Corteen
MANXMAN	Captain L Callow
PEVERIL	Captain H N Kinley
MONA'S ISLE	Captain W E McMeiken
CONISTER	Captain B C Corlett
SNAEFELL	Captain F Griffin

Captain G R Kinley was the Commodore of the fleet in 1962 and would remain so till his retirement in 1965.

He had joined the Steam Packet Company in 1923 and was made up to Chief Officer in 1928. He was Master of **RUSHEN CASTLE** in 1939 and served with the Company during the war, either on **RUSHEN CASTLE** or on **SNAEFELL**. After the war he became Master of **VICTORIA** although he did stand by **MANXMAN** at Harwich. From then on he worked his way up the seniority list, becoming Commodore and Master of **LADY OF MANN** in 1958. He passed away in 1986 aged 86.

It was on 24 February 1962 that the Company was informed that the builders of **MANX MAID** had received from Messrs Whittingham & Mitchell Ltd of Chertsey a tender for the supply of the car embarkation gangways and *"... hydraulic elevating device"* which for two 24 feet gangways for Douglas, one for each pier, and one 17 foot 6 inch gangway for Liverpool would cost £1,869. This was the cheapest quote received and the only one to fully fulfil the requirements and so Cammell Laird were instructed to accept the tender.

The Steam Packet Directors on 24 February 1962 also needed to discuss the situation at Llandudno. The Manager, Mr A J Fick, reported that he had received correspondence from the Isle of Man Tourist Board expressing concern that the Liverpool and North Wales Steamship Company would not be running their service from Llandudno to Douglas in 1962 as they had laid up and offered for sale their steamer **ST SEIRIOL**. The Tourist Board were hoping the Steam Packet Company might take over this service themselves. Even the Lieutenant Governor and his Executive Council had expressed concern and had requested a meeting with the Steam Packet Board.

*Above: In the Mersey in August 1954 - **ST SEIRIOL**.*

Author's Collection

The Manager briefed the Directors with the details of the number of passengers carried by **ST SEIRIOL** during recent years - more than 10,000 in 1961 - and then submitted details of how much it would cost the Steam Packet to operate a service on certain dates during the summer season. Costs, he estimated, would be about £3,500 perhaps rising to £5,000 if more sailings were offered. The situation was discussed and it seemed that the costs would be easily accounted for with healthy ticket sale revenue and so, subject to Full Board approval the next week and assuming the berthing facilities at Llandudno were satisfactory, a service between Llandudno and Douglas would be operated on Tuesdays from 26 June to 28 August and on Wednesdays from 18 July to 22 August. It was decided a one class fare would be charged at 25/- for the day return. The Full Board Meeting on 27 February 1962 discussed the proposals at length and they were approved and the approval of the Pier Master at Llandudno would be obtained for the sailing dates the Company had in mind.

On 23 March 1962 a fire broke out in the hold of **CONISTER** among cargo stowed in the after end port side soon after the dockers had left the vessel at about 1600 hours. It was noticed by Mr G Kelly, the Chief Officer, the decks had dried out very quickly after they had been washed down by the crew and so he investigated and discovered the fire at about 1710 hours. The Fire Brigade were promptly called and the fire was soon brought under control and the ship suffered minor damage. However some cargo had been damaged. No cause for the fire could be established. The Board were impressed by the quick thinking and swift action taken by Mr Kelly and later gave him a gift of ten guineas.

Meanwhile there had been discussion for some time about the surfacing of the ramps and shelter deck forward on **MANX MAID**, mainly because the Company were not happy with the proposals of Cammell Laird, who had indicated two coats of red lead and a finishing coat on the car ramps would be adequate. The Company were concerned that this would not make the decks skid proof, a real concern on the outer ramps. The builders came back with an alternative, one of which involved coating the decks finally with a finishing coat that had originally been used on the flight deck of HMS **ARK ROYAL**, which of course had also been built by Cammell Laird at Birkenhead.

Worrying news was received by the Steam Packet Company Directors on 14 April 1962. A motion had been put forward at Tynwald the previous week on behalf of the Harbour Board that "...*from the 1st May 1962 there shall be charged 6d per ton (NRT) for every vessel entering a harbour (no such dues being applicable at the moment) while the dues on all goods landed or loaded be increased from 6d to 1/- per ton and the tax in respect of each passenger embarked or disembarked raised from 3d to 1/-.*"

These proposals, it was estimated, would cost the Steam Packet an extra £54,270 per year. The Directors decided to take steps to strongly object to these swingeing increases in harbour dues but if the Harbour Board were determined to proceed and impose them, then the Company would have no alternative but to recover its costs by increasing passenger and freight fares substantially.

A special Board Meeting of local Directors was convened on board **MONA'S ISLE** on 23 April soon after she had

Above: **CONISTER** *(I) at sea a year after the fire in the hold.*

Author's Collection

departed Douglas for Liverpool. The only item on the agenda was the increase in fares, both passenger and freight, that would be necessary to cover the extra costs imposed on the Company by the Harbour Board and these fare increases were formulated and approved. On the Liverpool, Ardrossan and Irish services the single fare would increase by 1/6d, the return fare by 2/6d and a day return by 1/-. Heysham and Llandudno fares increased by more, day returns increasing by 2/6d to reflect the large number of light sailings needed to carry out the services. Special fares, Conference fares and freight rates also increased substantially.

Above: **MONA'S ISLE** (V) leaves Liverpool on 24 April 1962, a year and a day after the special Board Meeting was held on board.

Author's Collection

The sea trials of **MANX MAID** took place on 18/19 May 1962. "*... A mean speed of 21.69 knots was attained at full power on the two double runs over the measured mile off the Isle of Arran. The wind prevailing at the time being moderate Northerly, force 4 to 5 with only slight sea.*"

Bow rudder tests were also carried out, stopping and starting tests and circling trials were completed and then the vessel "*...proceeded on a full power four hour endurance trial at approximately 21 knots with engine revolutions 271.2, the machinery proving in every way efficient...*"

MANX MAID returned to the Liverpool Landing Stage after the sea trials and the Superintendents were satisfied that the building of the vessel "*...had been carried out in accordance with the requirements of the Contract. ... MANX MAID was handed over by the Builders to our Superintendents on behalf of this Company at 10.45a.m. on Monday, 21st May, at the Liverpool Landing Stage.*"

The sale of **MONA'S QUEEN** however was still not going well. The Board were told that the brokers, C W Kellock had "*...very extensively brought this vessel to the attention of possible buyers in all parts of the world, but no real progress had been made.*"

The broker was of the opinion that the Steam Packet Company had overvalued her "*...particularly owing to the cost of altering the vessel to the requirements of any potential buyer.*" There was also the problem that the

Above: **MANX MAID** (II) berthed on the King Edward Pier at Douglas in the second year of her service on 23 June 1963.

Author's Collection

Greek Government were in the process of bringing in a law which would restrict the age of passenger vessels purchased for registration under the Greek flag to fifteen years which would of course rule out a sale of **MONA'S QUEEN** to Greek flag operators. Not to be deterred however, the broker was advised to keep the ship on the books at the original asking price and the Steam Packet would continue to hold her in reserve. The ship was insured for Port Risks only.

Passenger traffic continued to decline. Passenger arrivals on the Isle of Man between 1 May and 3 June 1962 were 24,906 (24,438 ordinary and 468 day returns) compared with 26,218 (22,863 ordinary and 3,355 day returns) during the corresponding period the year before, a large decrease of 1,312.

Traffic continued to decrease as the year progressed. Figures showed that between 1 May and 1 July passenger arrivals totalled 81,929 (69,220 ordinary and 12,709 day returns) compared with 111,333 the year before (88,652 ordinary and 22,681 day returns) a decrease of 29,404. A large decrease in day returns was again noted. The trend continued throughout the summer. Figures from 1 May to 2 September showed that passenger arrivals totalled 268,050 (223,440 ordinary and 44,610 day returns) compared with 333,772 the year before (264,361 ordinary and 69,411 day returns) a total decrease of 65,722.

The loss of the Fleetwood service had been a severe blow, especially for the day excursion market.

On 31 May 1962 **MANXMAN** had suffered a machinery breakdown at the worst possible time in the summer season. She had undocked from Cammell Laird after her refit and was proceeding to the Bar with the intention of adjusting compasses and undergoing bow rudder tests *"…but when going full astern a heavy vibration was induced by the starboard propeller as if contact had been made with a heavy object."*

The vibrations became even worse when the engines were put full ahead and so the ship returned to the Landing Stage at Liverpool. A diver's inspection later in the day reported that one blade tip on the starboard propeller had been damaged. The ship was drydocked to enable a spare propeller to be fitted and she undocked once more on 2 June for further trials. However the heavy vibrations persisted so the ship returned to Cammell Laird's Wet Basin but *"…on entering the dock in the charge of two tugs the starboard propeller was fouled by a heavy floating dockside fender."*

*Above: **MANX MAID** (II) with a good load of passengers powers away from Douglas early in her career.*

Author's Collection

*Above: **MANXMAN** (II) in dry dock later in her career in April 1972, in Langton Dry Dock, Liverpool.*

Author's Collection

Once **MANXMAN** had been secured in the Wet Basin the starboard high pressure turbine was opened up and it was found that there had been heavy rubbing on the gland strips which meant the rotor had to be removed and repaired. Meanwhile the ship herself was moved to dry dock and the original propeller, now repaired, was re-fitted. All work was completed by late evening on 7 June and after successful tests in the river, the ship sailed for Douglas where she arrived at 1100 hours on 8 June and resumed service. As to the cause:

"...*Indications are that the original cause of the mishap could be attributed to the propeller striking an underwater object when the vessel was going astern.*"

On 10 September Captain McMeiken, Master of **MANXMAN**, reported that while **MANXMAN** was moored at the Landing Stage at Liverpool preparing to take the 1030 hours sailing to Douglas the tug **STORM COCK** had collided with **MANXMAN**'s starboard bow "...*causing an indent in the shell plate between Nos 1 and 2 frames.*" The damage was not severe and would be dealt with at the spring overhaul but the Board made it quite clear that the Liverpool Screw Towing Company were liable.

Meanwhile the broker had finally received an offer for **MONA'S QUEEN** on behalf of Greek clients who had offered £120,000 for the ship but unfortunately not in cash but "...*on terms of payment against suitable securities.*"

The broker had informed the Steam Packet Board that they would see if they could get the Greeks to offer the same amount of cash for the ship but they had offered instead cash on £80,000 less 3% commission. The brokers considered this to be too low. The Steam Packet Board instructed the brokers to inform the buyer that the Company would accept £140,000 cash but they could negotiate to a minimum price of £120,000.

Later on Saturday 21 July in Douglas the Steam Packet Board was informed of an enquiry from Italians residing in Naples, as to the possible charter of the ship for 12 months with a view to outright purchase after that. They intended trade for the vessel would be between West Italy, Israel and Morocco. The Company thought about it but decided chartering **MONA'S QUEEN** was not an option. Later, permission was sought by a prospective purchaser to view the Lloyds Records of the ship to see if she could require the classification to trade between Miami and Nassau.

There was however progress to report by 1 September 1962. The broker informed the Company that an offer had been received from Messrs Chandris of £75,000 and also an offer of £80,000 from a Mr Typaldos who had inspected the vessel on 31 August. His offer was 10% down, £42,000 on delivery of vessel "...*with balance in one year against first mortgage, repayable in half yearly instalments with 5% interest.*"

Kellocks also suggested that a Swedish client was interested in the ship and there was a possibility of an inspection the following week. This last piece of information encouraged the Company to reject the offers of Chandris and Mr Typaldos in the hope of a better deal from the Swedes. However this did not materialise as when the Swedes inspected the ship they decided she was not suitable. Meanwhile Mr Typaldos had increased his offer to £90,000 but it was subject to the ship receiving a certificate for a voyage to Greece and of obtaining a license to operate in Greek waters within one month of arriving.

The brokers were of the opinion that the Chandris offer could be increased to £100,000. The Steam Packet Company agreed but the Chandris Group reiterated their offer of £75,000. It had also been discovered that **MONA'S QUEEN** needed some machinery repairs which included the emergency fire and bilge pump injection valve together with the port turbo generator turbine nozzle box...it sounds very complex but most worrying was that these repairs involved lifting the turbine itself and it could only be done in dry dock. This was a blow as the usual terms of the sale included the conditions "*free of recommendation*" and "*usual dry dock clause.*" All this might very well have a detrimental effect on the eventual sale price. Mr Typaldos meanwhile had again offered £90,000 but with further conditions and instalments so the Company once again rejected his offer.

By Saturday 22 September 1962 it was clear to the Steam Packet Board that Messrs Chandris would only offer £75,000 for the vessel considering the work that needed to be done. The broker was told by the Steam Packet Board to let Chandris know £100,000 was now the asking price, considering the repairs, although they would accept £90,000. Chandris failed to increase their offer however so the Steam Packet Board came up with an interesting alternative. The broker was instructed to offer Chandris **KING ORRY** instead, which at the time was free of "*recommendations*" and had a valid trading certificate for the sum of £80,000.

Subsequently Mr Chandris and his Marine Superintendent, Mr Clarke inspected **MONA'S QUEEN** at Barrow and then **KING ORRY** at Liverpool. They came down in favour of **MONA'S QUEEN** and this time offered £60,000, outright sale with immediate deliver 'as lying at Barrow.' The Steam Packet considered this far too low an offer and rejected it. They instructed the broker to offer both **KING ORRY** and **MONA'S QUEEN** for sale.

MONA'S QUEEN was offered at £75,000 for an outright sale and immediate delivery. There would be a dry dock clause included in the sale (the Steam Packet accepted they would have to pay for the machinery repairs) and that a spare tail end shaft, a spare bow anchor and a spare propeller would also be included. **KING ORRY** was offered at £82,000 for an outright sale and immediate delivery, her Class would be maintained without recommendations, all her trading certificates were valid and the same spares would be included in the price. The Steam Packet Board were told on Saturday 29 September that after extensive negotiations with Chandris

they had accepted **MONA'S QUEEN** at £68,500 as an outright sale with immediate delivery at Barrow and both parties would share the cost of the machinery repairs. The ship initially would be transferred to the Liberian flag and would enter dry dock at Barrow on Monday 1 October for work to be carried out. Various formalities regarding the sale and transfer of flag were ongoing during October but surprisingly on 13 October Chandris had enquired whether the Steam Packet Company might be prepared to sell the **KING ORRY** as well for prompt delivery. The Steam Packet responded that until the sailing programme was finalised for the forthcoming season it would not be clear whether the sale of a further vessel was possible. Undeterred Chandris offered cash of £70,000 for immediate delivery of **KING ORRY**. The Board of the Steam Packet discussed the proposal at length and at one stage were inclined to accept the offer, with conditions. However eventually they decided that they were not able to sell another ship at this time and the offer was rejected. Chandris upped his offer to £80,000 a month later but the sailing programme by then had been finalised and **KING ORRY** had a full role to play. Mr Chandris however really wanted **KING ORRY** and enquired again in June 1963 whether the Company would consider a private sale to him, personally. The Company however informed him there was no change in the situation and that **KING ORRY** was still needed in the Steam Packet fleet. Not to be put off Mr Chandris tried again in September 1963 but this time he offered only £68,000 as the cost of refitting and converting **MONA'S QUEEN** to his requirements had been a lot more than he had anticipated. His offer was rejected.

Above: **KING ORRY** *(IV) was also offered for sale in 1962 as negotiations to sell her sister kept stalling. Here she is in April 1960, still with her cowl, leaving Liverpool.*

Author's Collection

Meanwhile **SNAEFELL** had been damaged while at the coaling berth at Ardrossan on 24 June. Captain Craine reported to the Steam Packet Board on 21 July that during a severe westerly gale "...*despite the use of two offshore ropes in an endeavour to prevent the vessel from falling on the piles* **SNAEFELL** *had received an indent in way of the boiler room, starboard side, together with slight damage to the main belting, while damage was also sustained to the piles on the quay.*"

Unfortunately the damage was more severe than at first thought. Once back in Liverpool she was surveyed and it was found that the bilge plates had also been damaged. **SNAEFELL** was drydocked immediately and essential repairs had been carried at a cost of £1,150. Repairs to the piling at Ardrossan amounted to about £80.

Above: **SNAEFELL** *(V) on No 1 berth Victoria Pier, Douglas, on 28 August 1963, about a year after her incident at Ardrossan.* **BEN-MY-CHREE** *(IV) can be seen on No 3 berth.*

Author's Collection

Proposals for the 1963 passenger services were submitted to the Steam Packet Board at Douglas on Saturday 27 October 1962. There was a full discussion as to whether the proposed services could be operated by seven vessels rather than eight...the possible sale of **KING ORRY** to Chandris was still a possibility. However it was decided that if passenger numbers were more or less the same as in 1962 it would not be wise to try and manage with one vessel less but a further review could be undertaken at the end of 1963.

The 1963 passenger services were agreed as follows:

Liverpool and Douglas:
Double daily sailings from Friday 31 May to Monday 9 September
Ardrossan and Douglas:
Sunday 2 June to Friday 6 September
Belfast and Douglas:
Friday 31 May to Friday 6 September
Dublin and Douglas:
Thursday 30 May to Tuesday 10 September
Heysham and Douglas:
Every Wednesday from 10 July to 21 August and Thursdays 1 and 8 August
Llandudno and Douglas:
Wednesdays 26 June to Wednesday 28 August inclusive

On 3 November 1962 the Steam Packet Company Board were informed that the Liverpool and North Wales Steamship Company was to cease trading. The Steam Packet Company were aware of the passenger numbers carried by **ST TUDNO** during her final year of service and of the costs of providing a possible service in 1963 by Steam Packet vessels. It would not be possible due to the size of the Manx vessels to operate to Menai Bridge but it was decided to offer an experimental service between Liverpool and Llandudno during the 1963 season. Sailings would be as follows:

Every Sunday from 2 June to 1 September inclusive
Every Tuesday from 16 July to 27 August inclusive
Every Thursday from 13 June to 29 August inclusive
Whit Monday 3 June and Bank Holiday Monday 5 August

Fares on the new Liverpool to Llandudno sailings would be a one class day excursion fare of 21/-, a return fare of 25/- and a single of 15/-.

Inevitably there was great disappointment at Menai when it was learned that the Steam Packet vessels would not be operating to Menai Bridge. The Menai Bridge Urban District Council wrote to the Steam Packet suggesting that they should take over **ST TRILLO** and operate her, or failing that operate the Packet ships to Menai when "...*the tides would be such that any anticipated hazards could be overcome.*"

When Mr Alexander of the Steam Packet Company met with representatives of the Liverpool and North Wales Steamship Company at their offices in Liverpool on 9 November and examined the passenger carryings of **ST TRILLO** in 1961 and 1962 it was deemed uneconomic for the Manx Company to operate her on a service between Llandudno and Menai Bridge. The Council were also informed that the Steam Packet Company were not inclined to risk their vessels at Menai. In the event **ST TRILLO** was bought by P&A Campbell Ltd and enjoyed a further successful few years sailing for that Company in the Bristol Channel and along the North Wales coast on some of her former routes.

Above: **ST TRILLO** *in August 1961 off Llandudno Pier. 1961 was the only year she sported the light green hull colour.*

Author's Collection

ANOTHER NEW VESSEL AND A MAJOR MISHAP AT PEEL

The Manager had reported to the Steam Packet Company Board on 3 October 1962 that the cargo vessel **PEVERIL** (II) was due a special survey in January 1964 and that to pass this survey she would need to be re-boilered and that "...*very extensive repairs carried out on the whole of the Boat Deck and on the Main Deck adjacent to the engine and boiler casings.*"

Due to the expense and age of the vessel it was decided that **PEVERIL** would need to be replaced by the early part of 1964 and that second hand tonnage would be sourced to replace her. If that proved not to be possible then a new build would have to be considered. By 6 December it was clear that no suitable second hand tonnage was available and so a specification for a new vessel had been prepared by the Superintendents and Management. Tenders would be invited from:

Ailsa Shipbuilding Company, Troon
Blyth Dry Docks and Shipbuilding Company, Blyth
Caledon Shipbuilding and Engineering Company Ltd, Dundee
Cammell Laird and Company, Birkenhead
Hall, Russell and Company Ltd, Aberdeen
Harland and Wolff Ltd, Belfast

By 2 February 1963 tenders had been received from Ailsa, Blyth, Caledon and Cammell Laird. There was also a tender from Burntisland Shipbuilding Company, Harland and Wolff having decided not to tender.

Full consideration of the proposed new cargo vessel was given at a full Steam Packet Board Meeting on Tuesday 26 February and it was "...*agreed that the new vessel would be fitted with British Polar engines sited aft, 2 cranes (for speedier working) and 2 derricks all on centre line...MacGregor steel hatches and the hull riveted up to the water line.*"

The Blyth Company and Burntisland had not quoted for a vessel with engines aft so the issue rested with Ailsa Shipbuilding Company who quoted £273,500, Cammell Laird who quoted £342,970 and Caledon of Dundee who quoted £377,500.

It transpired that Ailsa Shipbuilding were the only ones to offer two cranes and two derricks (the other two had specified four cranes). Thus Ailsa's tender was accepted with delivery within 12 months.

*Above: **PEVERIL** (II) berthed at Douglas in August 1963.*

Ships of Mann Collection

Meanwhile the age of another of the Company's cargo vessels, **CONISTER**, was causing concern as she was approaching 43 years of age and was due a Lloyd's Special Survey at her next overhaul in February 1964. The Manager anticipated that major repairs might be necessary, especially to the hull and decking and that the cost would not be justifiable on such an elderly vessel. The question was if she was sent to the breakers, should she be replaced by second hand tonnage? It was decided to get the brokers, C W Kellock and Company to attempt to source suitable second hand replacement tonnage. On 24 July **CONISTER**'s fate was sealed when it was decided to definitely sell her to the breakers at the appropriate time. Kellocks had come up with some second hand vessels in the meantime, but none were suitable.

Meanwhile on 5 September 1963 it was decided to name the new cargo vessel **PEVERIL**, subject to Ministry of Transport approval. The Ministry informed the Company that naming the new ship **PEVERIL** was fine but their present ship of the same name would have to be renamed. Thus it was decided to rename the old steamer **PEVERIL II**. The new ship was launched on 3 December 1963 at Troon. The Board also decided a new build to replace **CONISTER** would also be preferable and invited the Troon Company to tender for a replacement vessel to the cost of about £150,000. Ailsa came up later with the proposal to build a vessel to the Steam Packet's specification for £155,000, fitted with British Polar oil engines situated aft.

On Thursday 6 February 1964 the Superintendent Engineer reported to the Board that **BEN-MY-CHREE** was suffering from badly leaking boiler tubes and consideration should be given, considering her age, to her being replaced by new tonnage. Her turbines were also showing signs of severe wear. The badly leaking boiler tubes had caused concern on two separate occasions during the 1963 season. Furthermore "… *From investigations carried out during the vessel's current overhaul the Superintendent Engineer has come to the conclusion that although repairs can be effected when necessary, the time has come when he feels consideration should be given to the replacement of the* **BEN-MY-CHREE** *by other tonnage.*"

There was evidence on the water side of the tubes of pitting and corrosion and there were two cracks in one of the inside seam plates. Furthermore one large rivet head had dropped off! As far as the turbines were concerned there was evidence of wear on the impulse wheels of each of the high pressure turbines due to steam erosion. Retubing of the boilers was not an option as the Ministry of Transport and Lloyds Surveyors were of the opinion that the rest of the boiler structures would be under considerable pressure because of the "*…new material values stressing the older metal construction of the boilers which have become fatigued with age.*" There was however no reason why the ship could not remain in service during the 1964 and 1965 seasons as long as

it was realised that she might have to be taken out of service from time to time for 'running repairs.'

Above: **BEN-MY-CHREE** *(IV) on 14 August 1965, in her final year of service. She has just come in from Liverpool with the 0900 sailing and later in the day she sailed for Ardrossan.*

Author's Collection

On 9 January 1964 it had been decided to build another cargo vessel to supplement the services provided by **FENELLA** and the soon to be in service **PEVERIL** which was completing at the Ailsa Shipbuilding Yard at Troon. After negotiation the Company accepted Ailsa's offer of building a new, smaller vessel for the sum of £155,000. **PEVERIL** had cost £273,500. The new vessel was to be paid for in six instalments. Meanwhile with the delivery of the new **PEVERIL** imminent, the board decided on 13 February 1964 to place the old steamer **PEVERIL II** in the hands of C W Kellock & Co Ltd for disposal any time after mid-March preferably for further service.

Meanwhile the new **PEVERIL** underwent her sea trials on Wednesday 4 March 1964 departing from Troon at 0830 hours. It was reported on 12 March that these had been successful. A mean speed of 13.047 knots was attained on the first double run over the Skelmorlie Measured Mile after which further runs were successfully carried out at reduced power. D F calibration, steering, manoeuvring and anchor trials were carried out off Cumbrae. She was taken over by the Company at noon on Thursday 5 March and arrived in Douglas on Saturday 7 March at 0400 hours.

It was not surprising that the old **PEVERIL II** could not be sold for further service given her age and so the Company resolved to sell her for breaking. They were informed on 23 April 1964 by the broker, Kellock, that several firm offers had been made from shipbreakers but a firm decision was deferred until 30 April when it was decided to accept an offer from Belcon Shipping and Trading Co Ltd of London for the sum of £8,000, "… *vessel to be in condition to be taken away by crew and bunker coals to be included in the price.*" The ship was handed over to her new owners on Friday 22 May. She ended up at Glasson Dock, just south of Heysham, for scrapping.

*Above: **PEVERIL** (III) in Coburg Dock, Liverpool in April 1965. She is in her original condition.*

Author's Collection

*Above: **PEVERIL II** at Glasson Dock prior to breaking.*
Author's Collection

Meanwhile by the time the Board of Directors met on 27 August 1964 the completion of the new smaller cargo vessel was imminent and so it was decided to offer **CONISTER** for sale at the end of the year. On 3 September at a Steam Packet Board Meeting in Douglas it was resolved to name the new cargo vessel **CUSHAG** and that Mrs W E Costain be invited to launch her at Troon on 5 November 1964. Sadly the name **CUSHAG** was not available so on 24 September it was resolved to name her **RAMSEY** and failing that **BARRULE** or **GREEBA** in that order. **RAMSEY** was successfully launched at 1225 as planned on 5 November.

Surprisingly a possible purchaser of **CONISTER** for further service inspected the ship at the beginning of November 1964 but it came to nothing. She was therefore offered to shipbreakers on 7 November 1964 and by 9 January there had been progress in disposing of her. Offers had been received from Irish, Scottish and English breakers for the ship but the offer from the Scottish Breakers, who were Arnott Young & Co of Greenock was accepted - they paid £4,325 for the old vessel which was the last single hatch cargo vessel operating on the Irish Sea.

Meanwhile **RAMSEY** had undergone sea trials in the Firth of Clyde on 25/26 January 1965. These were reported to have gone well despite fog on the 25th having curtailed the trials early. A double run over the Skelmorlie Measured Mile on the 26th produced a speed of 10.872 knots. The vessel was accepted by the Company and on 27 January she sailed from Troon and then proceeded to Ramsey where she loaded cargo and sailed for Liverpool on 28 January - her maiden voyage.

On 20 February 1964 the Steam Packet Board were given details of a major incident involving **MONA'S ISLE** which was her grounding at Peel on Friday 15 February 1964, which became a major problem for the Steam Packet Company and resulted in the ending of the career of a fine Master and in the event could have led to the scrapping of the ship herself. The unfortunate incident had happened on St. Patrick's Isle at Peel where she had been diverted to from Liverpool as an ESE gale had made entry into Douglas untenable the day before. The next morning "…*when leaving there…for Douglas - where conditions were then favourable for berthing - in order to take up the 9 a.m. sailing to Liverpool, going astern and swinging when clear of the breakwater the vessel grounded at the stern on the rocks on St. Patrick's Isle at 6.37 a.m.*"

Two local fishing boats helped to tow the vessel off the rocks and she went to anchor in Peel Bay. Damage was at once thought to be serious and two tugs from Alexander Towing Co Ltd of Liverpool, **NORTH END** and **NORTH WALL**, were engaged to tow the stricken **MONA'S ISLE** to Liverpool leaving Peel at 1000 on Saturday 16 February. She berthed alongside the Princes Landing Stage at 1730 on the Sunday and entered dry dock at Cammell Laird later that same evening. In the meantime her Master, Captain Clucas had been relieved of his command and Captain Griffin was put in temporary charge for her tow

to the Mersey. As expected the damage was extensive. Her rudder had been broken off and was missing and the stock was twisted and bent. Her sternframe was broken and the lower portion was missing. Both propellers were badly damaged as were both tailshafts. It was anticipated that the steering gear had also suffered severe damage. The rudder, both propellers and tailshafts were beyond repair and would have to be replaced and the stern frame would have to be repaired and renewed. As well as all this, it was anticipated that both port and starboard turbines would have to be opened up for inspection along with thrusts and gearing. Costs of repairs were estimated at a minimum of £30,000 and this did not include fees to the owners of the two fishing vessels and to Alexandra Towing. This eventually increased to £61,000. It was thought two dry dockings would be necessary and the ship would not be back in service before June. Captain Clucas had been interviewed but "…*beyond stating that he must have turned the vessel too sharply after leaving Peel Breakwater and could not see land because of the darkness - in fact he was unaware of the danger even up to the moment of impact - he could throw no light on the matter.*"

Captain Clucas was asked to prepare as extensive a report as possible as were the other Officers of the ship and they were to be interviewed at a later date. The standing down of Captain Clucas from command was

*Above: A repaired **MONA'S ISLE** (V) arrives at Douglas from Llandudno in August 1965.*

Author's Collection

confirmed and he was instructed to undergo a medical examination by his own doctor. Since the mishap *MANXMAN* had maintained the service on her own, sailing from Liverpool at 1100 hours and Douglas at midnight. However *TYNWALD* had been awakened from her winter slumbers to join *MANXMAN* on the winter service.

At a Board Meeting on 25 February 1964 the reports from the Captain and the other Officers were read out as well as statements from various seamen on deck at the time. Both the Marine and Engineering Superintendents were questioned but were both at a loss to understand how it had happened. It was established however that the Captain had called the Chief Officer to the Bridge just before the impact and "*...the latter was on his way there when he observed the proximity of the vessel to the land although it was then too late for him to do other than to call out to the Master to go ahead on the engines as the vessel grounded immediately afterwards.*"

The Marine Superintendent was of the opinion that Captain Clucas must have been feeling unwell and that he had always found him to be a most careful Master. The Board decided to give consideration to requiring all Masters to undergo a medical examination every twelve months. The subsequent medical reports concerning Captain Clucas revealed that he was suffering from high blood pressure and was taking medication to control this problem. He stated that as *MONA'S ISLE* swung in Peel Bay he had begun to feel unwell and had called for the Chief Officer but after that he could remember nothing. He had not been aware that his medication, especially the amount he had been prescribed, had the effect of slowing him down and thus could not appreciate at the time of the accident, what was going on. The Chief Officer, Mr Kennaugh, was of the view that the Master had "*...suffered a complete mental blackout.*" He had seemed incapable and dazed and could not take in the information that the ship had grounded. It was the Chief Officer who had ordered the starboard anchor to be let go and who had ordered the closure of all the watertight doors and then inspected the vessel to make sure she was not taking in water. Mr Kennaugh was thanked by the Board of Directors for the way he had handled the situation.

After further reports were subsumed by the Steam Packet Board of Directors decided the following course of action:

1)   The Master was negligent in that he was not on the flying bridge when proceeding astern
2)   The Master, soon after leaving port, became medically unfit to command his ship
3)   On medical grounds the Master cannot be considered fit to resume command
4)   At all times when a vessel is proceeding astern a lookout must be established on the stern

It was decided that Captain R Clucas should be suspended on full pay and then retired on a disability pension.

On 7 May 1964 it was reported that repairs to *MONA'S ISLE* had been held up by strikes by shipwrights at the Cammell Laird Yard. A new rudder and stern frame had been manufactured in Holland and various other repairs to damaged components had been completed. However it was decided to "*...place the MONA'S ISLE in the hands of Gordon Alison & Co of Birkenhead for the completion of the repairs and fitting of the new sternframe, rudder, propellers, tail shafts, gear wheel and pinions. All new materials will be available by early June, the two new propellers will be delivered about the middle of June (spare propellers from the SNAEFELL are available if necessary) while Cammell Laird expect to complete the work on the tail shafts, gear wheel and pinions by the end of this month. Gordon Alison & Co have indicated that they hope to carry out all the work in time to enable the vessel to be on service at the end of June.*"

In the event repairs went well and *MONA'S ISLE* undocked on 10 July after the completion of the sternframe and rudder replacements. Dock trials in the East Float at Birkenhead of the propelling machinery on 13 July were satisfactory and the ship proceeded to sea the next day for further trials which were also satisfactory. She resumed service on 15 July 1964. However at one time, before repairs were authorised, consideration was given to withdrawing *MONA'S ISLE* and disposing of her for breaking, the damage was considered to be so severe.

MORE NEW TONNAGE

The condition of **BEN-MY-CHREE** was further discussed by the Steam Packet Directors on 26 February 1964 and although it was probable she could be kept in service for another two seasons, the issue of her replacement was now becoming pressing. The Management of the Company presented a report to the Board of Directors highlighting the fact that the conveyance of motor vehicles was increasing substantially following the introduction of **MANX MAID** in 1962 and that advance bookings for the 1964 season were 50% up on 1963. It was decided that a second passenger/car ferry was desirable and that Cammell Laird be approached to build a duplicate of **MANX MAID** which would be cheaper than going through the usual tendering process with other builders as long as the Cammell Laird quote was reasonable. On Thursday 19 March it was revealed that Mr Johnson of Cammell Laird had written to the Company to say they could build a repeat of **MANX MAID** and give delivery by April 1966 and that an assessment of the cost would be between £1,250,000 and £1,270,000. By 9 April certain amendments to the design of **MANX MAID** had been put forward by the Marine and Engineering Superintendents and the Company decided to ask Cammell Laird for a firm quote and not put the new ship out to tender.

The firm quote from Cammell Laird was presented on 7 May 1964. For a repeat of **MANX MAID** it was £1,268,000 but Cammell Laird emphasised that increased costs and improvements to the original design would result in a 3% increase to this figure to £1,306,040 which if accepted would be a firm price and "*...not subject to variation.*"

Matters were discussed further in Douglas on 27 May 1964. On the advice of the Marine and Engineering Superintendents it was decided to incorporate into the new vessel additional private cabins and increased passenger accommodation on the Bridge Deck and in the Dining Saloon. It is interesting to note that the Company saved £3,418 by a reduction in the thickness of the teak deck by half an inch to two inches as compared with **MANX MAID**. However the stabilisers on **MANX MAID** had been found to be unsatisfactory when the ship was sailing at less than 14 knots and Cammell Laird had been asked to investigate improvements to the design. On 18 June 1964 it was decided to fit a larger type of stabiliser on the new vessel at an extra cost of £5,000. A further proposal to reduce the number of lifeboats from six, as on **MANX MAID**, to four was rejected by the Ministry of Transport. By 15 October 1964 it had been decided that the seating capacity of the First Class Lounge on the new vessel compared with **MANX MAID**, would be increased to 136 and that of the Second Class Lounge to 155 and the Dining Room to 61. The additional cost of these measures was £3,100.

The fate of **BEN-MY-CHREE** was sealed on 3 December 1964. As long as construction of the new car ferry was progressing satisfactorily it was decided that the old ship would be offered for sale at the end of the 1965 season around mid - September. It was intended to take the inflatable liferafts from **BEN-MY-CHREE** for use on the new car ferry and buoyancy seats, certain items of upholstery "*...for other of our vessels whilst brass fittings will also be withdrawn if the vessel is sold for breaking up.*"

*Above: Fate sealed in 1964 but **BEN-MY-CHREE** (IV) makes a wonderful sight a few years earlier taking the 1030 sailing to Douglas from Liverpool on 27 July 1959.*
Author's Collection

At a Board Meeting in Douglas on 27 August 1964 the Steam Packet Company decided that it was important that they keep abreast of developments concerning hovercraft and hydrofoils. A subsidiary Company was formed called Manx Sea Transport Ltd with a capital of £10,000 with the purpose of "*...investigating, developing and operating new forms of sea transport...*" By October they were informed that a hydrofoil was available for purchase from Norwegian interests. She would be able to carry about 130 passengers at a speed of 35 knots at a consumption of about 380 litres of gas oil per hour. The purchase price was £180,000 with delivery in late February or March 1965. The Steam Packet asked for more information - and a photograph! Eventually, once plans and photos were perused, it was realised that the vessel was designed for operation in calm inshore waters and would be unsuitable for service in the Irish Sea.

The dates of the 1965 season passenger summer services were as follows:

Liverpool and Douglas:
Double daily sailings from Friday 28 May to Monday 13 September

Ardrossan and Douglas:
Sunday 6 June to Friday 10 September
Belfast and Douglas:
Friday 4 June to Friday 10 September
Dublin and Douglas:
Thursday 3 June to Tuesday 14 September
Heysham and Douglas:
Every Wednesday from 7 July to 18 August and Thursdays 29 July and 5 August
Llandudno and Douglas:
Wednesday 16 June to Tuesday 7 September
Liverpool and Llandudno:
Sunday 6 June to Sunday 5 September

It was reported to the Directors on 7 October 1965 that from 1 May to 30 September passenger arrivals at Douglas totalled 298,027 (232,445 ordinary and 65,582 day) compared with 298,185 (233,792 and 64,393 respectively) in 1964 a decrease of 158. Motor vehicles landed at Douglas numbered 10,569 compared with 9,423 the year before.

Before the main season started in 1965 another mishap to **MONA'S ISLE** was reported to the Board on 11 March. It had occurred on 3 March when she was berthing at the South Edward Pier at Douglas. The vessel, under the command of Captain W E McMeiken had left Liverpool at 1100 hours but on arrival in Douglas Bay at 1445 hours a severe snowstorm had reduced visibility to one cable and the ship was unable to enter the Harbour. About an hour later, after the ship had been steaming around Douglas Bay the visibility improved enough for her to attempt to berth. As she was approaching the South Edward berth she was caught by a severe squall of wind causing a wire mooring rope to part and the ship fell heavily on to the south east corner of the pier. The starboard anchor had been deployed and fenders placed over the side but damage nevertheless was caused to the top belting on the starboard side for about thirty feet. A gangway door on the shelter deck was also damaged as was some maindeck belting. With difficulty the ship was moored on the north side of the pier, bows to seaward (an unusual sight at the time). The thirty passengers were disembarked but it was found to be impossible to take off the motor cars, parcels and deck traffic. The vessel thus put to sea again and sailed round to Peel Bay, the weather conditions being still severe, a SE storm force gale with heavy seas, snow and poor visibility. The following day the weather improved enough for the ship to sail back round to Douglas and then sail to Liverpool at 1745. Temporary repairs had been undertaken at Douglas and the ship remained in service until just prior to the Easter Holidays when she was replaced by **KING ORRY**. Repairs to **MONA'S ISLE** eventually amounted to £3,750.

Above: **MONA'S ISLE** *(V) seen later in 1965 (11 September) in Morpeth Dock, Birkenhead, in the company of* **KING ORRY** *(IV) and* **SNAEFELL** *(V).*
Allan Jones

The Steam Packet Board were also informed that on 9 March while at Liverpool under the command of Captain L Callow and whilst she was moored alongside the Princes Landing Stage, **MANXMAN** was struck by the Mersey Ferry **ROYAL DAFFODIL** during a sudden dense fog "*...the point of contact being somewhere between the port shoulder and amidships.*" There was no evidence of any damage but at 0810 hours the same day the tug **CEDARGARTH** also collided with **MANXMAN** in the way of the main deck doors aft on the port side. This time there was damage to the doors and the belting as well as "*...considerable distortion of the frames and shell plating in the 2nd Class Lower Lounge and after end of the Engine Room.*" Damage was not sufficient for her to be taken out of service, temporary repairs were affected at Douglas and permanent repairs were to be carried out during her annual refit after Easter. Repairs were estimated at £2,750 and the Steam Packet held Rea Towing responsible.

There was another collision that the Steam Packet Directors were informed about which had taken place on 19 March involving the cargo vessel **PEVERIL**. She "*...sailed from Douglas at 2pm...and proceeded to enter the East Brunswick Lock...at 10.10pm. **PEVERIL** struck the west half of the inner gates with her stem at about 10.15pm displacing them and was swept stern first into the river by the onrush of water from the dock. During this period the **BOSCO** which was in the Brunswick Dock waiting to sail from Liverpool was also swept out into the river and the two vessels came into collision.*"

This was a serious incident and there was of course damage to **PEVERIL** and she entered Cammell Laird at Birkenhead soon afterwards for repairs to her stern and starboard side which were estimated to cost £3,125. The Company feared they might be responsible for damage to **BOSCO** and the lock gates and several other vessels in the dock system had been damaged due to the sudden escape of water through the lock. The Master, Captain A W G Kissack was asked for a full report and the Steam Packet Company's solicitors were advised of the situation.

Above: **PEVERIL** *(III) working cargo at the Office Berth, Douglas, in July 1965, a little time after she had had an altercation with the East Brunswick lock gate at Liverpool.*

Author's Collection

In the event the Mersey Docks & Harbour Board let it be known they would claim in excess of £200,000. Moss Hutchison Line claimed £4,500 for damage to their vessel **KARNAK**.

For many years it had been the custom to lay up some vessels at Barrow and some at Morpeth Dock Birkenhead. On 3 June 1965 the Company learned that the Mersey Docks & Harbour Board were to remove a veranda in the Morpeth Dock which would leave room for the berthing of an additional vessel during the winter. This meant that it would be possible to berth five vessels in the Morpeth Dock and one at the Vittoria Cross Berth. It was thus decided to berth all of the vessels at Birkenhead during the winter and so the long association with Barrow was nearly at an end. However **LADY OF MANN** was laid up at Barrow during the winter of 1965, the only vessel of the fleet to be there.

It was resolved by the Directors on 19 August 1965 to name the new car ferry **BEN-MY-CHREE** and that Mrs Brownsdon had accepted an invitation to perform the launching ceremony. The old **BEN-MY-CHREE** was to be renamed **BEN-MY-CHREE II**. Surprisingly considering her age, the Company were informed by the shipbroker on 16 September that several enquiries had been received from Greek and English interests with a view to purchasing the vessel for further service. However

nothing came of these and the broker was eventually instructed to offer the ship for demolition on 21 October 1965.

However no sooner had this been decided then the Directors of the Steam Packet Company were informed, on 28 October 1965, of problems in the construction of the new vessel which up to then had been progressing well. The builders informed the Steam Packet Company that there had been difficulties with the fabrication of the boiler drums resulting in a delay of eleven weeks in delivery from the manufacturers Babcock and Wilcox. Pre-Easter delivery of the new ship was not now going to happen and the earliest sea trials would be possible was estimated to be 9 May 1966. The Steam Packet were most perturbed by this and other construction problems related to the boilers which had only just come to light. The Board decided to inform Cammell Laird that delivery of the vessel by mid-May was essential and failure to do this would result in serious difficulties. In the event sea trials for the new ship were scheduled for 9/10 May 1966.

On 18 November 1965 the Company accepted an offer from Van Heyghen Frères of Belgium of £35,600 for **BEN-MY-CHREE II** 'as is, where is' at Birkenhead. There had been three other offers for the ship including one of £27,000 from Thos W Ward Ltd.

Above: Winter lay-up in Morpeth Dock, September 1965. **SNAEFELL** (V), **TYNWALD** (V), **KING ORRY** (IV), **MONA'S ISLE** (V) and the withdrawn **BEN-MY-CHREE** (IV). Mersey ferry **OVERCHURCH** is also in the picture.

Author's Collection

Above: **BEN-MY-CHREE II** seen in Morpeth Dock, Birkenhead, in October 1965.

Author's Collection

Meanwhile on the Firth of Clyde, there had been developments at Ardrossan, at the beginning of February 1966, which could impact on the Steam Packet's service to Douglas. It transpired that Montgomerie Pier Station at Ardrossan was due to close following the recommendations of Dr Beeching. Objections were made and it was unclear whether the pier and its station would be available to the Steam Packet for the 1966 season. Arrangements were put in hand to berth the Manx steamers at Winton Pier and the Harbour

Company were carrying out structural alterations at this pier to make it suitable for berthing. It was stated however that "*...the quay at South Montgomerie Pier will still be available whether or not the station closes and our Glasgow Agents are examining with the Harbour Co. the possibility of berthing the car ferries there when they visit Ardrossan during the coming season.*"

It was revealed at a later date that Burns and Laird had decided to introduce a new car ferry service between Ardrossan and Belfast and they would need all the adjoining land next to the Winton Pier as well as the permanent occupation of the berth that the Steam Packet wanted. This was coupled with the decision of the Caledonian Steam Packet to remain at Ardrossan having earlier considered Fairlie as an alternative for their service to Arran. It was feared that the Steam Packet may well incur substantial extra costs if berthing arrangements were constantly changed and steamers had to leave the port to go out to anchor at various times... this was in addition to the considerable inconvenience for Steam Packet passengers.

Further news from the Clyde was more welcome in early May when the results of the sea trials of the new **BEN-MY-CHREE** on 9/10 May were presented to the Steam Packet Board on 19 May. She had left Cammell Laird's Wet Basin early on Monday 9 May and had proceeded to Douglas after anchor trials had been satisfactorily concluded. A fault with a manoeuvring valve had curtailed further trials. She sailed into Douglas Bay around 0830 hours and carried out main bow and rudder trials and then set sail for the Skelmorlie Measured Mile on the Clyde where on the morning of 10 May on a double run a mean average speed of 21.472 knots was achieved - the wind at the time was southerly force 3 with a slight sea. After further trials full astern using the bow rudder and then full ahead with the stabilisers deployed the ship set a course back to Douglas at 1100 hours via the south of the Island and commenced a four hour full power endurance trial. The average speed on this was 21.2 knots and the machinery proved satisfactory in every respect. **BEN-MY-CHREE** arrived in Douglas at 1815 hours.

During the trials smoke and fumes from the funnel had been observed descending on to the boat deck and car ramps before clearing the vessel and "...*panting was noticed in the funnel uptake causing considerable vibration.*" Cammell Laird officials were informed of these faults with a view to remedial action being taken when the vessel returned to their Wet Basin the next day. Apart from this the Steam Packet regarded the new ship as having come up to all expectations and she was handed over to the Company at 1630 hours on Wednesday 11 May in the Wet Basin at Birkenhead. The maiden voyage of **BEN-MY-CHREE** took place from Liverpool to Douglas

on Thursday 12 May departing at 1430 hours. During this sailing it was noted however that fumes from the funnel were still descending to the car ramps when the ship was heading directly into the wind and also the main siren of the ship was not working properly. These were to be investigated at the earliest opportunity by the builders.

There was another cause for concern however. The National Seaman's Strike was due to begin three days later on 15 May 1966.

*Above: Making smoke - **BEN-MY-CHREE** (V) begins her maiden voyage on 12 May 1966.*

Author's Collection

*Above: **BEN-MY-CHREE** (V) at the Landing Stage Liverpool, prior to her maiden voyage on 12 May 1966.*

Author's Collection

STRIKES, BOXES, PIERS AND COMPETITION

The Seaman's Strike of 1966 was a major concern for the Steam Packet in particular and the whole of the Isle of Man in general. The TT was postponed as a consequence. A special Board Meeting in Douglas on Saturday 14 May 1966 made the following arrangements:

"*Although none of our deck, engine room or catering ratings had given notice to terminate their employment as from midnight, Sunday 15th May, it is understood they will, of necessity, withdraw their labour as all are members of the National Union of Seamen. Accordingly, arrangements for the safe berthage of those of our vessels in service has been completed as follows:*

BEN-MY-CHREE *and* **MANX MAID** *- Buccleuch Dock, Barrow in Furness*
MONA'S ISLE *- Morpeth Dock, Birkenhead*
PEVERIL *- Coburg Dock, Liverpool*
FENELLA *- Inner Harbour, Douglas*
RAMSEY *- Inner Harbour, Ramsey*
The **LADY OF MANN**, *at present in Langton Dry Dock, Liverpool, will be transferred to the Morpeth Dock, Birkenhead, where the* **SNAEFELL, TYNWALD** *and* **KING ORRY** *are berthed. The* **MANXMAN** *is in Vittoria Wharf, Birkenhead…*"

During the strike the National Union of Seamen were asked to agree at various times that one of the Company's cargo vessels could be permitted to sail to and from the Island to bring in essential foodstuffs and essential goods such as medical supplies and animal foodstuffs. The Company tried on Tuesday 17 May to get **RAMSEY** to sail from Liverpool but the NUS refused permission as in their opinion the Island was not short of anything so soon after the strike had begun. Passenger arrivals on the Island during May 1966 of course plummeted because of the strike. It was reported on 2 June that a total of 3,115 passengers had been landed at Douglas during May 1966 compared with 11,974 in May 1965 and cars had decreased from 852 to 458.

An intriguing suggestion was made by the Manx Government to the NUS and other Trade Unions concerning the TT Races. The Steam Packet Company was asked if it would be possible to bring one of the Car Ferries into service during the weekend beginning Saturday 4 June and the other car ferry to be brought into service the following weekend and a service to be operated by the two vessels in the hope of saving the TT Race Festival. All profits from the operation would be donated to charity. The Steam Packet immediately agreed to the proposal but unfortunately the NUS were having none of it and refused to co-operate. They also refused a request by the Tourist Board for the Company to convey 1,200 old age pensioners to and from Douglas in connection with their holiday scheme. By 9 June the NUS had softened a little. It had been agreed that **PEVERIL** would be allowed to operate a weekly essential cargo service from Liverpool but the cargo each time would have to be vetted by the Union and the Seamen would donate their wages to Union Funds. The first of these sailings was during the evening of Monday 6 June when a total cargo of 550 tons, consisting mainly of foodstuffs and mail was transported to the Island. It was agreed that Company profits from these sailings would be donated to the Merchant Navy Seamen's War Memorial Society. No cargo was allowed to leave the Island except for empty containers.

In view of the strike and the new proposed dates for the TT and MGP Races (depending of course if the strike had been settled), which were 28 August to 2 September for the TT and 13 to 15 September for the MGP, it would become necessary to extend the main passenger sailing season and so it was decided on 16 June that the Liverpool to Douglas double service would continue until Saturday 17 September and the Ardrossan and Belfast sailings would be extended until Friday 16 September. However, in addition, an extra Ardrossan sailing rotation from Ardrossan on Friday 23 September and a return from Douglas on Monday 26 September to take advantage of a long weekend holiday in Glasgow was agreed to. Furthermore it was decided to keep the Dublin service operating until 21 September and Belfast to the 22nd.

By Sunday 26 June there was, at last, cause for some optimism that the strike would soon be settled. There had been various moves to settle the dispute locally (the NUS had come to a separate agreement with Townsend Brothers Ferries Limited) and it had even been mooted that the Manx Government might possibly requisition the Company's steamers if the strike lasted much longer. However now a national settlement looked a distinct possibility and all masters were instructed to rejoin their vessels. In the event the strike was called off on Wednesday 29 June but the NUS instructed their members not to re-join their ships until after midnight on Friday 1 July.

The first sailing by a Manx steamer after the strike was from Liverpool to Douglas at 0930 on Saturday 2 July. It was taken by **MANXMAN**. Most of the ships had undocked at the same time as **MANXMAN**, that is the day before, but **SNAEFELL** only undocked on Tuesday 5 July and **KING ORRY** two days later on 7 July.

all considered. By 9 November the Port of Runcorn had contacted the Steam Packet Company and the Board were very impressed with the possibilities that Runcorn could offer. Services were diverted to Runcorn but costs were found to be 50% higher than at Liverpool. However on 4 January 1968 the Steam Packet Board were informed that in 1967 53,471 tons of cargo was carried by the Company's ships, compared with 60,174 tons the previous year.

Meanwhile problems that had been developing at Llandudno for some time had come to a head at the end of 1966. The Steam Packet Directors were informed on Thursday 17 November 1966 that it was most likely, because of the condition of the Berthing Head at Llandudno Pier, that it would not be possible for ships of the size of the Company's vessels to berth there in 1967 and that the Pier Company would not be rushed into a decision regarding repairs or replacement. This was of concern to the Company of course as it impacted on two routes, those from Liverpool and from Douglas. The Company had decided however to keep this matter confidential, apart from, of course, informing the Isle of Man Government. On 24 November the Board was informed that two schemes for repairs to the Pier had been put forward. The first envisaged spending £55,000

repairing and renewing the existing pilings while the second scheme suggested spending £35,000 on building two dolphins suitable for mooring ships of the size of the Manx Steamers. The Steam Packet Company was of the opinion that the Pier Company did not have the necessary money and were trying to off-load the whole enterprise on to Llandudno Urban District Council. What was clear however was that it was very unlikely that Llandudno Pier would be available for sailings in 1967.

In early December it transpired that winter gales had further damaged Llandudno Pier and that it was probable that even **ST. TRILLO**, now operated by P&A Campbell, would not be able to berth at the Pier in 1967. The Steam Packet Company agreed to have meetings with the Llandudno Pier Company, Llandudno Council and Mr Smith-Cox of P&A Campbell to try to find a way forward. Later meetings with various parties came to the conclusion, long suspected by the Packet, that the Pier Company did not have the money to effect repairs and that even if they took out a loan, the pier dues would be insufficient to service that loan. Even the offer of increasing landing dues from 8d per passenger to 2/- per passenger was not acceptable to the Pier Company. The Council indicated that they were unable to help financially.

Above: **FENELLA** *(III) and* **RAMSEY** *in Coburg Dock, Liverpool in 1967.*

Author's Collection

*Above: The bow of **MONA'S ISLE** (V) berthed at Llandudno.*

Allan Jones

Over the next few months, negotiations between the Steam Packet Company and the Pier Company continued, focused mainly on loans, security and repayment. On 6 September 1967 the Steam Packet were informed that the Pier Company had accepted the offer of an interest free loan of £35,000 from the Manx Company and "... *while no security could be given on the loan, to repay on the basis of allocation of 50% of the passenger dues to be imposed on passengers landing at Llandudno.*"

It was hoped that repairs to the Pier would be complete by the end of May 1968.

Further complications arose late in 1967 when it was discovered that Fortes were preparing a bid to take over the Pier Company at Llandudno and would not guarantee continuing with the repairs. However the Steam Packet Board were informed on 1 February 1968 that the new piling of the Pier's berthing head would commence on 26 February. However as with all this type of work, estimates of cost increased as time went on. Fortes, who now owned the Pier, estimated in March 1968 that costs for completion would be over £58,879. The Steam Packet agreed to increase their advance to £45,000 once again of course to be offset by the landing dues. Although there was much further negotiation and suggestions regarding the Pier at Llandudno the Steam Packet Company were delighted when sailings resumed to North Wales in June 1968.

On 17 November 1967 it was revealed to the Steam Packet's Directors that the cargo vessel **FENELLA** had had her crankshaft condemned during her overhaul at the Ailsa Yard, Troon and it would take five months to manufacture a new one and a further month to fit it meaning the ship would be laid up for six months, resulting in the Company incurring substantial fees for chartering another vessel to take her place. The Company asked Lloyd's surveyors if it would be possible to temporarily repair the crankshaft to enable the ship to continue in service until a new one could be fitted but at first this was turned down. However after much negotiation, including

*Above: **MONA'S ISLE** (V) off Llandudno Pier on a beautiful summer's day.*

Allan Jones

going over the heads of the surveyors in Scotland and appealing directly to Lloyds at London, permission was eventually given for the repairs which would take about two weeks. Meanwhile British Polar Diesels had suggested to the Steam Packet that instead of a new crankshaft they might like to consider a new engine for the vessel. They had one available and it would be quicker than waiting for a new crankshaft. The Company decided to consider this proposal. In the event, after the temporary repairs, *FENELLA* conducted sea trials on 28/29 November and re-entered service soon afterwards.

Some weeks later quotes for a permanent repair to the crankshaft and bedplate came out at £30,400 which included rebuilding the engine. A new engine would cost £52,100. The Engineer Superintendent was of the opinion that a new engine was not necessary and once the repairs were completed the ship should be good for another 15 years.

The future of hovercraft and hydrofoils was never far from the thoughts of the Steam Packet Company Directors at this time and on 24 November 1967 in Douglas Company officials were appraised of the latest developments and discussions concerning the development of these vessels. The Chairman and others had met with a Mr H H Radcliffe and Mr W E Quayle of the Transport Commission. The Commission had made reference to the four SRN4 hovercraft currently under construction, three of which had been earmarked for service in the English Channel. Mr Radcliffe wondered if the Steam Packet would be interested in the other one. The Steam Packet Company was dubious. Firstly they were not sure how such a craft would cope with the heavy seas that often prevailed in the Irish Sea and the question of cost of operation was also a worry. The latter was such a concern that the Board suggested that they would need the help of the Government if they were to pursue the hovercraft option. As the subsidiary Manx Sea Transport was the Company set up to look into hovercraft and hydrofoils it was decided to discuss the matter at the next Board Meeting of that Company.

The future of the Centenary Steamer, *LADY OF MANN*, was discussed for the first time at a Board Meeting in Douglas on 13 April 1967. It transpired that the Board of Trade, referring to the current survey of the ship, had asked how much longer the Company were going to keep her in service. They had informed the Company that future requirements regarding fire and lifesaving appliances might be difficult and the ship would have to have a full hydraulic test on her main boilers at the next survey. The Company decided to inform the Board of Trade that *LADY OF MANN* would only be in service for another four, possibly five, seasons.

Above: ***LADY OF MANN*** *at Douglas on 23 June 1964. By 1967 the Board considered she would have another four or five seasons.*

Author's Collection

It was not only *LADY OF MANN* which was of concern to the Company at the beginning of 1968. On 27 February 1968 the Board of Directors was informed of a number of difficulties with some of the other vessels. *MANX MAID* had suffered a breakdown on 17 February. She had been on passage from Douglas to Liverpool and was in the Queen's Channel when her main engines suddenly stopped and her steering became ineffective. This occurred at 1157 hours. The ship collided with Q17 buoy and the starboard anchor had to be dropped to arrest further drifting of the ship. Although thirteen minutes later the engine room had indicated that the problem had been solved, she got underway again only for the anchor having to be deployed once more at 1237 hours when both main engines stopped again. It was a fuel supply problem and the Captain decided to request tug assistance; *NORTH WALL* and *TRAFALGAR* towed *MANX MAID* to the Landing Stage where she arrived at 1523 hours. This resulted in a bill from Alexander Towing and it cost £90 to repair the shell plating of *MANX MAID* which had come into contact with Q17.

Meanwhile on 19 February *MANXMAN* also broke down at the Princes Landing Stage at Liverpool. It was the port main engine turning gear at fault and although Cammell Laird had carried out a temporary repair, *MANXMAN* was unable to take her 1100 hours sailing to Douglas. It was thus decided to transfer passengers from this sailing to one at 1430 hours by *MANX MAID* which had been scheduled to sail back to Douglas light after her recent repairs to her fuel system and shell plating. However *MANX MAID* once more failed (fuel supply problem once more) so *MANXMAN* was ordered to raise steam immediately, as her fault had been temporarily repaired and she sailed at 1455 hours for Douglas.

There was better news about *FENELLA* - she had returned to service after having her crankshaft renewed at Troon, on 26 February 1968.

*Above: **MANX MAID** (II) departs Liverpool for Douglas in the late 1960s. Shell doors wide open!*

Author's Collection

The Board of Trade continued to be concerned about **LADY OF MANN**, especially the fire protection systems and in February 1968 had insisted that a full sprinkler system be fitted throughout the ship. In fact all ships built prior to 1952 would have to comply with new regulations concerning fire protection and of course this would now include **KING ORRY**, **TYNWALD**, **SNAEFELL** and **MONA'S ISLE**. The cost to the Company was estimated to be not less than £100,000. The Board appreciated that they would have to comply as far as these ships were concerned but decided to ask for an exemption for the older **LADY OF MANN** as she might only be in service for a further two seasons "*…on the understanding that we comply with the other regulations regarding stairways and fire curtains in the alleyways on the Bulkhead deck.*"

The Board of Trade agreed to the Company's request regarding not fitting a sprinkler system to **LADY OF MANN** with the following conditions:

1)   She would not be granted an international certificate so would be unable to service sailings to Dublin in future.

2)   She would only be able to do a maximum of six night sailings per season and on these there would have to be special crew fire patrols on duty.

3)   Emergency lighting on stairs and in alleyways must be fitted. (This applied to **KING ORRY** also)

4)   The Board of Trade requested an indication from the Company for a reduction in the number of passengers carried on day and night sailings.

5)   The ship must only be in service for three more years at the maximum.

The Steam Packet accepted the recommendation of the Marine Superintendent that the Board of Trade had been fair and their conditions for the granting of a further passenger certificate would be accepted. The passenger certificates for **LADY OF MANN** were reduced to 2,400 passengers on day sailings and 2,000 at night from the current 2,873 passengers on all sailings. In fairness however the subsequent survey of **LADY OF MANN** found that her hull was in good condition and that ultrasonic tests had been satisfactory. However it was pointed out that some of the belting was in need of "*…extensive strengthening in the future.*" Meanwhile the sprinkler system work on the other four vessels needed to be tendered for.

The Steam Packet Company had learnt in the autumn of 1968 about the establishment of Norwest Hovercraft Ltd by Sir John Onslow, who intended to set up a service between Fleetwood and Douglas. At a Steam Packet Board Meeting on 5 December 1968 it was learnt that Norwest had chartered a car / passenger ferry, **STELLA MARINA** (1,400grt) to begin the service in 1969. Norwest were of the opinion that it would be another five years before hovercraft would be viable for Manx routes. A meeting was held between the Steam Packet's Manager, Mr A J Fick and Sir John, during which, the latter expressed the view that his proposed service would not be a rival to the Steam Packet as fares charged would be considerably higher and that they were mainly aiming for the day excursion traffic from Blackpool. Norwest Hovercraft, it was stated, wished to work with the Steam Packet Company and requested that they act as Norwest's agents in the Isle of Man. The Steam Packet Manager and his assistant who was also at the meeting were not to be persuaded by such conciliatory arguments and informed Sir John that his new venture was certainly a rival to the Isle of Man Steam Packet Company and no co-operation would be forthcoming. As is well known, Norwest Hovercraft began their service during the summer season of 1969 using *STELLA MARINA* as planned which of course was passenger only as *STELLA MARINA* was a stern loader and no linkspan was available at Douglas which would have enabled her to carry vehicles to and from the Island. During the year however they became more ambitious and had been in discussion with the Isle of Man Harbour Board about the possibility of installing stern loading facilities at Douglas so their ship could be used to her full potential. The Steam Packet Board were horrified when they heard about this, especially as Norwest Hovercraft had said that they were prepared to pay for any new docking facilities at Douglas. The Steam Packet Board surmised, correctly, that as Douglas was a fairly open port the only safe place for the proposed linkspan would be on the north side of the King Edward Pier. This would probably mean that Steam Packet vessels would in future be unable to use that berth. The Steam Packet Board decided that they needed to meet with the Harbour Board, more so since there were rumours that Norwest Hovercraft were attempting to charter a larger vessel named *BORNHOLM*. As we now know, nothing came of these proposals.

Above: STELLA MARINA berthed on the north side of the King Edward Pier, Douglas, on 4 June 1969.
Allan Jones

The first discussion by the Directors of the Steam Packet Company regarding the possible replacement of *LADY OF MANN* took place at a meeting in Douglas on 20 February 1969. The Board realised that the replacement was a matter of urgency and in addition they also informed the company broker, G W Kellock and Co *"...of our possible interest in charter should a suitable vessel, capable of carrying cars and a minimum of 1,400 passengers become available."*

LADY OF MANN herself was damaged on 25 May 1969 whilst lying starboard side to on the Vittoria Wharf at Birkenhead. She was hit by a vessel called *MANSOOR* of Karachi, which was swinging in the Float with the assistance of two tugs. Chief Officer of *LADY OF MANN*, Mr J E Ronan reported that damage *"...consisted of the Counter Rubber aft end shattered for a length of ten feet: the shell plating frames and angle bars in way of the main steering compartment buckled and set in and the rivets and paintwork disturbed. The taffrail, guardrails and ensign flagstaff at the aft end were badly damaged for a distance of eighteen feet."*

In addition, four mooring wires were carried away. However the rudder and propellers had not been damaged and the ship would be able to enter service as scheduled.

On 15 July *LADY OF MANN* was leaving Belfast in dense fog and collided with No 21 Buoy. Captain Callow reported no damage to the vessel but the buoy/beacon 29, according to Belfast Harbour Commissioners would cost £3,000 to repair.

A full discussion as to the replacement of *LADY OF MANN* took place at a Steam Packet Board Meeting on 24 July 1969 at Douglas when it was confirmed that her load-line certificate would expire on 30 June 1972. However the Marine Superintendent did not anticipate any problems in obtaining dispensation for the ship so she could operate in 1971.

But what to replace her with? Hovercraft were discussed again but it was felt that *"...owing to the present limited capacity of present available hovercraft, this type of craft could not replace the carrying capacity of one of our vessels."*

The Steam Packet Board decided that they needed another passenger/car ferry capable of carrying 1,400 passengers and 80 cars with side loading ramps would be the best solution...in other words, another *BEN-MY-CHREE* and *MANX MAID*.

As the matter was further discussed on 29 August 1969 the Marine Superintendent requested that special consideration should be given to the following when asking for tenders for any new vessel:

1)   Improved crew accommodation
2)   Composition and teak deck coverings
3)   Fibre glass lifeboats
4)   Bow thrust
5)   Improved seating for passengers
6)   Increased lounge space

The Engineering Superintendent asked the Board to consider:

1)   Pielstick oil engines instead of Steam Turbines
2)   Two engines to each shaft

Above: Her days were numbered. **LADY OF MANN** (I) off Douglas Head in the late 1960s.

3)   Variable pitch propellers, made of stainless steel
4)   AC electric power

After lengthy discussion it was decided to ask the following Companies to tender for the new vessel:

Cammell Laird, Birkenhead
Harland and Wolff at Belfast
Ailsa Shipbuilding Troon
Swan Hunter on the Tyne
Vickers Armstrong at Barrow
Robb Caledon and Scott Lithgow

In the event Harland and Wolff, Scott Lithgow and Vickers Armstrong asked to be excused tendering due to their current commitments. The Board were also disappointed to hear, at a Meeting on 27 November 1969, that Cammell Laird had also withdrawn from the tendering process as they would be unable to meet the delivery date required. The three remaining shipbuilders submitted tenders for the proposed new vessel:

1)   Swan Hunter Shipbuilders Ltd
        £2,600,000. Delivery by February 1972
2)   Robb Caledon Shipbuilders Ltd
        £2,432,000. Delivery by March 1972
3)   Ailsa Shipbuilding Ltd
        £2,145,000.
        Delivery 27 months after acceptance of tender

Ailsa of Troon also *"...incorporated in their tender certain suggestions regarding modifications of original requirements which, if adopted, would result in a reduction of their quoted figure..."*

It looked like Ailsa Shipbuilding were the cheapest but later they advised the Steam Packet that *"...certain additional items costing in total £12,175, which shipbuilders were prepared to include in their specification without change in the price quoted in the original tender."*

The Steam Packet Company duly gave the contract to Ailsa Shipbuilding and a detailed discussion of requirements and amendments took place in Douglas on 8 January 1970. The vessel was to be powered by two Pielstick oil engines of 5,000 BHP each but the builders were to ensure a service speed of 21 knots was possible. She was to have retractable stabilisers as fitted to **MANX MAID**. Many other details were discussed and decided upon such as the installation of two emergency generator sets, each of 80 KW in lieu of the originally proposed one only which would have been 120 KW - this added an extra £3,000 to the cost and an extra £4,200 was to be expended on a spare tail end shaft.

A NEW QUEEN, DIFFICULTIES AT LIVERPOOL AND A RETURN TO FLEETWOOD

The final contract with Ailsa Shipbuilders at Troon was signed off at a Board Meeting of the Steam Packet Company on 24 February 1970 - the cost would be £2,019,350 with delivery scheduled for March 1972. As a new vessel was on her way, an important part of the Steam Packet infrastructure was on its way out. On 8 January 1970 it was noted that the demolition of the old Imperial Buildings, formerly the Imperial Hotel, had started, at a cost to the Company of £2,000.

It would hardly be conceivable that Mersey Ferries would ever be in direct competition with the Isle of Man Steam Packet Company but this unlikely event could have materialised in the summer of 1970. The Steam Packet Directors were made aware on Thursday 12 February 1970, that Wallasey Corporation Ferries had expressed an interest in running excursion sailings from Llandudno Pier to Menai Bridge. The Steam Packet Company agent, Mr Bouwman, wanted to know what the attitude of the Steam Packet would be to such a proposal. After discussion it was emphasised to Mr Bouwman that the agreement with the Pier Company guaranteed the Steam Packet exclusive use of the pier for sailings between Llandudno and the Isle of Man and between Llandudno and Liverpool and whatever Wallasey Ferries were doing, a berth had always to be available for Steam Packet vessels at Llandudno. With this in mind it was decided that no review of the proposed 1970 timetable to and from Llandudno was necessary. In the event the proposal by Wallasey Ferries did not come to fruition.

It was brought to the attention of the Steam Packet Board on 19 February 1970 that both *KING ORRY* and *LADY OF MANN* required re-equipping with a new type of lifejacket before the coming season. In a further indication that *LADY OF MANN* was on her way out the Company had successfully applied to the Board of Trade for an exemption for her as she was only expected to be in service until the end of the 1971 season. *KING ORRY* however was another matter and the Company had to spend over £4,151 on the new regulation lifejackets which comprised of 2,062 adult ones and 273 for children.

Meanwhile the list of Masters and Chief and Second Officers was being formulated for the 1970 season. Captain T H Corteen was master of *LADY OF MANN* and Fleet Commodore and Captain Harry Kinley was the new Master of *MANXMAN* having previously been with *MONA'S ISLE*. Peter Corrin, at the age of 21, had been appointed as Second Officer of *KING ORRY* having been with *FENELLA* the year before. Peter became Marine Superintendent in later years. Andrew Douglas, at the age of 27, became Chief Officer of *PEVERIL*, having previously been with *FENELLA*. Andrew in later years became Master of *MANX VIKING* and eventually became editor of the magazine *Sea Breezes*. He was

instrumental many years later, in partnership with Steam Packet Managing Director Hamish Ross, in the successful campaign to restore the anchor of *MONA'S QUEEN*, sunk at Dunkirk, to the Isle of Man. A new appointment to the Company was S Cowin as Second Officer of *PEVERIL*. Ken Bridson was Chief Officer and Alan Bridson (no relation) was Second Officer of *MANX MAID* while J E Ronan, aged 41, was the new skipper of the cargo vessel *RAMSEY*, having been Chief Officer of *LADY OF MANN* the year before. J R Kinley was Captain of *SNAEFELL* while Vernon Kinley, aged 33, was Chief Officer. Both of them had previously been with *TYNWALD*.

Captain Thomas Corteen, the Fleet Commodore on *LADY OF MANN* in 1970 had joined the Steam Packet in 1932 as a seaman but by 1934 he was Second Officer on *RUSHEN CASTLE*. By 1939 he held the same rank on *MANXMAN* and was present at Dunkirk but for the rest of the war he was seconded, as many officers were, from the Steam Packet and served in many theatres of the war including the Far East. Rejoining the Steam Packet in 1946 he served on *BEN-MY-CHREE* and, once appointed Master in 1960, commanded most of the passenger ships, finishing in 1972 after *LADY OF MANN* had left the fleet.

Meanwhile the new vessel began to be known by her yard number, Hull No 533. On 5 March 1970 Ailsa Shipbuilding had suggested some improvements to the design of Hull No 533 which included siting the engines further aft than in the original plans and "*...after a full discussion several improvements were agreed which will be communicated to the shipbuilders to be embodied in fresh plans and submitted to the Board for further consideration and approval.*"

Ailsa's proposals were finally accepted by the Directors on 23 April 1970. These included not only siting the engines further aft but also a re-arrangement of cabins, bars and lounges. This involved additional expenditure in some areas but a reduction in others. For example £5,000 was to be saved by having a shorter propeller shaft than originally intended. However later in the summer of 1970 Ailsa informed the Company that a larger diameter fin stabiliser than that fitted to *MANX MAID* would be required by the new vessel. In addition the larger fin could not be a retractable one and the Steam Packet Company was urged to consider a folding type instead. The problem had occurred because the weight of the oil engines on the new ship, as compared with the heavier steam turbines of the older ships, would need to be compensated by adding about two feet to the beam of the ship compared with *MANX MAID* or *BEN-MY-CHREE*. Consequently the draught would be slightly reduced and this in turn would require a wider stabiliser fin at 45 square feet compared to 35 square feet on the steamers. The Steam Packet were concerned that the larger fin area might have a detrimental effect on the speed of the vessel and they were also concerned at the performance of the larger fin at slower speeds. It was decided that further discussion was needed.

By 1 April the Steam Packet Board was informed that the engines were to be tested by Crossley Bros on 20 April and would be fitted into the ship in May and all other machinery and fittings would be installed to enable the launching of the vessel to take place during the first two weeks in November 1971. In addition however the Chairman of the Steam Packet "...*informed Ailsa officials that we will require their firm assurance regarding delivery date in time for the Board to arrive at a decision in August this year in connection with the future of the* **LADY OF MANN**."

The Chairman of the Steam Packet together with the Marine Superintendent and the General Manager visited the Ailsa yard on 27 June. They were concerned that many deliveries from sub-contractors had been delayed but Ailsa were convinced it would not delay the launch of the vessel. However the Kamewa propellers would not be delivered until December so it meant launching the new ship minus her propellers. Enquiries were made to the Yard as well about building a scale model of the new ship "...*preferably cut away, to give a profile of all its facilities and suitable for mobility in connection with travel exhibitions.*"

(This model was in fact built and for many years was in the window of the Company offices in Liverpool in Water Street. In later years it has been on display at Port Erin Railway Station.)

On 9 March 1970 **SNAEFELL** had a damaging collision with the Princes Landing Stage at Liverpool. Captain Harry Kinley had the daunting task of explaining what happened to the Board of Directors on 12 March. **SNAEFELL**, while leaving the South Berth at the Princes Landing Stage at Liverpool stern first in thick fog, had been manoeuvring to avoid another vessel anchored nearby. The starboard anchor had been dropped immediately and the tug **HOLLYGARTH** was engaged to help **SNAEFELL** to berth at the north end of the Stage. Damage to **SNAEFELL** was considerable including "...*extensive concertinaing of stern plating below the main belting.*"

The Chief Engineer reported that fortunately both engines were able to manoeuvre normally after the accident, the boiler room and shaft tunnel were okay and the aft steering gear and rudder were still able to function. The ship entered No 3 West Float Drydock on 10 March and repairs were to be carried out by Messrs. Harland and Wolff Ltd but the full damage to the ship was not fully known at that stage. The Princes Landing Stage had suffered damage and Rea Towing, owners of **HOLLYGARTH**, had put in a claim for salvage. The Company decided that Captain Kinley might like to attend a future Board Meeting in the very near future but

Above: **SNAEFELL** *(V) approaching the Landing Stage at Liverpool at 1915 on 20 July 1972.*

Author's Collection

a later meeting rejected Rea Towing's claim for salvage as **SNAEFELL** had never been in any danger and all her machinery and navigational equipment were in working order. In the event, later in the year, Rea Towing accepted a cheque for £85 in respect of towing services. In order to maintain services **TYNWALD** was recommissioned to stand in for the damaged **SNAEFELL** on 12 March. In the meantime the passenger and car ferry **MANX MAID** operated the Liverpool sailings on her own.

Captain Kinley appeared before the Steam Packet Board again on 2 April 1970. It was noted that a survey of the vessel revealed that repairs, not yet finalised, were estimated to cost £15,500. Repairs, to be carried out to the Landing Stage by the Mersey Docks and Harbour Board would cost in the region of £14,000.

Above: **TYNWALD** *(V) at rest in Morpeth Dock, Birkenhead on 26 May 1971.* **SNAEFELL** *(V) is ahead.*
Author's Collection

Captain Kinley was given a thorough grilling by the Directors and was asked for detailed explanations of the cause of the accident and actions taken afterwards. He used charts and models to explain the circumstances and was asked for "*...full information regarding his seagoing and pilotage experience...*"

It must have been a considerably stressful time for Captain Kinley but his professionalism and clear explanations impressed the Company who decided that "*...his explanation was accepted by the Board, who appreciated that he had been called on to act in an emergency and that none of his actions taken were negligent. It was regretted that he had been involved in such a difficult situation and the anxiety this must have caused him. Captain Kinley thanked the Directors for their kind consideration of this matter and expressed his regret that it had occurred.*"

As well as being occupied extensively with the building of the new passenger car ferry the Directors of the Steam Packet Company were also anxious in 1970 to have a thorough review of the cargo services. It was proposed on 9 April 1970 that a Sub-Committee be set up to "*... consider all aspects of the Company's cargo services and make recommendations as to how they can be improved.*"

It was decided that several issues needed looking at including:

1) Consider ways of maximising the use of containers with recommendations of the best size of container for Manx routes.

Above: **RAMSEY** *at Douglas in the late 1960s. By 1970 her future with the Company was limited.*
Allan Jones

2)	Suitability of the current cargo vessels and how to improve them or replace them with more suitable tonnage.

3)	Reconsider the lay out of quay space at Douglas.

4)	Provision of door to door services for major customers.

5)	To offer attractive terms to attempt to procure cargo business from rival operators such as Ronagency.

It was decided later that 20 foot ISO containers were the best for the Company's needs and later in the summer 12 such containers were purchased.

The Sub-Committee reported to the Directors over two days on 9/10 December. Main recommendations were as follows:

1)	As much cargo as possible should be containerised in the future

2)	Only standard ISO containers should be bought in future

3)	A new Butters type crane should be bought for the warehouse berth at Douglas

4)	*PEVERIL* should be converted to container carrying with limited livestock accommodation

5)	*FENELLA* and *RAMSEY* should be sold and another more suitable cargo/container vessel chartered

6)	Liverpool should remain the main cargo port

The recommendations were accepted and the Sub-Committee was instructed to investigate how the plans could be best implemented.

In the event *PEVERIL* went back to her builders at Troon for the conversion work to be carried out, although the original estimate had to be increased, as the price of steel had risen 10%. Changes to livestock stowage were also required and these were more costly than anticipated. The new estimate was £66,400 which was approved on 3 June 1971.

It is interesting to note the cost of the winter overhauls of some of the vessels in 1969/70. For example Harland and Wolff had written to the Company stating that their gross expenditure from May 1970 had amounted to £61,000 of which £47,000 was apportioned to *SNAEFELL* (that included the repairs following her accident), £8,500 to *KING ORRY* and £5,500 to *LADY OF MANN*. They wanted a substantial payment on account. The Steam Packet Board were unhappy with the amount

Above: FENELLA (III) in Langton Dock, Liverpool in 1972. The containerisation of cargo services meant she had little time left in the Steam Packet fleet.

Author's Collection

apportioned to **SNAEFELL** and did not accept it, stating that they knew damage repairs amounted to £15,500 and £4,500 was needed to replace the cowl on her funnel. They considered the overall cost "...*inflated as a result of union pressure prohibiting engine overhaul work being carried out by our own engineers*." Harland and Wolff were informed that only £40,000 would be forthcoming for **SNAEFELL**.

Considerable alarm was raised in the new Imperial Buildings, Douglas, on 9 July 1970 when the General Manager advised the Board of a telephone conversation with Mr R D Roberts, the Passenger Development Manager of British Rail Shipping, Irish Sea Services. Mr Roberts "...*stated that his department is considering the possibilities of incorporating into their passenger/car ferry service between Heysham and Belfast an en route service to Douglas*."

Mr Roberts later confirmed to the Steam Packet that a scheme was being planned whereby their two vessels on the Heysham and Belfast service would call at Douglas during their daylight sailings during the summer of 1971. The catalyst for this plan was the fact that British Rail had spent a considerable sum of money converting two of their vessels to stern loading car ferries and providing the terminal facilities at Heysham and Belfast but traffic had not realised expectations and "...*the proposed service to Douglas is considered to be a possible means of increasing revenue*."

Mr Roberts was put in no doubt that the Steam Packet Company opposed such a development, which would possibly do irreparable damage to the good relations between them and that the Steam Packet Company would do everything they could to stop it. In the end British Rail dropped the proposal and the Manx Company breathed a sigh of relief.

It was reported to the Steam Packet Board on 16 July 1970 that **MANX MAID** had been damaged by the oiler **ASTRO** at the Princes Landing Stage the day before. **ASTRO** had been attempting to manoeuvre alongside **MONA'S ISLE** but had collided with the stern of **MANX MAID**. Captain Kissack had advised the Board of Directors by telephone that there was a hole in the stern of **MANX MAID** above the water line about 2' 3" in width tapering for a length of 6'. The vessel was attended to immediately by Cammell Laird and every effort was made to get her back into service to take the 1030 hours sailing from Liverpool to Douglas the next day.

Norwest Hovercraft had taken advantage of the Steam Packet's absence from Fleetwood and in 1969 successfully used their chartered vessel, **STELLA MARINA**, on sailings to Douglas. In 1970 however **STELLA MARINA** was not available and Norwest Hovercraft had bought from David MacBrayne Ltd their elderly vessel **LOCHEIL**, built in 1939, which had been sailing from West Loch Tarbert and Port Ellen and Port Askaig on Islay. As successful as this venerable old

*Above: **MANX MAID** departs Douglas in the summer of 1970.*

Allan Jones

vessel had been on her routes to the Hebrides, on the Irish Sea she was unfortunately a disappointment. The Ship was renamed **NORWEST LAIRD**. She had a number of machinery failures caused by engineers unfamiliar with her machinery and because of her certification was unable to sail directly from Fleetwood to Douglas but had to go via St Bee's Head which meant an extended passage time of about six hours.

In the minutes of the Board Meeting of the Steam Packet Company held in Douglas on 30 July 1970 the Board expressed concern over "… *repercussions in the future (could) prove detrimental to the Island in general and sea travel in particular which naturally causes grave concern to us, even though alternative arrangements were made for conveyance (of stranded passengers) by our vessels via Liverpool or by air.*"

The Steam Packet were also having great difficulty in obtaining payment from Norwest Hovercraft for the transfer of their stranded passengers and it was decided that no further credit would be extended to them in this regard. The Steam Packet had asked that the Manx Government assume responsibility for paying for the conveyance of stranded passengers but no guarantee was forthcoming. On 6 August 1970 it was reported that a cheque for £250 had been received from Norwest Hovercraft which went a little way to reducing the outstanding balance which stood at £1,108-12s. Further promises had been made but the Steam Packet decided that legal proceedings were necessary and instructed their solicitors accordingly. In the event however Norwest Hovercraft ceased trading before the end of the 1970 season and its debts were put into the hands of the Receivers.

Summer season 1971 sailings were the last when only two car ferries and six passenger ships were in the fleet. Arrangements for dates of sailings were approved on 15 October 1970 and were as follows:

Liverpool and Douglas double daily sailings:
Friday 21 May to Monday 13 September
Ardrossan and Douglas:
Saturday 22 May to Friday 10 September
Belfast and Douglas:
Friday 21 May to Friday 17 September
Dublin and Douglas:
Thursday 27 May to Thursday 16 September
Heysham and Douglas:
Wednesdays 7 July to 25 August and Thursdays 22 July to 5 August
Llandudno and Douglas:
Thursday 20 May to Wednesday 15 September
Liverpool and Llandudno:
Sunday 30 May to Sunday 12 September
Llandudno Cruises:
Wednesday 19 May to Sunday 12 September

The autumn of 1970 saw the beginning of a long running saga involving the Isle of Man Steam Packet Company,

the Mersey Docks and Harbour Board, the financial difficulties of the latter and the deteriorating condition of the Princes Landing Stage.

It was noted by the Steam Packet Board on 15 October 1970 that the Mersey Docks and Harbour Board were experiencing a "*cash flow*" problem and were intending to increase their harbour, wharf and dock dues which would add over £9,000 to the charges paid by the Steam Packet. They were also intending to increase their passenger tax levy by 50% which in a normal year would cost the Steam Packet an additional £77,800. The Steam Packet Company arranged a meeting with the Dock's Board where they put forward a strong case which stated that "*…the apparently discriminatory and unexpected announcement of passenger tolls increase…would cost us an additional £76,000 in 1971 based on 1970 passenger numbers carried. But if this additional charge be added to our already announced increased fares, the anticipated result must be adverse public reaction and diminishing numbers, consequently the desired increased revenue would not be forthcoming, as for instance it could well mean the elimination of the Liverpool/Llandudno service and Liverpool C.W.S. charter.*"

The Steam Packet also pointed out to the Harbour Board that they had and were continuing to commission car ferries that operated from the Princes Landing Stage, and stressed the harm that would be done to the Isle of Man's economy. The Harbour Board told the Company that because of the deteriorating state of the Princes Landing Stage berthing facilities they would be withdrawn after the 1971 season and the Stage demolished. The Harbour Board were in considerable deficit, the revenue from the Landing Stage was not sufficient to cover its operating costs and necessary maintenance and the Harbour Board could not contemplate replacing the Stage with a new one unless a certain level of income could be guaranteed. The Steam Packet Directors decided that a Landing Stage at Liverpool was essential and decided to appraise the Manx Government of the situation.

On 19 November the Steam Packet Directors were informed that the Harbour Board had decided that there was no alternative to their plans to increase charges. The Steam Packet had been in early discussions with representatives of the Manx Government and although it did not seem likely they would be able to help with the increased dues imposed by the Harbour Board it was thought they might look more sympathetically at the future of the Landing Stage at Liverpool as this was a matter which affected not just the Steam Packet Company but the entire Manx economy.

The Steam Packet Company decided that for the 1971 season they would have to increase fares on the Liverpool routes to Douglas and Llandudno to cover at least some of the extra costs. Increased charter fees from Liverpool were also approved. On 26 November the Manx Company were informed that they had an ally in the form of the Merseyside Passenger Transport Executive who were against the proposal from the Dock Board to cease to provide accommodation for the Mersey Ferries at the Landing Stage - the Mersey Ferries of course would be unable to operate if the entire Landing Stage was taken away. A joint approach with MPTE was approved.

Further meetings discussed the fact that the Harbour Board, by Act of Parliament, was obliged to offer berthing facilities for the cross river ferries free of charge plus offer berthing facilities for sea going vessels as well. It was noted on 17 December that the Harbour Board was trying to promote a Private Member's Bill in Parliament which would repeal these obligations. By this time the Manx Government had discussed the situation with the UK Government and stressed the vital needs of the Isle of Man with regard to suitable berthing facilities at Liverpool.

A meeting of interested parties took place on 15 January 1971 to look at ways forward. Engineers confirmed that the old stage was irreparable and would need to be replaced. It was agreed that if a new stage was to be built the Steam Packet Company would require a minimum of 800 feet of stage for two berths. The UK Government was not represented at this meeting as their view was that the Mersey Docks and Harbour Board would have to at least part finance any new facilities itself. Unfortunately the Harbour Board's credit rating was not good so it all seemed to be pointing in the direction of the Isle of Man Government which might consider providing the necessary finance which would be paid back over a number of years. And of course there was the question of new passenger waiting facilities as it was proposed to demolish the old waiting halls as well.

On 18 February the two possibilities for the Landing Stage at Liverpool were discussed by the Steam Packet Directors at Douglas, that is either repairing the old stage at a total cost of £792,000 with annual costs for 15 years of extra usage being £159,000 or building a new stage at a cost of £1,118,000. Unsurprisingly the Directors favoured the cheaper option of renovating the old stage. However the situation had changed by 29 July as the Dock Board had proposed that "...the Isle of Man Government should pay for the reconstruction of the Landing Stage (in other words, a new one) and recover the interest charges and capital sums direct from this Company, spread over 15 years. In addition, the Company would pay an annual charge to the Dock Board for services and maintenance. Government would have no charge on the Stage or on any of the assets of the Company, but were prepared to agree the proposals, their security for the cash advanced being the continued operation of the Company."

The Isle of Man Steam Packet Directors agreed to it. Proposals submitted by the Harbour Board on 12 August envisaged a 1,250 foot landing stage which included 350 feet for the Mersey Ferries, 800 feet including the floating roadway for the Steam Packet and 100 feet for pilot launches and tugs. Negotiations continued over berthing fees, the Steam Packet considered the £75,000 annual berthing charge fee to be rather high.

Earlier in 1970 another berthing facility had been giving cause for concern. Tynwald had decided to close Ramsey Pier to passenger traffic and Ramsey Town Commissioners had written to the Steam Packet with a view to objecting to the closure. However on 5 November the Directors replied to the Commissioners along the lines that although the Company did not wish the Pier to close they had to abide by the decision of Tynwald and, in addition "...the usage, economic and safety factors offered no grounds on which to oppose the decision, and consultation with Isle of Man Road Services Ltd has assured express bus services with Ramsey to connect with our sailings."

After the salutary experience of Norwest's competition from Fleetwood in 1969/1970 the Steam Packet, in early 1971, decided to revisit the possibility of a return to the port themselves. The Marine Superintendent, Captain Griffin and his deputy, Captain Kissack, had visited Fleetwood on 28 January 1971 to discuss with the British Transport Docks Board modifications needed to berthing and dredging which would enable vessels to return to the port. The Marine Superintendent was of the opinion that, following modifications to the berthing facilities "... it would be possible to operate daylight sailings into Fleetwood by our **KING ORRY** class vessels and that a limited number of medium sized cars could be handled."

Above: **KING ORRY** (IV) departs Fleetwood on 28 August 1971.

Author's Collection

The Steam Packet were minded to return to Fleetwood, but they emphasised that under no circumstances whatsoever would they ever enter into negotiations with the Receivers of Norwest Hovercraft and they did not want to be involved in terminal or ancillary services at the port. Fleetwood representatives supplied information to the Steam Packet Company regarding Norwest Hovercraft's former leases at the port and assured the Steam Packet that they could provide satisfactory arrangements for the return of the Steam Packet. They even suggested that the Steam Packet may wish to increase the number of sailings through Fleetwood, considering the current difficulties with berthing at Liverpool but the Steam Packet informed them that even so, Liverpool had to remain their main UK port. In the event the Steam Packet agreed to fund 50% of the money needed to make berthing possible again at Fleetwood (but not exceeding £15,000) which would be deemed "...as advance payments of passenger tax and vessels' harbour dues..." The Steam Packet, for their part, guaranteed at least 10 years usage of the Fleetwood berth.

Much further discussion ensued over the coming weeks and months regarding costs of dredging, berthing alterations, income from passenger operations, investments and possible loans. Representatives at Fleetwood were confident that they could have the port ready for sailings by Steam Packet ships possibly by the end of June 1971 but certainly sometime during the 1971 season. However an intriguing note in the Minutes of the Board Meeting of 4 March 1971 states that "...they had costed out a Fleetwood/Douglas service and in view of the estimated traffic potential from that Port, are of the opinion that such a service could not financially justify either the purchase or charter on a seasonal or long term basis of a special vessel smaller than those operated by this Company."

It would appear that Fleetwood representatives had suggested using a smaller ship for Fleetwood, no doubt mindful of the extensive dredging needed at the port.

After various negotiations throughout the summer of 1971 the Steam Packet Company were able to announce that they would be able to recommence sailings from Fleetwood to Douglas from Wednesday 25 August departing Fleetwood at 1030 and Douglas at 1700. It was agreed to operate a total of 11 round trip sailings on the route. In addition to 25 August there would be sailings in August on the 26th, 27th, 29th, 30th and 31st, as well as September 1st, 2nd, 12th, 13th, and 14th. It was decided to hold a cocktail party on board the vessel at Fleetwood prior to the service resuming, on Tuesday 24 August. Invited guests were to be civic dignitaries as well as other stakeholders. **MONA'S ISLE** took the first sailing on 25 August which was fitting as she had closed the route by taking the final sailing into Fleetwood in 1961. **MONA'S QUEEN** had taken the final sailing out of Fleetwood in 1961.

Fleetwood was not the only dredging concern in 1971. It was reported to the Steam Packet Company that soundings done back in 1968 had revealed a shoal patch in the direct line of approach to Llandudno Pier. Westminster Dredging suggested the shoal might be a rock pinnacle covered with sand but offered to dredge the shoal on a "no cure-no pay" basis at a cost, if successful of £2,500. The Marine Superintendent advised that "... the work be put in hand as soon as possible to minimise delayed sailings and obviate some of the propeller damages now incurred." The Steam Packet Company agreed but asked the General Manager to write to the Llandudno Pier Company to see if they would contribute to the cost.

In the event, in co-operation with Llandudno Pier, two hydrographic surveys were carried out on the approach to the Pier as the Pier Company were surprised at the shoaling of the approach since the survey carried out in 1968. Both surveys indicated the presence of large boulders in certain areas. The Marine Superintendent informed the Board that the more dangerous area so far as the propellers were concerned was now North North East and East of the berth. The latter was a considerable hazard if there was a strong wind blowing the ship on to the pier. In the event the Company advised Westminster Dredging that "...our minimum requirements, dredging down to allow a minimum depth of 11 feet at low water, spring tides."

Above: **MANXMAN** (II) at Llandudno Pier in May 1973.
Author's Collection

Westminster Dredging advised it would cost £12,000 and unless they could charter a grab dredger would be unable to do the work until mid-July. This however did not include dredging the shoal patch which had been the original concern but only the build up of silt and stones around the pier itself.

It was reported to the Board on 12 August 1971 that **KING ORRY** had impacted heavily on the Pier several times on 10 August, due to an exceptional sea swell and North Easterly winds Force 5/6. Damage had been caused to the piles. Llandudno sailings the next day were cancelled as a precautionary measure but damage to the vessel herself was very slight.

A note in the Board Minutes of 15 April 1971 suggest that there was some concern about the effects of corrosion on some of the ships which had been pointed out by surveyors. These concerns included:

"**MONA'S ISLE** - severe corrosion on shell plating under windows on the after shelter deck.
SNAEFELL - has had new plates each side of the fore peak. On the promenade deck under the windows there is deterioration for examination next year.
TYNWALD - corrosion from inside in the Engine Room stores has been temporarily covered by a cement box, with Surveying Officer's approval. The deck above port emergency generating room will require extensive

renewal this year in addition to that already carried out on the starboard side. Bow rudder will require major repairs. KING ORRY - corrosion from inside the chain locker has been temporarily attended to by fitting two doubling plates. Deterioration in Shelter Deck Head Stringer plating will entail considerable expense as extensive interior stripping of cabins etc will be required."

And then rather wistfully this section of the Minutes concludes with the statement: *"All these defects are entirely due to the age of the vessels and consequently Surveyors are more stringent."*

An unusual incident occurred on the Mersey on Sunday 13 June 1971 which impacted on the sailings of the Steam Packet vessels. The Port of Liverpool was completely closed at 1100 due to a spillage of 500,000 gallons of naphtha from a tanker into the river. This coincided with the end of the TT fortnight and no less than five Steam Packet vessels were heading for Liverpool and another two were ready to sail, all with full complements of passengers, motor bikes and cars. As there was no indication as to how long the port would be closed all vessels were diverted to Ardrossan which was the only port that could handle the large volume of traffic and offer bunkering facilities for the ships. However Liverpool reopened after only two hours and all ships reversed course back to the Mersey. However the Board were concerned that in anticipation of an event like this happening again the Company should have an alternative port to use and the Manager and Marine Superintendent were instructed to look into the matter.

Ardrossan was of course a main Scottish terminus for sailings to Belfast in the 1970s. Damage to the gear box of Burns and Laird's vessel **LION** on Friday 25 June 1971 resulted in a request from them to charter some Steam Packet vessels to help to maintain their sailings between Ardrossan and Belfast until at least 12 July. Burns and Laird received **BEN-MY-CHREE** for double daily trips on

28, 29 and 30 June and on 5, 6 and 7 July. **SNAEFELL** and **KING ORRY** undertook some sailings between them during the remaining period Thursday 1 July to Sunday 4 July and further sailings were planned by **MANXMAN**, **KING ORRY** and **LADY OF MANN** from 8 July to 12 July but in the event LION returned to her duties with the 1630 sailing out of Belfast on 8 July and therefore **MANXMAN** which had taken the morning sailing was stood down. In all twelve single sailings were made by **BEN-MY-CHREE**, six by **SNAEFELL**, six by **KING ORRY** and one by **MANXMAN**. It cost Burns and Laird £800 per trip which resulted in a charter fee for the Steam Packet Company of £20,000.

As the 1971 season wore on, the entry into service of the third car ferry and the demise of the Centenary Steamer **LADY OF MANN** came into a clearer focus. On Sunday 15 August a group of Steam Packet Directors accompanied by the Superintendent Engineer visited the Ailsa yard to be appraised of the progress of the new vessel. They were assured that the new ship would be ready as planned for delivery sometime in April 1972. Even though there were continuing delays (the propellers were still not fitted) the Directors came to the decision that it would be far too costly to retain **LADY OF MANN** even if the new ship was delayed past the start of the 1972 season. The brokers therefore, C W Kellock and Company, were instructed to offer **LADY OF MANN** for sale on an *"as is, where is basis and with the usual proviso that the name must be changed and buyer must give a written guarantee that the vessel will not be used for trading in competition with this Company."*

Meanwhile the builders had given a target date for the launch of hull No 533 as Friday 3 December. The Directors decided to invite Mrs K C Cowley to perform the launching ceremony and it was decided to seek the permission of the relevant authorities to name the new ship **MONA'S QUEEN**.

MONA'S QUEEN

The final entry for the Minutes of the Board Meeting on 19 August 1971 reports a letter submitted by Director Mr Rae:

"*Mr Rae stated a perusal of our weekly sailing schedules indicated an under-utilisation of the fleet for a large part of the year. Whilst appreciating nothing further could be done in the winter months, the high cost of lay-up and operation and the fall in passenger numbers suggested a reduction in the size of the fleet by at least three vessels over the next three years. This would necessitate greater utilisation of the other units.*"

Mr Rae's far reaching suggestions were thoroughly discussed by the rest of the Directors and it was concluded that "*…both from the financial and service to the public point of view…it was agreed eight units are required if we are to maintain the present standards of service. The position is however, one which will be reviewed in the future when replacement has to be considered and in the light of traffic pattern at that time.*"

However most attention over the next few months would centre around the new ship and on 26 August 1971 the Company were told that the Board of Trade had approved the name **MONA'S QUEEN** for the new vessel and they were informed on 4 November 1971 that the new ship would be launched at Troon on Tuesday 21 December 1971 at 1330 hours and that the official party would fly from the Isle of Man to Prestwick Airport on a charter plane for the occasion. It is interesting to note that after the launch while the ship was fitting out, the Ailsa Shipbuilding Company billed the Steam Packet for an extra £27,000 for agreed additions and modifications to the original specifications. The Steam Packet Board noted the cost of £1,993 for the supply of a 3/16" scale/foot model of the vessel and demanded a much lower quote for this. In addition the Company were informed that the Sunderland Model Company Ltd had suggested a model of 24" in length which would be more than suitable for advertising displays and the like. Cost would be £365 for one or £665 for two. The Steam Packet Board were pleased to order two! In addition Ailsa Shipbuilding Company came back with a lower quote for their larger model as well (£1,550) which was accepted by the Company.

On 22 February 1972 the Steam Packet Board was informed by the builders at Troon that because of various labour disputes at the yard, including one involving floor layers employed by sub-contractors, delivery of the vessel was about two weeks behind schedule. It was beginning to look like delivery would now be after the TT fortnight and the new ship would be unavailable for the busiest part of the season. The Steam Packet Board was later assured by the builders, on Thursday 4 May, that the vessel should be ready for trials on 15/16 May followed by delivery on or about 18 May 1972. Tentative arrangements were made for Directors and Officials to attend the trials and also arrangements were made for invited guests to travel on her maiden voyage.

These arrangements were not to come to fruition. It was reported on 11 May that **MONA'S QUEEN** had entered dry dock as sea water had been found to have entered both tail shafts and this had caused corrosion to the flanges. The time taken to remedy these defects would result in sea trials being put back to 21/22 May with delivery as soon as possible thereafter. More delay occurred due to work being necessary on the tail shaft flanges due to the inadequacy of drilling equipment needed for the repairs but Ailsa had assured the Company that repairs would be completed in time for **MONA'S QUEEN** to leave dry dock by 22 May and sea trials would likely take place on Sunday/Monday 28/29 May with delivery on Wednesday 31 May. It was decided that the Chairman, Manager and Marine Superintendent would visit the shipyard on 21 May in order to get a timetable firmed up and the Steam Packet Board were beginning to think about compensation from Ailsa of Troon for the late delivery of the vessel.

At the visit to Troon the Steam Packet representatives were pleased to see that… "*Progress on the crew and passenger accommodation was well advanced and very little work remained to be done.*"

Meetings during the day suggested that the vessel would undock the following morning and subject to no major alterations being required to the engines, sea trials would commence on 29 May. Unfortunately once the ship was out of dock it was found that the port engine was out of alignment and it would need to be "*…re-chocked, such work, on a 24 hour working basis, to take about 9 days.*" It was not clear as to why the port engine was so out of alignment but "*…it was felt that this might have been occasioned when the vessel had grounded in the fitting out berth.*"

It was now obvious that sea trials would be delayed until about 7/8 June and the vessel would be late in arriving in Douglas thus missing the TT fortnight period.

The Steam Packet Board was told on 26 August that passenger arrivals, excluding charters, from 1 May to 22 August 1971 were disappointing at 249,150 (197,791 ordinary and 51,359 day returns) compared with 280,212 (217,658 and 62,554 respectively) in 1970 which was a decrease of 31,062. During the same period motor vehicle arrivals totalled 14,134 compared with 14,815 in 1970, a decrease of 681. These were not the results the Company had been hoping for and when the figures

*Above: **MONA'S QUEEN** (V) when she did finally enter service. Her maiden voyage from Liverpool on 9 June 1972.*
Author's Collection

were produced from 1 May to the end of September at a meeting on 7 October there had been no great improvement. From 1 May to 30 September 1971 there were 299,995 passenger arrivals (230,537 ordinary and 69,058 day returns) compared with 323,472 (247,191 and 76,281 respectively) a decrease of 23,877. Car traffic for the main season had however totalled 17,659 in 1971 compared to 17,349 the year before, which was a small increase of 310 - positive news which a third car ferry, it was hoped, would surely build upon.

Meanwhile the use of the proposed new Princes Landing Stage at Liverpool was once again causing concern. The Steam Packet had for some time been worried about the costs involved in using the new Landing Stage at Liverpool and had held numerous discussions with the Mersey Docks and Harbour Board over the previous few months about the matter. The cost to the Steam Packet of using the facilities at Liverpool had been estimated at £166,250 per annum which was seen as reasonable. However the cost of manning arrangements were high - £25,000 for port manager costs, manning and rates, another £25,000 for engineering services, maintenance and insurance and a further £23,000 for overheads, including profit and police services. All this came to an extra £73,000 which the Steam Packet considered excessive.

The General Manager had written to the Harbour Board asking for a more detailed breakdown of the extra costs and he had received a telephone call from a Mr Evelyn of the Harbour Board who said he "...*accepted the said letter as fair criticism, but as his Board is now asked to approve expenditure of £89,700 for the engagement of Harrison Sutherland as Consulting Engineers, he required assurance that this Company is still desirous of continuing the project. He was reminded that our*

Chairman had stated that Liverpool must remain our main terminal and this fact is unchanged. However we were so alarmed at the high cost and its effect on fares and traffic that we had advised the Manx Government of the present situation."

The Steam Packet Board had earlier been concerned that, since the new Stage would only be used by Steam Packet vessels and the Mersey Ferries, plus some harbour vessels, the Steam Packet would not be subsidising the cost of the Stage for these other vessels. On 28 October 1971 it was revealed to the Steam Packet Directors that Tynwald had approved the agreement and financial arrangements with the Dock Board at Liverpool. The Manx Government agreed to pay for the "...*capital cost of reconstructing 800 feet of the Princes Landing Stage estimated at the sum of £800,000.*" In return the Dock Board agreed to maintain, operate and make available the Landing Stage for the use of the Steam Packet for a period of not less than 15 years while the Steam Packet in return had to agree to use the new stage as their main terminal for not less than 15 years and of course to repay the Manx Government in respect of capital and interest which was estimated at £77,000 per annum.

The Steam Packet Board was informed on 1 June 1972 that the Mersey Docks & Harbour Board had decided that the new Princes Landing Stage would be built over pre-stressed concrete pontoons and that work would commence in October 1972 and be completed in January 1974. This was a slightly different system to the one originally envisaged and would increase the cost of the Isle of Man contribution to £935,000. However it was expected that it would result in an increased working life from 15 years to 25. The Steam Packet looked upon this development favourably.

On 16 September 1971 it was announced that Her Majesty the Queen had granted permission for the Red Ensign flown by the vessels registered in the Isle of Man to be defaced by the emblem of the Three Legs of Man. The Board of the Steam Packet thus decided that Steam Packet vessels would fly the new ensign in accordance with the authority now granted.

With so much attention being given to the new **MONA'S QUEEN** and the problems being caused by the new Landing Stage at Liverpool the fate of the Centenary steamer, **LADY OF MANN**, was still undecided. However, on 7 October 1971, the progress with the sale of **LADY OF MANN** by the brokers C W Kellock & Co, was explained to the Steam Packet Board of Directors. They were informed that there had been an offer of £35,000 from British Demolition Merchants but Arnott Young at Dalmuir had only offered £26,000 less 4% commission plus some other costs for towage etc. The Company dismissed the Arnott Young offer but expressed the hope that British Demolition Merchants might increase their offer. Surprisingly, given the age of the vessel, Greek interests had offered £37,000 and they "*...intend to operate the vessel for trading and impose conditions and stipulations which render their offer unacceptable.*"

The Steam Packet made it clear they would want at least £50,000 if the vessel was sold for further service. At a later stage it was revealed that Spanish shipbreakers had offered £37,750 but this offer depended on how much it would cost to tow the ship to the breakers yard. This offer fell through later as did another offer from a different Spanish shipbreaker. In the end the Steam Packet, on 2 December 1971, were informed four further offers had been received for the old ship including one from Van Heyghen Frères of Ghent. However Arnott Young of Dalmuir had come back with an improved offer of £36,000 less 4½%, "*as lies*", at Barrow. This was accepted and **LADY OF MANN** was broken up at Dalmuir on the lower Clyde, arriving there in January 1972.

Above: **LADY OF MANN** *(I) preparing for her final season, at Vittoria Wharf, Birkenhead, on Whit Monday, 31 May 1971.*

Author's Collection

Meanwhile there were further developments towards the end of 1971 with regard to the cargo handling facilities used by the Steam Packet Company. On 7 October 1971, the Board of Directors were appraised of a scheme put forward for their cargo vessels to use the new B&I Terminal at Liverpool between midnight and 0400. The Irish vessels would use the Terminal during the day. The Waterloo Dock Entrance would be available and the scheme would operate at a fixed rate per ton and loading/unloading at a fixed sum per lift. The Dock Board would furnish the necessary labour. There were some attractions for the Steam Packet in these proposals but further investigation was agreed upon before coming to a final decision. The problem was of course that the South Docks at Liverpool, where the Steam Packet cargo operations were based at this time, were due to close to commercial traffic in the Autumn of 1972. However, after due consideration, it was decided the B&I Terminal offer was not suitable for the Manx Company.

It was not just the Liverpool end of the cargo business that was causing concern. With the decision to go over to Unit Load cargo handling rather than the traditional break bulk system, the purchase of new cranes at Douglas and substantial warehouse alterations, plus the conversion of **PEVERIL** so she could handle containers came to £168,800 by January 1972. The Steam Packet Company were informed in December 1972 the Registrar of Shipping had decided that as the conversion work on **PEVERIL** had been so major she was now regarded as a new ship and would need to be re-registered as such.

The proposed sale of both **FENELLA** and **RAMSEY** was confirmed to the Board of Directors on 13/14 December 1972. The Company were advised that **FENELLA** was only capable of conveying nine ISO units (containers) and **RAMSEY** was only capable of carrying seven. This made them both completely uneconomic to load, convey and discharge. **FENELLA** was to be offered for sale immediately followed by **RAMSEY** once the rebuilt **PEVERIL** was commissioned. The conversion of **PEVERIL** had cost £66,400. The Steam Packet Board was informed of a firm offer for **FENELLA** of £30,000 from a Mr Emmanuel Mastichiades of Piraeus which was accepted. The sale was executed on 30 January 1973.

Above: **FENELLA** *(III) in her last days as a Steam Packet vessel. Berthed at Langton Dock, 5 October 1972.*

Author's Collection

On 16 March 1972 the Steam Packet Board provided details of the new cargo facilities at Liverpool. The Company and their stevedoring firm Ireman were offered Bramley Moore Dock but this was rejected as being totally unsuitable for the Steam Packet's needs. The Company really wanted berths at Langton Branch Dock deep water berth but were offered Carriers Dock instead which was adjacent to Langton. It was decided that "...subject to certain alterations to existing shed and quay space..." this might be a suitable berth. Princes Dock was also inspected for possible use but this was rejected as unsuitable. By July the Steam Packet had been informed that the Dock Board were desirous of the Company relocating their cargo operations to the North Docks at Liverpool as early as 14 August and that temporary arrangements could be implemented at West Shed, North Langton Branch, at the west end of North Nelson for unit loads with other facilities at West Shed, South Bramley Moore Dock. After a great deal of wrangling over terms, fees and conditions and Trade Union concerns the Steam Packet eventually decided to accept the offer of the use of North Langton Branch Dock for its cargo operations. The Steam Packet Board was then informed that a further offer had been received from the Dock Company of a cargo berth at Hornby Dock instead, on a short 12 month contract for the Packet's stevedoring firm Ireman which the Steam Packet decided to accept, despite their concern at the short tenure. However facilities at Hornby were better and the £60,000 per year fee included the use of a 35 ton Butters Crane which was already on the site.

Meanwhile arrangements for the passenger services for 1972, the first season with three car ferries in the fleet, was confirmed on 14 October 1971. They also took into account the provision of the reinstated service from Fleetwood and were as follows:

Liverpool and Douglas double daily service:
Friday 19 May to Sunday 10 September
Ardrossan and Douglas:
Saturday 20 May to Friday 15 September
Belfast and Douglas:
Friday 19 May to Friday 15 September
Dublin and Douglas:
Thursday 25 May to Thursday 14 September
Heysham and Douglas:
Wednesdays 28 June to 23 August and Thursdays 20 July to 10 August
Llandudno and Douglas:
Tuesday 23 May to Wednesday 13 September
Liverpool and Llandudno:
Sunday 28 May to Sunday 10 September
Llandudno Cruises:
Sunday 28 May to Sunday 10 September
Fleetwood and Douglas:
Sunday 28 May to Sunday 17 September

At a meeting of the Steam Packet Board of Directors on Tuesday 8 February the Directors were informed that **MANXMAN** had sustained damage at 0200 hours on 31 January while she was "...securely moored at

South Princes Landing Stage, port side to and lighted throughout, a tug contacted heavily with the main belting starboard quarter in way of the after lower lounge. At the time of the incident the Watchman was at the mid-ships gangway and he immediately ran to the scene where he sighted a tug backing off, but was unable to identify the vessel."

Repairs to the vessel (shell plating, frames and fender) at the next general overhaul were estimated at £1,000 and the Steam Packet Board expressed concern that they couldn't identify which tug was responsible.

It was next reported that while **MANXMAN** was on passage from Douglas to Liverpool on 27 January she had been struck by a very heavy sea on her port quarter and even though she was steaming at reduced speed there had been damage to her port quarter shell plating and frames, which the cost of repairing would be about £1,200.

It was reported to the Board of Directors on 22 February 1972 that the Fleet Commodore, Captain W E McMeiken would be retiring at the end of March. It was decided to appoint Captain A W G Kissack as the new Fleet Commodore and he would fly his flag in the new **MONA'S QUEEN**. Captain Kissack had previously been in command of **MANX MAID**.

Other appointments for the 1972 season were:

BEN-MY-CHREE	Captain Harry Kinley and Chief Officer D C Hall
MANX MAID	Captain J S Kennaugh and Chief Officer T V Kinley
MANXMAN	Captain J R Kinley and Chief Officer T K Crellin
MONA'S ISLE	Captain J B Quirk and Chief Officer A C Douglas
SNAEFELL	Captain C H Collister and Chief Officer J D Clugston
TYNWALD	Captain J E Ronan and Chief Officer J M Collins
KING ORRY	Captain E C Fargher and Chief Officer R A L Bridson
PEVERIL	Captain M Maughn and Chief Officer J W Woods
FENELLA	Captain B H Moore and Chief Officer A Bridson
RAMSEY	Captain K Bridson and Chief Officer J Costain

Captain William Ernest McMeiken had been one of the longest serving Masters in the Steam Packet fleet, joining the Company as a seaman in 1928. By 1939 he was Chief Officer of **SNAEFELL** and was present at Dunkirk (not on board **SNAEFELL** which remained on Manx routes throughout the War) and he was also present at the Normandy Landings. He was Chief Officer of **BEN-MY-CHREE** after the War and stood by **MANXMAN** as Master for a while in 1948 whilst she was laid up at Harwich. He was then Chief Officer for three years on **LADY OF MANN** before his first permanent command, **CONISTER**, in 1952. He commanded most of the Company's ships from then on, his last command being the passenger car ferry **BEN-MY-CHREE**, as Fleet Commodore, between 1970 and 1972.

Just before the start of the main summer season in 1972 **KING ORRY** was involved in a collision in the Mersey. The ship, under the command of Captain E Fargher, had just left the Alfred Dock, Birkenhead, at 1400 on Friday 19 May, after having completed her annual overhaul. She was testing her bow rudder and steaming stern first in the River Mersey when she collided with the Mersey Ferry **EGREMONT** which had left Seacombe for Liverpool. The collision happened despite Captain Fargher taking "…*what he considered to be the appropriate navigating actions…*"

Damage to **KING ORRY** consisted of "*… an indent on starboard quarter at 17 feet draught mark in way of No.1 trim tank aft, also some slight internal damage in that area…*"

She proceeded to the Princes Landing Stage and after inspection by Board of Trade and Lloyd's surveyors she sailed from Liverpool to Douglas as arranged. **EGREMONT** was damaged on her port side amidships but she was able to continue in service for the rest of the day. However the Steam Packet Company were informed that the Mersey Passenger Transport Executive held **KING ORRY** responsible for the accident and estimated repairs to **EGREMONT** were in the region of £4,000 whilst estimated repairs to the Manx ship were only £400.

The sea trials of **MONA'S QUEEN** were undertaken on a continuous basis on the Skelmorlie Measure Mile on Sunday 4 June and Monday 5 June. Speeds both forward and astern were in excess of those stipulated in the contract and the vessel was handed over on Wednesday 7 June. She arrived in Douglas at 0100 hours on Thursday 8 June and she commenced her maiden voyage at 1030 hours from Liverpool to Douglas on Friday 9 June 1972.

Above: **MONA'S QUEEN** *(V), maiden voyage from Liverpool, 9 June 1972.*

Author's Collection

The Steam Packet Board was informed on Thursday 22 June that although the new ship had performed reasonably well, several adjustments were necessary and she would have to be taken out of service the following week between Monday and Thursday inclusive. Ailsa Shipbuilding was informed about this and also the probability of the Steam Packet claiming compensation under the Contract Penalty Clause. An oil leak had also been reported by Captain Kissack which had developed in the control box of the starboard propeller and this required the shaft being disengaged. This had occurred whilst on passage between Douglas and Liverpool on Thursday 15 June and the ship had completed the sailing on her port engine only needing the assistance of two tugs to berth at the Princes Landing Stage. She was subsequently moved to a berth in Gladstone Dock to await the delivery of a new seal from Sweden which once fitted allowed the ship to return to Douglas. This problem was only one of several worries that the Steam Packet Company had regarding the reliability of the shafts and engine alignments of **MONA'S QUEEN** and the resultant vibrations felt whilst the vessel was under way. The builders were told by the Steam Packet Board that the vessel would be made available to them between 8 and 30 September and that the Company expected that two new tail end shafts be supplied and fitted and that "*…the oscillation in the oil distribution boxes must be obviated, even if new shafts are required.*" Ailsa were also told that any delay in the completion of this work would result in a claim by the Steam Packet against loss of earnings and that the Steam Packet would pursue a claim for compensation for the lost period between 18 May and 7 June.

On Thursday 3 October the Manager reported that "*… during the guarantee drydocking and overhaul of the vessel in the period 11th to 28th September, the tail shafts were examined and no further corrosion was found, thereby permitting the D.O.T.I. to approve the vessel continuing in service subject to annual examination.*"

It was also reported that the cause of excessive vibration of the oil distribution boxes had not been established as everything had appeared to be true and correctly aligned. However once an additional bearing had been fitted on each shaft and reassembled and the couplings adjusted the vibrations considerably lessened. The Steam Packet Company still wanted the builders to replace the two tail end shafts and a further problem had also been identified with the noise level coming from the air intakes on the aft part of the promenade deck. Rubber baffles were to be tested to solve the problem.

On 8 March 1973 Mr Sydney Shimmin, the General Manager reported to the Steam Packet Directors a meeting he held with representatives of Ailsa Shipbuilding and representatives of Kamewa of Sweden, who were the suppliers of the faulty tailshaft equipment which had caused the severe delays to **MONA'S QUEEN**. This meeting resulted in Kamewa agreeing to extend their guarantee against corrosion and to fitting without charge any replacement flanges needed plus other obligations regarding repairs to existing tailshafts and associated equipment including the provision of a spare tailshaft. This last item was later disputed by Kamewa. A small amount, £630 as per contract was offered by way of compensation by Kamewa and the builders also agreed to meet various expenses that the Steam Packet had made.

The question of how many ships were needed in the Steam Packet fleet was revisited by the Board of Directors on 24 August 1972. Costs were rising with proposed increases in port charges at both Douglas and Fleetwood. The Steam Packet Company were particularly concerned that the Isle of Man Harbour Board exempt all light sailings from port charges completely and that passenger tax on day excursionists should be lowered, "...stating that unless some permanent alleviation was forthcoming in these two directions, there was the probability that the number of early and late season day trips would be curtailed with a resultant reduction in their revenue."

The Steam Packet Board made it clear that they did not see any reason for an increase in port charges at Fleetwood. The port dues on vessels here were to be increased by 1p per NRT to a new charge of 11p per NRT. The Steam Packet expressed their disappointment that after going to the trouble of re-opening the Fleetwood service new charges were to be imposed at such an early date.

With all this going on two statements were examined by the Steam Packet Board which analysed the estimated annual savings and effect on the season's sailing patterns if one of the five **KING ORRY** class vessels was taken out of service and the passenger fleet was reduced to seven vessels. It was decided once again to retain a passenger fleet of eight vessels but the Steam Packet Company decided to review the situation once again the following year.

There had been better news initially about the financing of and contractual details concerning the new Landing Stage at Liverpool and these were discussed by the Steam Packet Directors on the 10 May 1973. The General Manager reported that recent meetings with the Mersey Docks and Harbour Board had gone well and all difficulties had been resolved in principle and it was anticipated that contracts would be signed "...within the next two weeks." Many difficulties however were to arise over the coming months in both the construction and financing of the Landing Stage and by 20 June 1974 the costs escalation of the project was causing great concern to the Steam Packet Company and the Manx Government.

Meanwhile the Steam Packet was eager to introduce a car ferry service on the Douglas to Dublin route in 1973. However it appears that "...the meeting arranged for the 8th May at which it had been hoped to resolve the labour position had now been cancelled by the Union." It appeared now there was little hope for 1973.

At the beginning of the main summer season in 1973 two of the Steam Packet Company's steamers had suffered breakdowns. The Directors of the Steam Packet Company were informed on 31 May 1973 that **MANXMAN**, while approaching Dublin from Douglas on 24 May at 1300 hours, had suffered a loss of vacuum in the condensers of both engines which "...necessitated anchoring in Dublin Bay until repairs were effected, permitting the vessel to berth at 1605 hours. In the meantime **KING ORRY** was ordered to Douglas in order to undertake **MANXMAN**'s next scheduled sailing to Belfast on the Friday and **BEN-MY-CHREE** was placed on stand-by to proceed to Dublin light to uplift the Dublin/Douglas passengers and solos."

In the event the problem with **MANXMAN** was found to be a sticking valve which was repaired and she was able to sail from Dublin at 1815 hours and made the passage back to Douglas at full speed. **BEN-MY-CHREE** did not sail. Meanwhile **MONA'S ISLE** had undocked on Friday 25 May from Birkenhead and had undertaken the Liverpool to Douglas sailing at 1530 hours that day in place of **KING ORRY** which had gone to Belfast in place of **MANXMAN**. As for **MONA'S ISLE** "...an armature on a condenser burnt out and in order that repairs could be affected more quickly than at Douglas the vessel was ordered to Liverpool immediately on discharge." Repairs were carried out the next day at Liverpool.

Once again it was reported to the Board on 14 June 1973 that early season passenger traffic was down a little over the previous year. During the period 1 May to 10 June 1973 passenger arrivals, excluding charters, totalled 59,087 (46,786 ordinary and 12,301 day returns) compared with 61,824 (51,812 ordinary and 10,012 day returns) in 1972. This was a decrease of 2,737. However motor car arrivals had increased from 4,653 in 1972 to 4,957 in 1973.

Happily however, by the end of the season the situation had improved as far as the passenger carryings were concerned. It was revealed on 4 October that passenger arrivals (excluding charters) during the period 1 May to 30 September 1973 totalled 337,827 (239,244 ordinary and 98,583 day) compared with 320,982 (227,877 ordinary and 93,105 day) from the year before, an increase of 16,845. Motor car arrivals totalled 21,686 compared with 19,601 an increase of 2,085.

The Palace Hotel and Casino had several gaming machines on the Steam Packet vessels at this time but profits generated by them were not as much as the Palace Hotel had hoped for. They suggested in a letter to the Steam Packet Board on 14 June 1973 that perhaps the machines could be located in other places on board the vessels, not just in the bar areas. Minimum rental on these was £5,000 per machine (payable to the Steam Packet Company) and the Palace Hotel said that unless profits improved the situation was unsustainable. The Steam Packet Directors were not keen on the machines being anywhere but in the bar area of the vessels but after negotiations, a compromise was reached where instead of the rental charges it was agreed that a 50/50

*Above: Classic shot of **MONA'S ISLE** (V) off Douglas, late May 1973.*

Allan Jones

split of the profits might be more equitable. However, by the end of 1973 the Palace Hotel felt that the returns on the machines did not even justify capital needed for servicing and repair or the wages of staff needed to maintain them. They once again suggested moving the machines out of the bar areas of the vessels and on to the decks and into other lounges, but this was rejected by the Steam Packet Board. The Steam Packet did however agree to split the total receipts 50/50 instead of a 50/50 split on profits alone, and the annual rent of £5,000 per machine was waived. The Palace Hotel agreed to these proposals.

Meanwhile the Steam Packet Company was still anxious about their cargo services and their freight handling capacity. To increase the cargo handling capacity since the advent of containerisation the Company had been looking at acquiring some second hand tonnage and the Coast Line's vessels **SPANIEL** and **POINTER** seemed suitable vessels to improve the freight handling capacity of the Steam Packet Company. They had been inspected by the Marine and Engineering Superintendents and been visited by two of the Steam Packet directors. On 14 June it was reported that the vessels "... *though slightly smaller than **PEVERIL** were built in 1954 and 1955 and although not cellular, are capable of conveying 43 x 20' containers and would prove satisfactory for our service ...*"

Coast Line did not want to sell immediately but offered a charter instead with an option to buy later. It was agreed to pursue the charter option and on 21 June the Steam Packet were told that Coast Line was offering **SPANIEL** for charter for one month from 16 July at £290 per day with an option to purchase "...*in excess of £80,000.*" The Steam Packet decided to accept the one month charter and to offer the required £80,000 for the subsequent purchase of the vessel. She was available at Hornby Dock, Liverpool from 16 July. At the same time it was agreed to lay up **RAMSEY** and possibly offer her for sale if the evaluation of **SPANIEL** proved to be satisfactory.

The sale of **RAMSEY** was authorised on 16 July and she was moved to Morpeth Dock, Birkenhead and her crew were paid off. After one month **SPANIEL** was found to be satisfactory and a further charter for two more months was agreed and the Steam Packet Company stated it was keen to purchase. The memorandum to purchase the vessel was signed on 23 August 1973 and on 30 August it was decided to rename her **CONISTER**.

The importance of the passenger car ferries was evident at a Board Meeting on 28 June 1973 when the winter service arrangements were discussed. It was agreed that **MONA'S QUEEN** and **BEN-MY-CHREE** would operate the bulk of the service with **MANX MAID** relieving both for overhaul.

Above: **CONISTER** *(II) at Douglas in July 1976.*

Adrian Sweeney

The Directors received a report from the General Manager, Mr S Shimmin on 26 July 1973 concerning some of the incidents involving vessels during the early season period which necessitated some attention. It appeared that **TYNWALD** had bent one of her starboard propeller blades and tipped another whilst berthing at Llandudno on 12 July. It was high water and the wind was light. She had to be dry docked two days later at Birkenhead and was commissioned again on Monday 16 July without any loss of scheduled sailings. Divers had found nothing off Llandudno Pier that could have caused the damage.

Due to the weather on Monday 11 July **MANX MAID** had to anchor in North Bay but when she returned to the King Edward Pier at Douglas that evening "*...it was discovered that the port side bearing and half shaft of the windlass had fractured which necessitated immediate withdrawal from service.*" She sailed to Cammell Laird at Birkenhead for repairs only returning to service on 19 July. Resulting from her temporary withdrawal from service it was necessary to cancel the Liverpool to Llandudno sailing and cruise on 17 July and the Fleetwood sailings the following day.

Prior to taking the Douglas to Liverpool sailing at 1730 hours on Wednesday 18 July a fire was discovered aboard **MANXMAN** in the galley ventilator trunking. Fat had lodged in the trunking and caught fire. It was dealt with quickly and no sailings were lost. Meanwhile **MONA'S QUEEN** had a serious oil leak on Saturday 21 July in one of her stern tubes and dry docking was necessary as soon as "*...the weekend commitments were fulfilled.*" She dry docked on Monday 23 July and came out the next day at 0400 hours and no sailings were lost.

LOOKING TO THE FUTURE

In Douglas on 23 August 1973 a full review of the 1973 season to date was undertaken. It was decided that the Company could not operate their planned services in 1974 with any less than the current fleet of eight passenger vessels. (The same conclusion was also reached at the end of the 1974 season for the season of 1975). They also discussed "...the availability of craft other than conventional vessels for our services and it was agreed that neither hydrofoils nor hovercraft, with their necessary terminals were, at least for the foreseeable future, practical replacements, particularly in view of our commitments with the new landing stage at Liverpool."

The Steam Packet Directors however did look at the projected cash flow over the following three years and, with consideration given to the age of some of the current fleet, it was decided "...to proceed in principle with arrangements to invite tenders for a new passenger/car ferry, generally similar to MONA'S QUEEN, for delivery in the spring of 1976."

On the 6 September 1973 it was decided to invite the following shipbuilders to tender for a new vessel based on MONA'S QUEEN:

Ailsa Shipbuilding at Troon
Cammell Laird at Birkenhead
Harland & Wolff at Belfast
Swan Hunter at Newcastle
Vickers Armstrong at Barrow
Scott-Lithgow on the Lower Clyde
Robb-Caledon at Dundee

What was certain for 1974 was that fares would have to increase. Costs were rising, not least an extra £53,000 demanded by the Isle of Man Harbour Board for berthing dues at Douglas and an estimated extra £80,000 for the annual fuel bill as the cost of oil continued to rise. There was also interest of £30,000 to be paid on the loan for the construction of the Liverpool Landing Stage. It was decided that standard, mid-week and two day fares would increase by 60p per return journey and day excursion fares, except Fleetwood, would go up by 20p. Fleetwood would only go up by 10p. The Liverpool - Llandudno return fare would increase by 50p and cruises by 10p.

The standard fares for 1974 were:

Liverpool, Ardrossan, Belfast, Dublin, Heysham, Llandudno and Fleetwood to Douglas were £3.60 single and £7.20 return
Liverpool and Llandudno was to be £1.50 single and £3.00 return

Mid-week return fares were to be:
Liverpool, Llandudno and Heysham to Douglas were to be £6.20 but Fleetwood to Douglas was to be £4.40
Two Day Tickets and Day Excursions were to be:
Liverpool and Fleetwood to Douglas £2.60
Ardrossan, Belfast, Dublin Heysham and Llandudno to Douglas £2.40
Liverpool and Llandudno £2.00
Coastal Cruise from Llandudno or Douglas 90p

In addition Contract Tickets were to be increased by 10% and fares for solo motor cycles and combinations were to be increased by 50p to £4.50 and £6.50 respectively. Charges for motor cars were to be increased by £1 per single journey apart from Belfast where no increase was made.

Meanwhile there were further worries regarding Ardrossan. The Steam Packet Directors were informed on 11 October 1973 that the Isle of Man Tourist Board had raised concerns about the number of complaints they were receiving regarding the conditions for passengers at Ardrossan. The directors were "...well aware of certain shortcomings in the port when we are required to use freight berths for passengers and the Tourist Board are to be advised of the proposal by the Port Authority to reclaim land and build a better berth adjacent to Winton Pier and which would be available for our vessels on many occasions."

Early in her service MONA'S QUEEN was found to have suffered corrosion in her shafts and subsequently there had been a dispute between the Steam Packet Company and the manufacturers of the shafts, Kamewa of Sweden. The Steam Packet had claimed compensation in relation to loss of earnings. Kamewa informed the Steam Packet by letter, read to the Board on 1 November 1973, that the corrosion problem had now been solved although Lloyds were insisting on a further inspection of the shafts in the Spring of 1974 and others in two and four years time. Kamewa claimed that the amount wanted by the Steam Packet was far in advance of their normal maximum compensation arrangements but as a gesture of goodwill they were prepared to "...keep in their workshop an unmanufactured shaft, valued at £4,000, during the three years covering the inspections."

Alternatively, Kamewa offered to make a manufactured spare shaft available during the three year period at a cost to the Steam Packet of only £3,000 if they decided to purchase it. However this offer was conditional on Kamewa getting the order for the shafts for the new vessel planned by the Steam Packet. The Steam Packet Directors advised Kamewa that any contracts for the new vessel would be awarded by tendering and that they would still pursue their original claim for compensation. In response the Swedish Company invited the Steam Packet to send representatives to a meeting at their headquarters at Kristinehamn to try to come to some sort of settlement. It was decided to send the General Manager, Mr Shimmin, to undertake this delicate mission but only in an observer's capacity accompanying the Ailsa Shipbuilder's representative Mr MacKenzie.

The meeting took place on 27 November 1973 and all parties agreed that because of the modifications to the flanges of the shafts the proposed regular inspections by Lloyds and the Board of Trade were now no longer necessary and the two relevant authorities should be appraised of this. The Steam Packet were claiming from Ailsa Shipbuilding £5,300 for delay in delivery and £1,600 for inspection charges whilst Ailsa Shipbuilding were claiming from Kamewa £7,150 for the cost of the remedial work. In the event Kamewa offered a joint compensation of 75,000 Swedish Crowns (about £7,150) to be split between the shipowner and the shipbuilder. Although both the owners and builders were a little reluctant they felt that this was the best that they could hope for. Ailsa Shipbuilders offered the Steam Packet two-thirds of the compensation and this was agreed by the Steam Packet Directors on 29 November 1973.

Despite several other shipbuilders having been asked to quote for the proposed new vessel the Steam Packet Board Meeting minutes suggests that Ailsa Shipbuilding Company at Troon was the preferred bidder for the new ship, despite the problems encountered with **MONA'S QUEEN**. As early as 11 October 1973 Robb-Caledon of Dundee had requested a list of the sub-contractors who had worked on **MONA'S QUEEN** and this had been given to them. However they also requested the detailed specification that had been prepared by Ailsa Shipbuilders for **MONA'S QUEEN**. The Steam Packet's Directors decided to treat this as confidential and it would not be loaned to any other shipbuilder but Robb-Caledon were told that they could inspect **MONA'S QUEEN** any time they wished.

The Directors of the Steam Packet were also informed on 15 November 1973 that Mr MacKenzie of Ailsa Shipbuilders had been in detailed discussions with the Steam Packet management and superintendents regarding the type, size and cost of engines that would be appropriate for the new vessel. Crossleys had quoted £474,000 for 12 cylinder engines but the 10 cylinder type (as on **MONA'S QUEEN**) would be £25,000 less and there was a proposal to fit four smaller engines from a different manufacturer which would cost about £375,000 but they would generate a similar amount of power as the two 12 cylinder machines. The Steam Packet thus asked Ailsa Shipbuilders to provide a list of types and costings of the various engines as soon as possible.

By 29 November 1973 two tenders for the new vessel had been received. Ailsa Shipbuilders had quoted £3,373,000 and Robb Caledon £4,375,000. The Troon company in addition had hinted at minor savings "...*if certain other makers' equipment had been specified and had presumed a 10% per annum escalation.*"

Above: **MONA'S QUEEN** *(V) arriving at Douglas from Liverpool at 1900 on 12 July 1972.*

Author's Collection

By 6 December Ailsa Shipbuilders had put further pressure on the Steam Packet as the Chairman Mr Brownsdon had been personally telephoned by the Chairman of Ailsa "...*requesting early information about their tender for our proposed new vessel in view of the Ailsa Yard having been advised of their success in tendering for two tugs for Cory Bros. Ltd.*" The upshot of this was that it would delay the delivery date for the new Steam Packet vessel unless they heard fairly swiftly that their tender had been accepted and they could then amend arrangements with Cory Bros. Mr Shimmin, the General Manager, was instructed to intimate to Ailsa Shipbuilders that their tender was being favourably looked upon.

In the event the tender for the new vessel was discussed at length on 13 December by the Steam Packet Directors and they accepted that the proposed 10% escalation clause was "...*a fair way of endeavouring to keep a price level in these inflationary times.*" The proposed engine types were considered but in the end it was felt it was better to have the 12 cylinder engines by Crossley rather than the four smaller engines due to the fact that the four smaller engines would have a total of 64 cylinders with a higher potential for breakdowns and increased refit costs as well as having more complicated couplings to the twin shafts. The tender from Ailsa Shipbuilders of Troon was thus accepted.

While the new ship's tender was being finalised the sale of **RAMSEY**, also required attention. The Steam Packet Board heard on 22 November that a Mr Milligan of Belfast had offered £70,000 cash for **RAMSEY** subject to inspection and dry-docking. The Steam Packet instructed the broker, S C Chambers Ltd to hold out for £80,000 if possible. At a later date, on 29 November, the Board heard that the offer had increased to £77,250 on an "...*as is basis...*" with extra payment for bunkers. The Steam Packet was at first minded to accept this offer. However Mr Milligan subsequently withdrew his offer for the ship as he found that it would be too expensive to convert her for the trade he had envisaged for her. By 13 December however an offer had been received from Lapthorn Shipping Ltd of Kent totalling £76,000 inclusive of bunkers and the Steam Packet accepted this offer.

The financing of the new vessel building at Troon was also causing the Steam Packet Board cause for concern and on 13 December it discussed at length how to finance the new ship as an alternative to direct borrowing and clear ownership of the vessel. Two leasing proposals had been put forward, one by Cripps Warburg Ltd and one by Edward Bates & Sons (Leasing) Ltd. The proposal by the former was to totally finance the building of the vessel and then charge a high rental for the first fifteen years. The proposal by the latter was along similar lines charging a high rental for the first fifteen years followed by a smaller annual rental for the following thirteen. Both proposals had some merit in the fact that the Steam Packet would not have to find money up front and would be free of interest charges on any loan.

Another proposal had been put forward by Bibby Line. They had offered to build the vessel and bare-boat charter her to the Steam Packet. There were tax advantages for both Bibby Line and the Steam Packet in this proposal but the difficulty was that Bibby Line only envisaged a charter period of eight years and the Steam Packet Directors realised that their cash flow over this short time period would not "...*be sufficient to meet the eight annual payments.*"

In the end the directors of the Steam Packet decided to stick with the financing method they were most comfortable with - direct borrowing, although they did agree to "...*consider any further information on the other schemes.*"

In the event the Steam Packet was advised on 7 March 1974 that the loan taken out for the construction of the new vessel was £2,698,400 (which was 80% of the whole contract price) at a rate of interest of 7% per annum.

On 10 January 1974 further progress with the construction of the new vessel was discussed by the Steam Packet Company Directors. The Ship Mortgage Finance Corporation had asked for information regarding the trading position of the Company in 1973 and this was provided. Ailsa Shipbuilders had provided the specifications and general arrangement of the new ship which with minor modifications had been approved by the Company. Crossley's had reduced the price of their 12 cylinder engines by £45,000 and Kamewa had been persuaded to reduce their price for propellers and bow thrusters by £8,000 with no delivery charges and their price would now include an electronic control system for the propellers.

However the whole side loading concept favoured by the Steam Packet Company for their passenger car ferries was once again under threat when the National Ports Council, late in 1973, had made recommendations as to the provision of Roll on/Roll off facilities at the port of Douglas and that the Executive Council of the Island, led by the Lieutenant Governor had been sympathetic to the recommendations. At a meeting of the Executive Council the Steam Packet Chairman stated that "...*while not disagreeing with the N.P.C. in the longer term, subject to the siting of a safe and efficient berth, the Company felt that with four car ferries by 1976, the needs of the Island would be well served by them in the most economic way in respect of tourists' cars and light commercial vans. He also advised on the spare capacity for cargo freight as a consequence of the **CONISTER**'s purchase to augment the **PEVERIL**. He stressed that the unanimous opinion of both the Board and the administration of the Company, including particularly the seafaring staff, that the first priority was to make Douglas a safe harbour by the extension of the breakwater and the second most important improvement would be to deepen the cargo berth to make it non-tidal.*"

The oil supply crisis caused by the Yom Kippur War in October 1973 hit the Steam Packet Company hard by the end of 1973 and the beginning of 1974 and the Company had reluctantly to add a fuel surcharge to its fares for 1974. For example from 1 March 1974 a surcharge of £1.40 was added to all return passenger fares apart from two day returns where the surcharge was 70p. Day excursion surcharges ranged from 20p to 60p depending on the route and for motor cars a surcharge of £1.00 was payable per single journey and motor cycles 50p per return trip. There were also surcharges on freight and an extra £1,000 was charged per charter sailing.

MANX MAID had suffered a feed pump failure as she approached Ardrossan on the 1500 hours sailing from Douglas on Saturday 25 May 1974 and this was reported to the Board of Directors five days later. The failure had necessitated starting the second feed pump but nevertheless the ship came to a temporary halt outside the port whilst filters were cleaned and it was made sure that the ship could berth safely at 2150 hours. It was necessary to install another feed pump aboard *MANX MAID* to act as a reserve; this equipment was already at Birkenhead as it had not been fitted at the ship's previous overhaul. It was sent by road to the Scottish port but then had to be fitted and balanced, all of which took time. *MANX MAID* was eventually able to leave Ardrossan on Tuesday 28 May bound for Liverpool. Whilst she was out of service *MONA'S QUEEN* and *BEN-MY-CHREE* had made extra sailings but nevertheless the Company were not pleased that "*...125 passengers and 70 cars and solos were delayed for about five hours at Liverpool on Tuesday.*"

The Board was informed on 25 July 1974 that *BEN-MY-CHREE* had, on Saturday 20 July as she was approaching the Princes Landing Stage at Liverpool on completion of the 0700 hours sailing from Douglas, come into contact with the oil barge *BLACKBURN* which had entered the river from Waterloo Dock. *BLACKBURN* had been unable to turn sharply due to the strong flood tide and had collided with the starboard side of *BEN-MY-CHREE*'s bow. *TYNWALD* was at the Landing Stage getting ready for her sailing to Douglas. The pilotage authority had accepted the reasons for the collision and no further action was expected from them but the Steam Packet Company was concerned at the lack of co-ordination between the Stage Master at Liverpool and the Masters of the Company vessels. The Steam Packet Company was of the opinion that *BEN-MY-CHREE* should have been instructed by the Stage Master to hold off until *TYNWALD* had departed and concern was also expressed at the lack of control of vessels exiting Waterloo Dock. In the event *BEN-MY-CHREE* could no longer operate her bow rudder and would need to go to dry dock, but because of an industrial dispute this would not be possible until 5 August.

On 22 August 1974 the Steam Packet Directors came to the conclusion that they would still need eight passenger vessels to carry out the proposed timetables for 1975. It was envisaged that "*The position will be reviewed at the end of the 1975 season in the light of the new vessel being due for delivery Spring 1976. The general feeling was that two of the older ordinary passenger vessels would be disposed of at the end of 1975.*"

*Above: **MANX MAID** (II) and **BEN-MY-CHREE** (V) together on the King Edward Pier, Douglas in June 1971.*
Author's Collection

THE FINAL PIECE

As the 1974 summer season drew to a close it was evident that the Manx tourist industry was in decline. Passenger figures for the period 1 May to 1 September 1974 revealed that passenger arrivals, excluding charters, totalled 282,248 (203,242 ordinary and 79,006 day returns) compared with 323,050 (230,435 ordinary and 92,615 day returns) in 1973. This was a decrease of 40,802 and in the same period motor car arrivals were 18,896 compared with 20,284 - a decrease of 1,388. However for the period between 2 September and 22 September the Directors were informed that passenger arrivals were 8,314 up on the same period in 1973 and car arrivals were also up by 1,278.

On 12 September 1974 Steam Packet Board was informed that **TYNWALD** had docked at Birkenhead on Tuesday 27 August for winter lay-up and her machinery was opened up for inspection as usual. Severe damage was observed on the astern turbine in the form of "...*16 damaged and distorted blades and 24 packing pieces were found underneath the condenser tubes. Western Shiprepairers were called in and on opening up the port L.P. Turbine for inspection found that the 8th and 9th rows of reaction blading were missing from the rotor with the 10th row intact but badly damaged. The remaining seven rows were damaged to varying degrees."*

The Chief Engineer of **TYNWALD** reported that nothing untoward had been obvious during the season. Replacing the damaged blades was estimated to be £40,000. She would have been allowed to operate with three blades missing as long as the rotor was re-balanced but even this would cost £20,000. It was decided to put off any decision regarding the vessel until fuller reports were to hand.

On 3 October 1974 the Steam Packet Directors were informed that Western Shiprepairers of Birkenhead had indicated that the minimum repairs, which the Surveyors would allow, would certainly cost in excess of £20,000. It was very difficult to source the materials needed for this sort of turbine repair although Hawthorn Leslie and Company on the Tyne had suitable replacement parts but not enough of them. **TYNWALD** also needed major work on her two aft trimming tanks and this would cost over £10,000.

*Above: In happier days, **TYNWALD** (V) departs Douglas at 1600 on 22 June 1965. Captain Corteen on the Bridge.*
Author's Collection

The Board of Directors went over all the relevant figures. The Chairman reported that "…*some £115,000 would be saved during 1975 by disposing of one of the passenger vessels now - reflecting 50p on a return ordinary fare.*"

It was also revealed to the Board that the price of fuel oil was due to go up by about £45,000 per year. The 1975 timetable was also uppermost in the minds of the Directors but it was seen that the same level of service could be maintained even if one passenger vessel was disposed of. The Company decided not to repair **TYNWALD** but to offer her for sale.

Captain Collister of **BEN-MY-CHREE** reported to the Steam Packet Board that whilst on passage between Liverpool and Douglas on Saturday 7 September at 1835 "…*in conditions that can only be described as being exceptionally bad, a larger than average wave broke aboard the fore part of the vessel, resulting in damage being occasioned to both vessel and fittings.*"

Damage included "…*the fore end of the promenade deck bulwarks on the port side and the bulkhead of the bridge house, the twin doors of which positioned on the weather side both burst inwards and being of teak wood were shattered. Several dual purpose deck seats and inflatable life raft covers were broken adrift and in some instances shattered beyond repair…*"

The vessel had hove to in order to re-lash some mooring ropes which had been washed to one side of the deck and it was noted the ship rolled violently. This had occurred six miles north-north-west of the Liverpool Bar Lightship and the wind speed was believed to be at Force 11. Although a slight ingress of water was noted in the shelter deck lounge, suggesting the bulkhead's integrity had been broken, her general seaworthiness was not in doubt and repairs were put off until her scheduled docking on 21 September 1974.

As **TYNWALD** was to be disposed of, the Marine Superintendent had begun to supervise "…*the removal from the vessel of many items of furniture and upholstery: life saving, galley, pantry and other equipment for use on other vessels, while the Chief Engineer at Birkenhead have taken off all Engine spares and certain pumps and machinery. They are also arranging for diesel generators to be landed. 160 tons of fuel oil is also being transferred to* **MONA'S ISLE**."

The Company were also concerned at the end of 1974 with the future of the Heysham - Douglas route. It had had a poor 1974 season and losses on the route amounted to £12,500 compared with a surplus of £5,600 the year before. The higher cost of fuel oil was considered to be the reason - fuel costs were £19,770 in 1974 compared with £4,090 in 1973, a substantial increase. The only way of solving this was to increase substantially the day return fare but even this was no guarantee of profitability and might reduce patronage. It was estimated each sailing had to carry 800 passengers to break even and this

was considered unlikely. The Steam Packet Directors therefore reluctantly decided to end the Heysham service and not operate it in 1975.

The following sailing arrangements for summer 1975 were agreed on 10 October 1974:

Liverpool:
Saturday 17 May to Tuesday 30 September
(All double sailings)
Ardrossan:
Saturday 17 May to Friday 12 September
Belfast:
Friday 23 May to Tuesday 17 September
Dublin:
Thursday 29 May to Thursday 11 September
Fleetwood:
Sunday 25 May to Tuesday 16 September
Llandudno:
Monday 26 May to Thursday 18 September
Liverpool/Llandudno and Cruises:
Sunday 1 June to Thursday 11 September

The Landing Stage at Liverpool was still causing anxiety, mainly because of escalating costs. The Isle of Man section had gone up from £1.2 million to £1.7 million. This was due to an increase in the work required and financial inflation. The cost of the demolition of the old stage was originally to have been shared with the Harbour Board but they were now reluctant to contribute. The Steam Packet Company wanted its costs reduced both in terms of fees payable to the Harbour Company and the consultants, the demolition costs and the overhead fees of the Harbour Company which were in addition to the original project cost. Meanwhile weather damage occurred to the current Princes Landing Stage on 9 and 10 December 1974.

The northern end of the Stage had suffered severe damage and had "…*started to sink when two pontoons floated away into the river. No. 12 Bridge collapsed and is suspended by the landward end, with weather conditions still not allowing the floating crane to move out of dock to lift the Bridge. At 1700 hours yesterday the Mersey Docks & Harbour Co. decided to cut away 270 feet of the northern end of the Stage which will leave us some 800 feet operational and they hope to move No. 12 Bridge to this area later in order to assist with vehicular traffic movement.*"

The viability of the old Stage was now becoming a matter of increased concern. The Company Directors thoroughly discussed the matter in Douglas on Wednesday 18 December and Thursday 19 December at a full Board Meeting and were updated on the situation. It was hoped that with the cutting away of a substantial part of the damaged north end together with the resiting of the No 12 Bridge (that had now been recovered) it would be possible to keep the vehicular traffic moving when the Floating Roadway was removed in preparation for it to be fitted to the concrete pontoons of the new Landing Stage.

If demolition for the time being did not progress past No 4 boom then 800 feet of berthing for the Manx vessels would still be available. However the Harbour Company were not sure whether the deterioration of the old stage could be halted until the new one was ready.

The Harbour Company at first proposed alternative berths at Brocklebank Dock but then said it might be possible to use the Princes Dock and the Waterloo Entrance subject to this being suitable for the Company's vessels. Locking in would incur delays, extra costs and greater hazards to vessels but Princes Dock was preferable to Brocklebank. The Steam Packet Company at this juncture had no alternative but to await further developments.

Meanwhile progress on the building of the new Landing Stage was being closely monitored by the Steam Packet Company. The life expectancy of the new Stage was considered by the Steam Packet to be well in advance of the 25 years quoted on the original building and construction contract. Consultants estimated that 40 years or more was a reasonable expectation as far as the main concrete work was concerned but a further consultation concerning the booms, bridges and floating roadway would be necessary. In short a tenancy of 40 plus years without further capital costs could be anticipated. The saga of the building of the new landing stage continued into the spring of 1975. A Progress Report (No 6) dated 24 April 1975 stated that the Isle of Man portion of the new Stage would not be ready for use until 30 November 1975 which was a further delay of four months. This was bound to cause commercial and political difficulties and together with the ever increasing costs caused by damage and subsequent redesign was a cause for concern.

Above: Fate sealed for **TYNWALD** (V) in 1974 as it would be for **KING ORRY** (IV) in 1975, both seen here in Morpeth Dock, Birkenhead in the late 1960s preparing for the season.

Author's Collection

TYNWALD of course was never to use the new Princes Landing Stage and on 14 November the Steam Packet Directors were told that seven offers had been made for her:

Cashmore, Newport	£75,250 less 1%
Belgian Buyers	£70,000 less 1%
Frangoulis, Greece	£94,000 less 5%
Henderson, Nottingham	£71,000 less 3%
Mayer Newman, Fleetwood	£60,500 less 1%
Greek Buyers	£70,000 less 4%
Phetouris, Greece	£75,000 less 4½ %

It was decided to accept the offer from Cashmore at Newport (scrap merchants), despite the higher offer from Frangoulis, difficulties in dealing with Greek companies in the past being mentioned.

There was a collision between **MANX MAID** and the Fort Anne Jetty on 13 November, 1974. Captain J Ronan "... *stated that when approaching the south side of the King Edward Pier, the vessel failed to respond to helm and engine movements and collided head on with the end of the Fort Anne Jetty. The stem of the vessel below the water line had been fractured consequent upon hitting the concrete base of the Jetty and the bow rudder had been damaged. There was only superficial damage to the upper shell plating and the fore peak tank showed no signs of damage. The weather at the time was strong S.E. with heavy S.S. Easterly swell at harbour entrance and very strong river fresh-water current was augmenting the ebb tide out of the inner harbour."*

Above: Passengers enjoying the stern ramps of **MANX MAID** (II) in June 1973.

Author's Collection

Dry docking for repairs was arranged for the night of Thursday 14 November 1974 and it was decided while she was out of service **MONA'S QUEEN** would do a double trip each day between Liverpool and Douglas until it was clear how long the repairs would take and whether **BEN-MY-CHREE** might have to be brought into service.

The Board was told on 16 January 1975 that two days earlier **BEN-MY-CHREE** had sustained damage "... *amounting to about 6 feet of belting set in below the forward port hydraulic door, also damage to one of the door hinges and part of a door frame. This was caused whilst approaching the berth at the South Edward Pier at 1510 with the main contributory factor being the ebb of a tide which at high tide, 1219 hours, was 2½ feet higher than predicted."* Temporary welding work was enacted and the vessel was able to continue in service.

During the latter part of 1974 progress in building the new vessel at Troon had progressed so that minor details such as fixtures and fittings could be discussed and acted upon, as well as whether passenger cabin windows should have clear or opaque glass, both with the Steam Packet Company motif engraved on them. The clear glass option was the preferred choice. However on 5 December 1974 the Steam Packet Company Directors learnt that Ailsa "...*were two months behind in their preparations for the construction of the new vessel and it was agreed that a letter should be sent...expressing their disquiet and pressing... to make all possible efforts to make good the lost time and emphasising how vital it was for us in our forward planning that there should be no delay in the delivery of the new tonnage as contracted for in the spring of 1976.*"

However the Company was informed by Ailsa Shipbuilders at the beginning of January 1975 that production on all their contracts was 2½ months behind schedule. Some of this was blamed on the three day week imposed at the end of 1973 but strikes and demarcation practices were contributory. Ailsa Shipbuilders now anticipated launch of the Steam Packet's new vessel might be possible in October 1975 with delivery in April 1976. The Steam Packet Company decided to keep up the pressure on the builders to deliver as soon as possible.

Meanwhile with **TYNWALD** now disposed of the Engineering Superintendent reported to the Steam Packet directors on 18/19 December regarding the condition of all the other vessels. It was Mr M Casey, Chief Engineer of **MONA'S QUEEN** who presented the reports as the Superintendent himself was unwell. Each ship was discussed individually as to their condition and it was decided that "...*subject to assurances from Ailsa Shipbuilding Co. of delivery of the new vessel for the 1976 season, it would be their intention to offer a vessel for sale in August 1975, and as it had been indicated to them that the fabric of* **KING ORRY** *is generally not as good as the other class vessels, the Superintendents should progress the* **KING ORRY** *1975 overhaul with her disposal in mind.*"

In the event **KING ORRY**'s final season began on Saturday 17 May 1975 with the Liverpool to Douglas sailing in the morning and in the afternoon she took the sailing to Ardrossan, the first sailing to Scotland that summer. She also opened the Fleetwood season in May 1975. She sailed on all the Steam Packet routes in 1975 and her final season ended on Sunday 31 August with a round trip sailing from Liverpool to Llandudno. The next day she laid up in Morpeth Dock in Birkenhead and she was sold in the autumn for breaking up at Glasson Dock. However as is well known, after being taken to Glasson Dock, before scrapping could begin she was freed from the wharf during a severe westerly gale on 2 January 1976 and grounded. She was not refloated until 14 April and she remained at Glasson for another twenty months until in December 1977 she was towed to

Above: **KING ORRY** *(IV) leaves Liverpool for Llandudno on 31 August 1975, her last day in service.*

Author's Collection

Queenborough, Isle of Sheppey. She was not broken up until 1979, thus outliving her younger sisters **TYNWALD** and **SNAEFELL**.

Above: **KING ORRY** *(IV) in Morpeth Dock, Birkenhead, on Saturday 20 September 1975 after her withdrawal from service.*

Author's Collection

On 16 January 1975 the Steam Packet Directors were appraised of a meeting held between the General Manager of the Steam Packet, Mr Shimmin and the assistant Marine Superintendent and representatives of Douglas Harbour Board regarding the development of Douglas Harbour. The plans of the Harbour Board were far reaching and substantial. These included:

*The extension of the Battery Pier Breakwater
*Conversion of South Edward Pier up to the swing bridge into four cargo berths with a new quay wall to permit deep water berths up to 15 feet
*A roll on-roll off linkspan and berth on the North Edward Pier
*Space between the Piers to be made into a cargo handling facility (The area known as Circus Beach)
*Inner Harbour beyond the swing bridge to be filled in
*Imperial Buildings, Peveril Hotel and Royalty Cinema to be demolished to allow access roads and a bus station
*A roll on-roll off linkspan and berth at Victoria Pier No 1 berth
*Demolition of the north side shelter on Victoria Pier
*Rock revetment in Douglas Bay from Conister Flakes to Peveril Steps
*Dolphins at the Battery Pier for two tanker berths
*Three other cargo berths along by the present Harbour Board Yard below Fort Anne with berthage for small boats between there and the swing bridge

The Steam Packet had been asked to comment on these proposals but they were so radical and complex that more time was needed to digest all that was proposed. In the meantime detailed drawings were to be requested from the Harbour Board.

As well as the concerns regarding the redevelopment of Douglas Harbour, the Steam Packet Company, on 30

January 1975, were informed that Copeland (formerly Whitehaven) Council were looking into the possibility of operating a hovercraft service between Whitehaven, Ramsey and Northern Ireland. They had contacted the Isle of Man Harbour Board with a view to approaching the Steam Packet to reveal sea passenger traffic details to and from the Island over the past few years. The Steam Packet Company informed the Harbour Board that passenger figures were already in the public domain anyway. Copeland Council however wanted more detailed figures together with a thorough analysis of them. Needless to say the Steam Packet refused firstly to divulge confidential information to the Council and in addition refused the Harbour Board permission to do likewise.

However the question of hovercraft and hydrofoils continued to be on the Steam Packet Board's agenda. On Thursday 20 February 1975 the Directors were informed of a meeting held on 4 February between Mr Shimmin, the General Manager and Mr G T Egee of Eire Vannin Line Ltd of Castletown. Mr Egee had furnished to the Steam Packet Copmany details and operating data of the *Kometa* M E hydrofoil vessel built in Russia. Mr Shimmin had also been in contact with the agents for the Russian vessel and had come to the conclusion that *"...in the period 1st May to 30th September with estimated utilisation, the average daily operating costs when divided into 4 trips per day would require a 5% pay load of 58 passengers necessitating a £5.75 single fare, with port charges at each terminal additional. It was felt this was not an economic proposition, particularly when Mr Egee's idea is that day excursionists would be part of the market."*

Mr Egee advised the Steam Packet Company by letter to the effect that Manx Sea Transport (owned by the Steam Packet) could take over the operations of the proposed Hydrofoil services between Liverpool, Menai Bridge, Holyhead and possibly Fleetwood and Ayr. He advised that the craft would run trials during the coming April.

Mr Egee's second proposal was a containerised freight service by a 33 unit vessel, costing £75,000 and financed by 33% down payment and the balance paid over 3 years. This service would run from Greenore in Ireland to Peel and on to Manchester and return. The Steam Packet resolved to look carefully into both of Mr Egee's proposals. A Board Meeting on 6 March 1975 was told that since the last meeting, Mr Egee had contacted Mr Shimmin to tell him that the Russian consultants for the hydrofoil had informed him that another Manx Company had expressed an interest in utilising the craft. In addition Mr Shimmin had received a telephone call from a Mr Goldsmith of Slater Walker Ltd enquiring as to the Steam Packet's position regarding Mr Egee and his Eire Vannin Line. It was clear that Mr Egee had approached Slater Walker for finance and they intimated to Mr Shimmin that this would be declined. Thus the Steam Packet resolved to have nothing more to do with Mr Egee and his Russian hydrofoil or his container vessel proposal.

Meanwhile consideration needed to be given to the supply of radio and radar equipment for the new vessel building at Troon. Tenders had been received for the annual rental and maintenance of radio and radar equipment plus the supply of a Radio Officer. Three firms had tendered, Marconi, ITT and Kelvin Hughes. Marconi's tender for the radio equipment was accepted. They had quoted for new equipment a rental of £2,427 per annum but there was a slightly cheaper option of £2,274 if the Company would accept reconditioned equipment instead…which they chose to do. Therefore their new ship would be equipped with a second hand radio. As far as the radar was concerned the quote from Kelvin Hughes was accepted at £656 which was considerably cheaper than the Marconi quote at £1,553. The Radio Officer was to cost £7,250 per annum.

During April 1975 there was an ongoing inter-union industrial dispute at Western Shiprepairers involving the Boilermakers Union which impacted on **MANX MAID** while she was being prepared for the coming season. The Steam Packet Board on 10 April were informed of meetings between Mr Shimmin and both sides in the dispute emphasising that it was imperative to the Steam Packet that **MANX MAID** was back in service by 17 May. Mr Shimmin reported to the Steam Packet Board on 24 April that no progress had been made and the ship was still in dry dock. The Directors were told that "…Mr Shimmin has at all times stressed the difficulties being experienced by this Company through this dispute also of the dreadful future if the **MANX MAID** and **MANXMAN** are not available for this season or even part of the season."

Although the language used by the Board, especially the term "dreadful future", may appear to be unduly alarmist, it illustrates how worried the Steam Packet Company were about how they would provide the scheduled services, especially over the TT fortnight, if two of their ships remained strike bound.

MANXMAN, as seen above, had been due to go to Birkenhead for her refit as well but to make sure she was not caught up in the dispute like **MANX MAID**, it was decided to send her up to Ailsa Shipbuilders at Troon for her refit and she in fact was out and ready for service by 8 May. In the event the dispute at Birkenhead was settled and **MANX MAID** completed her refit by Saturday 24 May and she entered service again on Tuesday 27 May.

The Steam Packet Company representatives who had been to Birkenhead on 28 April, over the next few days visited Fleetwood to inspect the new roll on-roll off berths for the service to Ireland and then called in at Ardrossan to inspect the new berth being constructed there. The main purpose of the trip north was however to visit Ailsa Shipbuilders at Troon to check on the progress of the new vessel. They were pleased to be informed that some of the time which had been lost had now been made up and the builders anticipated a launch in November and delivery in April 1976. The builders did report late delivery of components by contractors but the only

serious one was "…in respect of the gearboxes which had been scheduled for delivery in May, but now were for November."

In the event the last of the side loaders, the second **LADY OF MANN**, was eventually launched on 4 December 1975 by Mrs J E K Rae. Guests of the Company flew to Prestwick Airport on 3 December and stayed at the Marine Hotel Troon. The launch took place at 12 noon the next day and was followed by lunch in the hotel before guests were flown back to Ronaldsway at 1800 hours.

*Above: **LADY OF MANN** (II) at Liverpool just prior to her maiden voyage on 30 June 1976. Keeping her company is **MONA'S ISLE** (V). The building of the new Landing Stage is visible in the foreground.*

Author's Collection

The delay in launching **LADY OF MANN** was followed by delays in her fitting out and she missed the 1976 TT traffic. She only ran trials on the Skelmorlie Mile in the Firth of Clyde on 24 June 1976 and even then some adjustments were necessary before she could be handed over on 29 June at Troon and she arrived at Douglas for the first time at 2100 hours that day.

LADY OF MANN commenced her maiden commercial voyage from Douglas on 30 June 1976. Although the post war boom for Manx tourism had been on the wane for some years there did not seem to be any need for undue worry as regards the continued attraction of the Isle of Man as a holiday destination. The Steam Packet considered itself in a strong position as the principal carrier to the Island, despite the increasing popularity of the airlines. After all, the airlines could not convey cars and the Steam Packet felt at ease in the knowledge that they were the only Company who could.

However two serious issues soon emerged. In 1977 the Chairman of the Isle of Man Harbour Board announced that, subject to certain conditions, they were considering the provision of roll on-roll off facilities. The main conditions concerning this provision at Douglas were firstly the need to build a breakwater extension on the Battery Pier which was likely to cost over £5million and secondly the provision of a linkspan which would more than likely cost in excess of £2million.

In addition, of equally great significance, in 1977 two businessmen, Mr Geoff Duke, formerly of Isle of Man Ferry Services, and Mr John Counsell were drawing up, registering and incorporating a new Shipping Company with the name Manx Line to operate a passenger and vehicle ferry service between Douglas and Heysham.

The presumption that the glory years of the Isle of Man Steam Packet Company would be rolling on indefinitely was soon to be interrupted very rudely indeed. The Steam Packet would now have to focus very clearly on this new and emerging threat.

*Above: She's away - **LADY OF MANN** (II) begins her maiden voyage to Douglas from Liverpool on Wednesday 30 June 1976.*

Author's Collection

*Above: Tranquil summer scene at Douglas on 18 August 1976 with **LADY OF MANN** (II), **MONA'S QUEEN** (V) and **SNAEFELL** (V) on **VICTORIA** Pier.*

Adrian Sweeney

FLEET LIST 1935-1975

VIKING (I)
Armstrong Whitworth, Newcastle
Launched 7/3/1905
Three Steam Turbines Direct Drive
Service Speed 23 knots
Length 361 feet Gross Tonnage 1957
Broken up 1954, Barrow

PEEL CASTLE
Wm Denny & Co, Dumbarton
Launched 30/2/1894 as **DUKE OF YORK** for the
Lancashire & Yorkshire Railway Company
Acquired by Steam Packet 1912
Steam Reciprocating Triple Expansion
Service Speed 17½ knots
Length 321 feet Gross Tonnage 1531
Broken up 1939, Dalmuir

KING ORRY (III)
Cammell Laird, Birkenhead
Launched 23/6/1913
Four Steam Turbines Single Reduction Gearing
Service Speed 21½ knots
Length 313 feet Gross Tonnage 1877
Sunk 29/5/1940, Dunkirk

MONA (IV)
Fairfield Shipbuilders, Govan
Launched 13/4/1907 as **HAZEL** for Laird Line
Acquired by Steam Packet 1919
Steam Reciprocating Triple Expansion
Service Speed 16 knots
Length 268 feet Gross Tonnage 1241
Broken Up 1938, Llanelly

MANXMAN (I)
Vickers, Sons and Maxim, Barrow
Launched 15/6/1904 for the Midland Railway Company
Acquired by Steam Packet 1920
Three Steam Turbines, Direct Drive
Service Speed 22 knots
Length 341 feet Gross Tonnage 2030
Broken Up 1949, Preston

MONA'S ISLE (IV)
Wm Denny & Co, Dumbarton
Launched 11/3/1905 as **ONWARD** for South Eastern &
Chatham Railway Company
Acquired by Steam Packet 1920
Three Steam Turbines Direct Drive
Service Speed 21 knots
Length 318 feet Gross Tonnage 1688
Broken Up 1948, Milford Haven

SNAEFELL (IV)
Fairfield Shipbuilders, Govan
Launched 10/3/1906 as **VIPER** for G & J Burns Line
Acquired by Steam Packet 1920
Three Steam Turbines, Direct Drive
Service Speed 21 knots
Length 325 feet Gross Tonnage 1713
Broken Up 1945, Port Glasgow

CUSHAG
G Brown & Co, Greenock
Launched 23/9/1908 as **ARDNAGRENA** for J Watterson
& Co, Antrim
Acquired by Steam Packet 1920
Twin Cylinder Steam Compound
Service Speed 9 knots
Length 124 feet Gross Tonnage 223
Sold by Steam Packet, 1943
Broken Up 1957, Grangemouth

MANX MAID (I)
Cammell Laird, Birkenhead
Launched 14/9/1910 as **CAESAREA** for London & South
Western Railway Company
Acquired by Steam Packet 1923
Three Steam Turbines Direct Drive
Service Speed 20 knots
Length 298 feet Gross Tonnage 1512
Broken Up 1950, Barrow

BEN-MY-CHREE (IV)
Cammell Laird, Birkenhead
Launched 5/4/1927
Four Steam Turbines Single Reduction Gearing
Service Speed 22½ knots
Length 366 feet Gross Tonnage 2586
Broken Up 1965, Bruges

VICTORIA
Wm. Denny & Co, Dumbarton
Launched 27/2/1907 for South Eastern & Chatham
Railway Company
Acquired by Steam Packet 1928
Three Steam Turbines Direct Drive
Service Speed 21 knots
Length 322 feet Gross Tonnage 1641
Broken Up 1957, Barrow

RAMSEY TOWN
John Brown, Clydebank
Launched 22/4/1904 as **ANTRIM** for Midland Railway Company
Acquired by Steam Packet 1928
Steam Reciprocating Triple Expansion
Service Speed 20 knots
Length 340 feet Gross Tonnage 2083
Broken Up 1936, Preston

RUSHEN CASTLE
Vickers Sons & Maxim, Barrow
Launched 23/4/1898 as **DUKE OF CORNWALL** for Lancashire & Yorkshire and London & North Western Railway joint service
Acquired by Steam Packet 1928
Steam Reciprocating Triple Expansion
Service Speed 17½ knots
Length 321 feet Gross Tonnage 1724
Broken Up 1947, Ghent

PEVERIL (II)
Cammell Laird, Birkenhead
Launched 25/4/1929
Steam Reciprocating Triple Expansion
Service Speed 12 knots
Length 213 feet Gross Tonnage 798
Broken Up 1964, Glasson Dock

LADY OF MANN (I)
Vickers Armstrong, Barrow
Launched 4/3/1930
Four Steam Turbines Single Reduction Gearing
Service Speed 23 knots
Length 371 feet Gross Tonnage 3104
Broken Up 1972, Dalmuir

CONISTER (I)
Goole Shipbuilding Company, Goole
Launched 13/9/1921 as **ABINGTON** for G T Gillie & Blair, Newcastle
Acquired by Steam Packet 1932
Steam Reciprocating Triple Expansion
Service Speed 10 knots
Length 150 feet Gross Tonnage 411
Broken Up 1965, Dalmuir

MONA'S QUEEN (III)
Cammell Laird, Birkenhead
Launched 12/4/1934
Four Steam Turbines Single Reduction Gearing
Service Speed 21½ knots
Length 347 feet Gross Tonnage 2756
Sunk 1940, Dunkirk

FENELLA (II)
Vickers Armstrong, Barrow
Launched 16/12/1936
Four Steam Turbines Single Reduction Gearing
Service Speed 21 knots
Length 327 feet Gross Tonnage 2326
Sunk 1940, Dunkirk

TYNWALD
Vickers Armstrong, Barrow
Launched 16/12/1936
Four Steam Turbines Single Reduction Gearing
Service Speed 21 knots
Length 327 feet Gross Tonnage 2326
Sunk 1942, Bougie

KING ORRY (IV)
Cammell Laird, Birkenhead
Launched 22/11/1945
Four Steam Turbines Single Reduction Gearing
Service Speed 21 knots
Length 344 feet Gross Tonnage 2485
Sold 1975, Broken Up 1979, Queenborough

MONA'S QUEEN (IV)
Cammell Laird, Birkenhead
Launched 5/2/1946
Four Steam Turbines Single Reduction Gearing
Service Speed 21 knots
Length 344 feet Gross Tonnage 2485
Sold 1962 to Chandris Group, renamed **CARINA** then **FIESTA**. Broken Up 1981, Perama

TYNWALD (V)
Cammell Laird, Birkenhead
Launched 24/3/1947
Four Steam Turbines Single Reduction Gearing
Service Speed 21 knots
Length 344 feet Gross Tonnage 2493
Broken Up 1975, Aviles

SNAEFELL (V)
Cammell Laird, Birkenhead
Launched 11/3/1948
Four Steam Turbines Single Reduction Gearing
Service Speed 21 knots
Length 344 feet Gross Tonnage 2489
Broken Up 1978, Blyth

MONA'S ISLE (V)
Cammell Laird, Birkenhead
Launched 12/10/1950
Four Steam Turbines Single Reduction Gearing
Service Speed 21 knots
Length 344 feet Gross Tonnage 2491
Broken Up 1980, Netherlands

FENELLA (III)
Ailsa Shipbuilders, Troon
Launched 6/8/1951
Seven Cylinder British Polar Oil Engine
Service Speed 13 knots
Length 213 feet Gross Tonnage 1018
Sold 1973 for further trading, renamed **VASSO M**
Sunk 1978, Eastern Mediterranean

MANXMAN (II)
Cammell Laird, Birkenhead
Launched 8/2/1955
Four Steam Turbines Double Reduction Gearing
Service Speed 21½ knots
Length 344 feet Gross Tonnage 2495
Sold 1982 for static use, Preston. Further static use at Liverpool from 1990 and Hull from 1994. Laid up at Sunderland from 1997. Broken Up 2012, Sunderland

MANX MAID (II)
Cammell Laird, Birkenhead
Lainched 23/1 1962
Four Steam Turbines Double Reduction Gearing
Service Speed 21½ knots
Length 344 feet Gross Tonnage 2724
Broken Up 1986, Garston

PEVERIL (III)
Ailsa Shipbuilders, Troon
Launched 3/12/1963
Seven Cylinder British Polar Oil Engine
Service Speed 13 knots
Length 220 feet Gross Tonnage 1048
Sold 1981 for further trading, renamed **NADALENA H**
Broken Up 2001, Aliaga, Turkey

RAMSEY
Ailsa Shipbuilders, Troon
Launched 5/11/1964
Six Cylinder British Polar Oil Engine
Service Speed 12 knots
Length 156 feet Gross Tonnage 446
Sold 1973, renamed **HOOFORT** and renamed in 1982 **BOA ENTRADO**

BEN-MY-CHREE (V)
Cammell Laird, Birkenhead
Launched 10/12/1965
Four Steam Turbines Double Reduction Gearing
Service Speed 21 knots
Length 344 feet Gross Tonnage 2725
Sold 1985 for static use. Broken Up 1989, Santander

MONA'S QUEEN (V)
Ailsa Shipbuilders, Troon
Launched 22/12/1971
Two Ten Cylinder Pielstick Oil Engines
Service Speed 21 knots
Length 342 feet Gross Tonnage 2990
Laid Up 1990, Birkenhead. Sold for further service in the Philippines 1995, renamed **MARY THE QUEEN**. Broken Up 2008

CONISTER (II)
G Brown & Co Greenock
Launched October 1955 as **BRENTFIELD** for Zillah Shipping Company, renamed **SPANIEL** in 1959 for Coast Lines
Acquired by Steam Packet 1973
Seven Cylinder Sulzer Oil Engine
Service Speed 11 knots
Length 224 Gross Tonnage 891
Broken Up 1981, Aviles

LADY OF MANN (II)
Ailsa Shipbuilders, Troon
Launched 4/12/1975
Two Twelve Cylinder Pielstick Oil Engines
Service Speed 21 knots
Length 343 feet Gross Tonnage (as built) 2998
Sold 2005 for further trading, renamed **PANAGIA SOUMELA**. Broken Up 2011, Aliaga

SIGNIFICANT CHARTER VESSELS

SEAVILLE
A Jeffrey & Co Ltd, Alloa
Launched in 1918 as **CROSSHANDS**
One Three Cylinder Triple Expansion Steam Engine
Service Speed 9 knots
Length 190 feet Gross Tonnage 717
Foundered off Q15 buoy, Queen's Channel, Liverpool Bay 20/11/51
Chartered from John S Monks Ltd

ST SEIRIOL (II)
Fairfield Shipbuilding & Engineering Co Ltd Govan
Launched 5/3/1931
Four Steam Turbines Single Reduction Gearing
Service Speed 18½ knots
Length 269 feet Gross Tonnage 1586
Broken Up November 1962, Ghent
Chartered from the Liverpool & North Wales Steamship Co Ltd

Above: **SNAEFELL** (V) awaits departure time at Liverpool in the 1960s.

The late Laurie Schofield

Above: **LADY OF MANN** (I) getting ready for her final summer season at Vittoria Wharf, Birkenhead, on May 31st 1971. She is being kept company by several general cargo vessels of the day from Blue Funnel Line and Clan Line.

Author's Collection